sailing the pacific

sailing the pacific

A VOYAGE ACROSS THE LONGEST STRETCH

OF WATER ON EARTH, AND

A JOURNEY INTO ITS PAST

MILES HORDERN

ST. MARTIN'S PRESS ❧ NEW YORK

www.stmartins.com

ISBN 0-312-31081-1

First published in Great Britain by John Murray (Publishers) Ltd., under the title *Voyaging the Pacific*.

First U.S. Edition: March 2003

10 9 8 7 6 5 4 3 2 1

In memory of Lucy

Illustrations

The author and publisher would like to thank the following for permission to reproduce illustrations: Plate 4, courtesy of the New York Public Library; 10, 11, 13, 15 and 16 © Pete Atkinson. The remaining photographs were taken by the author.

THE SOUTH

10° North

0° — — — — — — — — — — — E

SOLOMON
ISLANDS   FUNAFUTI

10°   ×Macaw
                              Bank
                    ÎLES
VANUATU   WALLIS   SAMOA

              FIJI   MOOREA
20°   VAVA'U PALMERSTON TAHITI
NEW   TONGA   ×   HÉRÉHÉRÉTUE
CALEDONIA   Beveridge   NUKUT IP
              ATA   Reef   MU
AUSTRALIA   SOUTHERN   ÎL
                           COOK ISLANDS
30°

                                        ×Sophie
40°   Christensen
     TASMANIA   Shoal
                    NEW
                    ZEALAND

50° South

          160°   180°   160°
                     East | West

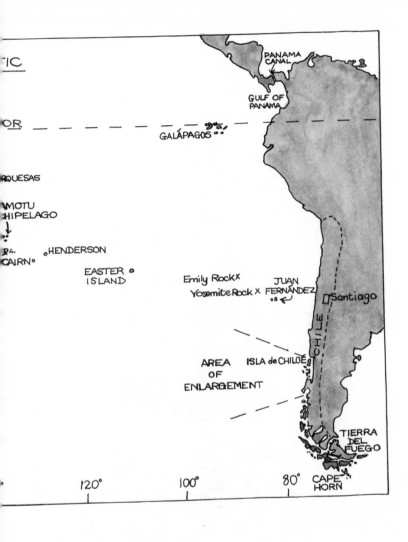

IC

OR

GALÁPAGOS

PANAMA
CANAL

GULF OF
PANAMA

QUESAS

MOTU
IPELAGO

HENDERSON

AIRN

EASTER
ISLAND

Emily Rock X

Yosemite Rock X

JUAN
FERNÁNDEZ

Santiago

CHILE

AREA
OF
ENLARGEMENT

ISLA de CHILOE

TIERRA
DEL
FUEGO

120°   100°   80°   CAPE
HORN

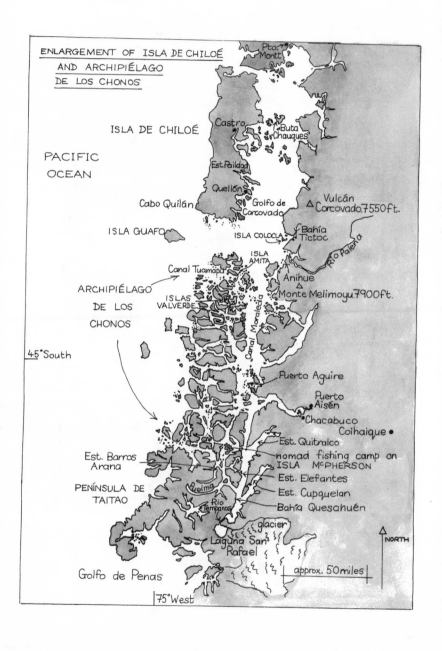

ENLARGEMENT OF ISLA DE CHILOÉ
AND ARCHIPIÉLAGO
DE LOS CHONOS

Pto. Montt

ISLA DE CHILOÉ

Castro

Buta Chauques

PACIFIC OCEAN

Est. Paildad

Quellón

Cabo Quilán

Golfo de Corcovado

Vulcán Corcovado. 7550 ft.

Bahía Tictoc

ISLA GUAFO

ISLA COLOCLA

Río Palena

ISLA AMITA

Canal Tuamapu

Anihue

Monte Melimoyu. 7900 ft.

ARCHIPIÉLAGO DE LOS CHONOS

ISLAS VALVERDE

Canal Moraleda

45° South

Puerto Aguire

Puerto Aisén

Chacabuco

Coihaique

Est. Quitralco

Est. Barros Arana

nomad fishing camp on ISLA McPHERSON

Est. Elefantes

PENÍNSULA DE TAITAO

Quelma

Est. Cupquelan

Bahía Quesahuén

Río Tempanos

glacier

NORTH

Laguna San Rafael

approx. 50 miles

Golfo de Penas

75° West

sailing the pacific

Prologue

An ordinary, quiet night at sea. No waves beat against the hull. No spray peppered the sky. The ocean rose and fell stiffly, the consistency of ash. A powdery wake spread behind the boat. There was a dryness to the silence. A breeze from the Colombian coast rippled the water, but was barely strong enough to heel the yacht. Thin cloud veiled the heavens, faintly back-lit by a quarter moon.

I sat down on the cockpit bench, rubbing my eyes. I was far beyond the coastline and dressed only in boxer shorts, but it was still hot. I'd spent the previous week trying to escape the fickle winds of the Gulf of Panama. Drifting on the calms, clumps of grass and dead branches floated beside the boat. Ships passed at times, steaming to and from Balboa and the first locks of the Panama Canal. Light, shifty winds had dogged me all the way. I was tired. I didn't know how many times I'd woken that night. It was a familiar routine: I'd climb leadenly to the cockpit, scan the horizon for ships, and return gratefully to bed. I followed my body through the process, an unconscious accomplice. Standing on deck at night was little different from the oblivion of sleep. Time was beginning to blur.

I sat a while longer in the cockpit. The horizon was a chalky line between water and sky, smudged and faded as if drawn in many years before. I checked around its length one more time.

There was nothing there. I climbed cautiously back down into the cabin, wary even of shifting my weight for fear the precarious balance might be lost. Then I lay lightly on the bunk and slept while the boat ghosted south-west, out into the empty Pacific.

It was probably only a short time later, but the next time I woke I saw the clear lights of a ship on the eastern horizon. There had been many ships on many nights, comfortless interruptions, engines grinding into the distance. I've never forgotten those lights on that night, though. There was something odd about them from the start. They were high up, very bright, and coming straight at me. There was no engine noise. Then the ship altered course, heading to pass behind my boat. But it got little closer, moving only very slowly towards me, being strangely attentive. Why was it taking so long? I turned on the radio in case there was a problem. No one called.

The ship closed on me for just under an hour. It seemed to be following me. I'd read stories of acts of piracy at sea, but never taken them seriously. Now I looked down at myself, my boxer shorts fluttering in a rising breeze, a few white horses tumbling nearby. This was a new sort of vulnerability: I'd never felt threatened by human beings at sea before.

Finally the lights passed close across my wake. I wondered if I were disappointed, or relieved. I climbed into the bunk and pulled a sheet over my head. What happened next was like the scene in George Orwell's *1984* when Big Brother's voice comes out of the painting.

Vessel on my port bow, vessel on my port bow, this is United States warship.

I sat bolt upright. I'd forgotten to turn off the radio.

Vessel on my port bow, vessel on my port bow, this is United States warship.

I jumped up and went back to the cockpit. The ship had altered course again and was now steaming parallel to my boat.

I tried to find the shadow of its outline against the horizon, but the ship was very unclear, except for its navigation lights.

Sailing vessel on my port bow, this is a warship of the United States Navy. Do you copy? The voice was sharp and clipped, fuelled with the authority of sitting atop thousands of tons of steel. I wondered what he saw when he looked down from his banks of screens and keyboards towards me: through the pale green twilight of the ship's bridge, could he see me, half-naked, staring back from the dark waters of the ocean? I stepped over the bridge-deck to the chart table, picked up the microphone and answered the call.

Sir, this vessel is part of an international patrol operating in Central American waters. What is your vessel's name and port of Registry?

I gave them both.

How many persons are there on board, sir?

'One.'

What was your last port, please?

'Panama.'

Where are you bound?

'French Polynesia.'

How many days at sea, sir?

'Six.'

ETA in French Polynesia?

'Four weeks, maybe five.'

Are you carrying illegal narcotics?

'No.'

Are there any firearms on the boat, sir?

'No.'

Sir, I'm requesting your permission to send over a boarding party.

I paused a moment here. The sailors I knew hated this sort of thing. Boardings cut deep into the notion of sovereignty that was sacrosanct on yachts. I felt a knee-jerk obligation to resist, but knew it wouldn't last. This was just the kind of alien visitation I'd always hoped to experience at sea. Still, I thought I'd keep my end up a little longer.

'Am I in international waters?'

Yes, sir. Sir, I have advance authority from your embassy in Washington to board vessels sailing under the British flag.

'What's the name of your ship?'

Sir, I cannot give you that information at the present time. I have identified myself as a United States warship. I have a coastguard unit standing by to board you.

I was growing into my role as David to this Goliath of the oceans. A dead night had come to life. I told the ship I'd been worried about pirates. They needed to identify themselves more clearly.

Sir, we will fly a US flag from the bridge and illuminate it with a spotlight.

They did this. I saw the Stars and Stripes high up in the sky, rich reds and blues against the colourless wastes of the night sky. Behind it were a fragment of superstructure and a cluster of aerials. But I could see nothing more of the ship. I said I still wasn't happy. Anyone can buy a flag. I wanted to wait until daylight.

Stand by please, sir.

Only a few seconds passed. I looked carelessly around the cabin, past shelves of books, nets of vegetables, soot stains above the cooker. Then, with a sudden *flash*, it appeared to be daytime. I scrambled, breathless, back onto the deck. The sea was molten white, the sky blinding. A hundred metres away there was a bloody great naval ship. They'd turned on all their deck lights, lit up the ship from stem to stern, hundreds of thousands of watts cutting into the night. Three powerful spotlights blazed down onto my boat. I went back to the radio. I tried to make a joke of it and muttered something about, 'Under the circumstances ...'

There was no hint of humour, nor any smugness. Just the same monotone drawl: *Yes, sir. The boarding party is on its way.*

It took a long time. The deck lights were turned off, but a single spot still played onto the boat. I made tea and sat self-consciously sipping it on deck. Finally a second spotlight picked

out a large inflatable leaving the ship and heading my way. There
were five figures on board, sitting astride a central seat. They had
their arms around each other's waists and lurched in unison as
the boat slammed into the small waves. As they drew closer a
robotic voice reached me through a megaphone. 'Are-there-any-
weapons-on-the-boat?'

'No.'

'You-are-not-armed-sir?'

I stood there in my underwear, my bare skin glowing in the
fierce spotlight.

'No, for Christ's sake!'

The launch fell heavily off the plane and slopped alongside beneath the surge of its own wash. I saw the black steel and honey-
comb barrel of a small machine-gun slung beneath an arm. A
squat man climbed over the rail and stepped into the cockpit. He
wore a heavy moustache, fawn fatigues, and a rubbery black flak
jacket with stub collar. He had a hand-gun on one hip and a
radio on the other.

'Evening, sir. Lieutenant Hough of the United States Coastguard operating as part of an international patrol. Our mission is
to curb the trade in illegal narcotics. Permission for my men to
come aboard?' Hough turned back to the launch. 'Hubba-hubba
Coastguards, let's see you on deck.' Three burly figures piled ox-
like into the cockpit. It was a hot night and they were sweating
hard. They shed their US Coastguard baseball caps, then their
flak jackets, and we stacked them on the coach-roof. I'd already
been deemed harmless. Ten bare legs filled the small cockpit, our
knees contorted for want of space. Their shirts and shorts were
starched and neatly pressed. I smelt aftershave. Their hair was
shorn down to stubble. Their cheeks were pink and scrubbed.

'Evening, sir.'

'Captain.'

'Sir', and they each stole a glance in my direction. Badges on
their chests identified them as Mitchley, Rosenthal and Randall.

Lieutenant Hough said, 'Captain, sir, requesting permission for my men to search the boat.'

Rosenthal and Randall went down into the cabin. Mitchley stayed with us in the cockpit. Lieutenant Hough pulled out a form. 'Mind if I ask you a few questions, Captain? What's the length of the boat, sir?

'And the beam?

'Draft, sir?

'Tonnage?

'Engine size?

'Engine make?

'Fuel capacity?'

Mitchley began vomiting.

Hough muttered darkly, 'Christsake Coastguard, we've only been here five minutes. Go do that in the launch. You're dismissed.' Hough summoned the launch on the radio and Mitchley moved uncertainly away. The lieutenant turned back to me. 'Apologies, Captain. Goddam rookies, all of them. So the fuel capacity was ...?

'Number of masts?

'Number of sails, sir?

'Water capacity?

'And how much food you got on the boat – approximately?'

I told him I had enough for six months.

The professionalism slipped for just a moment. Coastguard Hough stared back at me, his pen poised above the pad: 'Six goddam months? You're kidding! You gonna be out here alone for six months?'

'I hope not. It's just in case.'

Hough looked past me along the deck of the yacht, then down the companionway into the cabin, which was almost filled by the figures of Rosenthal and Randall. 'So,' he said, 'six months, then,' and he wrote the words on the page. We finished the form, only a few more questions. I asked the lieutenant if he would like a cup of coffee. I went down into the cabin to light the stove.

Hough shouted over my head, 'You guys nearly done down there?' The coastguards weren't having an easy time. Every locker was crammed to bursting. Whenever they opened a door the contents tumbled out: tins, jars, packets of pasta, dried beans, root vegetables. Searching a boat at sea was an impossible task. They knew this. I was just one more for the log-book. I asked if they wanted a drink too. They looked to Hough first, then nodded that they did.

We sat in the cockpit. The wind had fallen light again and the boat was barely making way. If the wind fell further still I'd need to take in the sails and drift. I was glad they'd seen my life this way, one of the ordinary, quiet nights at sea.

They were in no hurry to leave. I asked if they boarded many yachts. Hough said it was mostly small fishing boats. 'And if you find that they are carrying narcotics,' I asked, 'where are they headed?'

'Usually to a ship offshore. Some go direct to Mexico or the West Coast.'

Randall asked me, 'So where're you outa anyway, Captain?'

'I'm sorry?'

'Where're you *outa*? You know – where are you from, sir?'

I told him.

'Is that near the sea, sir?'

I said it wasn't, and that he should call me Miles.

'You always been interested in sailing, sir, Miles?'

Lieutenant Hough said, 'Say, Captain, you know we got a big ship over there. Workshop, hospital; you name it, we got it. You need any fuel, water, stores, spare parts for your boat, just let me know. I'll have them bring it over in the launch.' I thanked Lieutenant Hough, but said I had everything I needed.

Randall was looking at me again. He obviously had something to say. 'You know, Captain, sir, I don't get it. You all alone on this bitty boat. I mean, no offence, but, like – what the hell are you doing out here?' I'd forgotten how to answer this. I'd forgotten that I might need to, so soon. Randall said, 'I mean, it's kind of an adventure, right?'

'In many ways.'

'Lots of bad storms, I guess.'

The storms. They always wanted to know about the storms. 'Not as many as you think,' I said.

'Don't you get lonely?'

'Not really.'

'But you gotta miss seeing other people?'

'I see them when I get to land. It doesn't take so long.'

Randall still wasn't satisfied. 'I suppose so. But it's not the same, is it? I mean, you gotta miss having people around. You know, *close* to you. What about women? Jeez, I couldn't do that. You gotta miss women, Captain – the touch of a woman's soft body next to yours at night-time.' He paused for a moment. Then he gave me a sly look and leaned closer. 'Or maybe you prefer something different?'

Lieutenant Hough looked appalled. 'That's enough, Coast-guard. You stop right there. You're way outa line.'

'Hey, take it easy Lieutenant, will you? You did your bit for the guy, offered him any stores or spares from the ship. I'm just following your example, sir, asking if there's anything I can do for him while we're here.'

Hough rose abruptly to his feet. 'Christsakes, Coastguard, this has gone too far. Our mission here is completed. We're returning to the ship. Prepare to disembark.' I helped them back into their flak jackets, and to find their baseball caps, radios and machine-guns. We gathered on the side-deck as the launch approached. Lieutenant Hough said, 'Thank you for your co-operation tonight, Captain. Good luck on your voyage. Hope you find, you know, whatever.' They climbed into the launch and sat astride the central seat. Hough may even have given a prod with the spurs, then they galloped off over the swells and into the night.

One

MY BOAT WAS boarded by the US Coastguard in May 1991. As I had told Lieutenant Hough, I was on passage from Panama to French Polynesia. It turned out to be a long and slow trip, first through the equatorial doldrums, then running before patchy south-east trade winds to the Marquesas. I spent the next eighteen months following the wind and other boats between the islands of Polynesia. By late 1992 I had reached the northern shores of New Zealand. It was now two years since I had left my home in England. I needed to stop and work. I was twenty-six years old.

I lived on the boat in Auckland harbour for the first winter. Then I moved into a flat ashore. Gradually my life became removed from the sea. I had colleagues, then I made friends. At weekends we sailed to islands in the Gulf and ate picnics on the beach. When they asked me about the sea, I told what I now called the 'Coastguard Anecdote'. There were other anecdotes about my voyage to New Zealand, too: my life as a sometime teacher in island schools, the strange companionship of the circle of single-handed sailors I found myself a part of. My stories about the sea were traveller's tales, filled with people and events, and the occasional farce of voyaging under sail. These things were easy to describe. My friends and I shared the same terms of reference. These were stories *on* the sea, or *by* the sea, but not stories *of* the sea.

What I could never tailor to fit the confines of an anecdote was a description of a place without people or events: a place where the landscape was not simply a backdrop. Seven-tenths of my human body is water. I spent the first nine months of my life suspended in fluid. A journey over water is not the same as a journey on land. But in my anecdotes I never found a way to even begin to explain this. I could not describe the things at sea which had moved me. I believed that the sea existed only in the moment that one lived there; that no form of words could recreate the formless. As the years went by, the handful of anecdotes I told my friends became almost the only memories that I had of the voyage. When I tried to picture the sea, the water itself and the life I had led on it, I could conjure in my mind only the most simple impressions or routine details, like the earliest memories of childhood.

On the wall of my room in New Zealand there was a map. It was a small print of the Castiglione map, the first European map of the Pacific Ocean, drawn by Diego Ribeiro in 1529. Ribeiro based his work on reports by Magellan's survivors, who had recently completed the first circumnavigation. Magellan believed it would take three weeks to cross the Pacific and reach the Spice Islands; instead it took four months, while his crew ate sawdust and leather. Ribeiro's map shows the Pacific as endless, fading off the sheet and into emptiness, as if the cartographer did not really know what to do with it.

On the other side of my window was a copy of another work of art. This was a wooden globe carved by Ruth Watson. 'The Soul is the Prison of the Body' was inspired by Martin Waldsee-müller's wooden globe, made in 1507. Waldseemüller used the grain of the wood to portray waves on the oceans; in Watson's work the grain forms a huge fingerprint, representing the rotating flow of winds and currents around the ocean.

My desk was beneath this window and I often sat here in the evening when I got home from work. The other side of the house was sunnier at this time of day, with a view over several wild gardens and barely another building in sight. But, perhaps because of the time I had spent alone at sea, I preferred sitting at my bedroom window, because it looked out onto an ordinary suburban street, rather steep, descending from left to right. Kids trundled past on in-line skates, then toiled back up the hill for another run. It was while sitting at my desk, watching the street scene between these two representations of the Pacific, Ribeiro's chart and Watson's meteorological fingerprint, that I began to plan a second voyage.

I had been living in Auckland for five years, and had come to realise over that time that I now thought of the South Pacific as my home. It was a home that had found me, rather than the other way around. So this voyage would be different in a number of ways. For a start, I did not have two years – as had been the case for my previous voyage. I thought I could afford six months at the most. But, more importantly, this time I would be returning to my point of departure. I had never done that before – sailed back to a home port.

The South Pacific weather system is indeed a little like a fingerprint, winds and currents rotating anti-clockwise enclosed by New Zealand, Antarctica, South America and the equator. I thought that in six months I could complete a circuit of the South Pacific by taking the westerlies across the Southern Ocean to the coast of Chile, following the Peru Current north to the tropics, and then returning with the south-east trade winds through the Polynesian islands. Looking through my bedroom window at the children playing in the street outside, I believed I could jump on the back of the Pacific weather system, the most powerful thing on Earth, ride it round my own back yard for the summer, and then be carried back home before it got dark and cold.

Over the years I had lived in Auckland I had sailed my boat often, but made few changes. That boat and I have had an unsentimental relationship from the beginning. I cannot write, as is perhaps conventional at this point of a sea narrative, that I fell in love with my vessel the day I first saw her, pulling gently at her mooring against a backdrop of weeping willows and bulrushes, and so on. In fact, I bought the boat in Bradwell Marina, just next to the nuclear power station. The previous owner was a local Essex property developer. Once the deal was clinched he told me he thought the boat hopelessly small and old-fashioned, then drove off in a mauve Rolls-Royce.

The boat I bought that day was a twenty-year-old Twister, designed in 1963 by Kim Holman. I had sailed dinghies and dayboats since childhood, but knew little about yachts. I liked the Twister because I had never seen something so simple that could do so much: a marriage of the small Edwardian offshore yacht with the utility of the synthetic age. I guessed that this would be the perfect machine in which to make my way across the ocean in search of a place to live. I have never been disappointed with my choice.

The timing for this second voyage would be tight. I planned to leave Auckland in the late spring, making the high-latitude passage across the Southern Ocean to Chile in November and December. I would spend the southern summer cruising in Patagonia, then re-cross the Pacific in the tropics in the autumn, by which time the risk of a cyclone would be reduced. I anticipated meeting heavier seas in the Southern Ocean than I had on my trip to New Zealand, and over the winter months before I left Auckland I made a few alterations to the boat, beefing up the hatches, bolting a sheet of polycarbonate over each of the six cabin windows to reinforce the original glass, fitting custom-made bronze gudgeons on the rudder, putting up heavy rigging, ordering new sails. As the 1 November departure date drew closer, I started to shed the skins of my life ashore. I got rid of my car and quit my job. Then I started to say goodbye to friends. I tried to make it a clinical process, beginning on the outside with those people I saw only now and again. We met for a drink, or took a walk. I tried to be matter-of-fact, businesslike. I wanted no emotional baggage on the boat. But with each parting the enormity of the ocean came a little closer.

A week before I left I received a letter from one of my sailing friends, someone I had met on the passage out to New Zealand. I admired him, as a seaman, more than anyone else I knew. He wrote what was obviously a carefully considered letter. He said he believed my boat to be too small for such a passage, but I suspected that he was also questioning my abilities. He argued that it was unrealistic to hope to sail so far, in a small boat, in only six months. He was an underwater photographer: he suggested, as an alternative, that I should sail direct up to the tropics to join him – we could do some diving. I was hurt by his letter at the time, but tried to persuade myself I had shrugged it off.

The day before I left, I did not go down to the boat; I went to the nursery and bought a young kowhai tree, which I planted at the bottom of our garden. I spent the rest of the day weeding and turning the soil beneath the tree-ferns, bathing in the green-filtered sunlight. I wanted to cram my head with this image of the land, then feed off it over the weeks ahead. It was a hollow exercise. Preparing a boat for the sea is easy. There is nothing you can do to prepare yourself.

On the last evening my house-mates drove me down to the boat with their two-year-old son, Ben. Ben loved the boat. Everything was his size. He jumped around the bunks and made dens beneath the cushions. I tried to chat breezily to his parents. When they left, Ben cried and wanted to run back down the pontoon to the boat. It was a scene that came back to me many times.

I left Auckland at dawn the following morning. It was a warm and soft spring day. The waters of the Hauraki Gulf looked green and furrowed, an extension of the rolling farmland all around. I found a path between the islands, then among inshore craft that would be tied up at home that evening. In the distance I could see ruffled headlands and lonely villages. I wondered why I had never been to these places, when for five years I had lived so close. It was one of those days when the land and sea present themselves as one inseparable view, and it was hard to choose between them.

I passed through Colville Channel, then sailed south of Cuvier Island. There it began to change. A longer, slower sea spread beneath the boat, like a sheet billowing in slow motion. The rise and fall was measured, smoothly oiled and unstoppable, as if a great engine were working beneath me or the boat were sailing across the chest of some planetary creature lost, for the time being, in the deepest sleep. I had never begun an ocean passage in this way before. In the past there had always been a period of transition: I had followed a coastline or hopped between islands before heading onto the open sea. The Southern Ocean was different from the start. I was in the city one minute and the next, when I could still taste espresso, I was sailing out into the blue.

I have never been able to quantify distance properly at sea. I knew that it was five thousand miles to South America; I told myself that the passage should take six weeks. But it was rather like being told it was so many million light years to a far-off star: the distance was so great that it became meaningless, and in my mind I left the city with no destination other than the sea.

For me, the sea represented an empty space. When I read about the history of human attitudes to the ocean, I had realised what a commonplace belief this was. The idea that the sea could be used as a thoroughfare to connect a home port with far distant continents only gained acceptance in the sixteenth century, after the voyages of the Age of Discovery. Until then, Europeans often believed the sea to be an alien dimension. Early Mediterranean societies saw it as a barrier which marked the limits of the human world. Exactly what, if anything, lay beyond the ocean was unclear. Some believed that the sea was infinite, others that voyagers risked falling off the edge of the earth. There were those who claimed that beyond the ocean lay a burning fire. Water itself was clearly an essential element of life, but the sea was a mystery. The early Egyptians saw the Nile as the centre of the world, with its rich farmlands on either side. The river divided their world in two, then swept round it in the Great Circular Ocean. The Egyptian world was a disc floating on the sea. Heaven was an island of reeds. Beyond that there was nothing.

The ancient Chinese had similar ideas. The Chinese believed that the universe was a great sphere with a pool of water at the bottom. The earth floated on the water. Beyond the sky, water vapour filled the empty reaches of space.

The good weather did not last. Grey crept over the ocean on the south wind until it coloured everything – the sea, the sky, the clouds; soon it began to colour my mood, too. It is very hard truly to remember a piece of ocean – the shape and texture of the water itself, the sounds, the smell – for more than a few days. That is part of its mystery. What fixes itself most easily in my memory is the colour of the sea. Colour has the power to transport me back many years, tens of thousands of miles, to a certain stretch of water on a certain day. I remember the burnished silver of dawn in mid Atlantic; emerald pastures in the Caribbean; piebald mirages among equatorial squalls; that deep, eternal blue of the Pacific trade winds; turquoise shoaling hundreds of miles from land; the navy-blue monotony of temperate gales. On my earlier passages colour had changed, bringing character to an otherwise anonymous ocean. But in the south these separate identities had been drained from the water. There was just this one great, grey, monolithic sea, that might last forever. Grey clung to the ocean world with a viscosity such that no wind could clear it, no optimism pierce it. It could get inside the boat, into my food, and into my dreams.

Those first days of the passage were plagued by setbacks and frustration. The weather was shifty and obstructive. I bustled about the boat, thinking that this was all something I understood. But it was five years since I had been to sea, and I was out of touch. The fickle wind forced sail changes several times a day, but still I never got it quite right. There was no pattern to tap into, and I blundered clumsily around the deck in thick boots and heavy clothing, while the ocean rubbed me raw. Working the ropes and sails left my hands red and sore. When I warmed them over the kettle, the tips cracked and bled. As the wind rose I hauled down the sails, shrinking the exposed surface area so as to maintain control. Then I sat numbly in the cockpit, nursing bruises and aching limbs, feeling sick.

I spent as much time as possible in the cockpit. At the start of a passage it is the easiest place to be. I had not yet learnt to turn my back on the sea and create my own world in the cabin. So I sat there watching it, distrustful. Flocks of shearwaters wheeled overhead, hundreds of plaintive cries filling a cold and flat sky. They circled, crazy and disoriented, as if something had gone wrong with whatever drove them. Waves climbed into the sky as the birds dropped vertically towards the water. They appeared indifferent to the boat. Once I saw a pair of humpback whales barging through the swells. Seas broke heavily across their backs and the wave pattern was cut up all around. I tried to conjure up the image of an old whaling ship: the call from the lookout, the rush to lower the boats, the single-minded faces at the oars, the oblivion of the chase. I wanted to fill the emptiness with imaginary characters.

After a couple of hours in the cockpit I felt cold and stiff. I took cover in the hatchway, with my head beneath the spray-hood and the washboards in place, the opening sealed to chest height. Sometimes I stood there for hours. From the hatchway my view was always over the back of the boat, past the tiller and self-steering gear and down the boat's wake. It was easier this way, to look back at what had been accomplished. As the wind settled in the west the view behind the boat was always uphill. I was chased across the bottom of the earth by a single wave.

At first I woke often during the night. The night was the happiest time. Half-asleep, in the darkness, I found my way around the boat more easily, and I ate a lot of chocolate. But at dawn I woke feeling despondent, willing my eyes to close again so I could hide in sleep. I climbed from my bunk, knowing that by nightfall it would have grown heavy with damp. As I pulled back the hatch, the first impression was always the same: it's not so bad here, this is manageable. Only after a few minutes did I feel the heat of unease begin to creep back through my body. The swells were not *big* so much as *long*. There was an energy here, a sense of exposure I would have felt even if I had never seen the size of the Southern Ocean on a map. I watched ashen seas rise up fully formed from a point beyond my horizon. The sky, with scarcely a pocket quarried from its slate-grey surface, pressed down with unnerving uniformity. Everything was empty and wasted, devoid of detail. In the south there was a different scale, and after so long ashore I had forgotten how to live exposed to an infinite space. I wanted to know if it had always been this way. Did everyone who came here first have to accept that this ocean was different? Polynesian legend tells of a canoe ranging far to the south, sometime around the fourteenth century. The navigators describe what seems to be ice, perhaps the first ever seen in the Southern Ocean. I wondered if these Pacific voyagers had needed to make a transition each time they went offshore. Or, if you devoted a whole culture to the quest for land in the ocean, as the Polynesians had at times done, could you call them both 'home', at will?

My course was south-east. After a week at sea I crossed the fortieth parallel for the first time. Sailors call these waters the Southern Ocean, or else personalise each latitude: the Roaring Forties, the Furious Fifties, the Screaming Sixties. These names are not strictly authentic. Most charts refer only to the parent oceans, Pacific, Atlantic, Indian.

The area that I was travelling through has gone by many other names. Most of them refer to the vast land mass that was supposed to exist here. The Great Khan told Marco Polo this place was called Lokak. It was rich in gold, elephants and game, but the people were savages. Fra Mauro, cartographer to the Court of Venice, believed it was called Patal, and that the inhabitants painted their bodies with maps of the land as they walked through it. Cartographers in Dieppe named it Java La Grande. French explorers called it Gonneville Land. English privateers called it Davis Land and wanted to loot it; colonists called it the Great Southern Land; the whimsical preferred more colourful titles, such as the Painters' Wives' Island, the Lands of Chivalry or the New World in the Moon. The grey waters around my boat were laced with the dreams of imaginary new homelands.

In November 1726 Jonathan Swift received a letter telling of an old man who, on reading *Gulliver's Travels*, went immediately to his map to search for Lilliput and Houyhnhnm Land. But Swift had redrawn the waters of the Pacific as an imaginary landscape, and the old man found nothing. Gulliver made sea-voyages through what are, in fact, inland deserts. On his fourth voyage his crew mutiny and he is cast away in the country of the perfectly rational Houyhnhnms. From here he sails for only sixteen hours and reaches the 'south-east point of New-Holland'. In Swift's day the south-east point of New Holland

(Australia) was not a cartographic certainty. On Herman Moll's map of the East Indies, which Swift is believed to have consulted, New Holland is vastly bigger than the real Australia. It is a continent that dominated the South Pacific, though Moll, wisely, drew the boundary of his sheet at about 180° longitude, leaving most of this to the imagination. The south-east point of New Holland is far off Moll's map, somewhere in the South Seas. It is 'no-where', which is the origin of 'utopia'. When Gulliver is expelled from the uncharted Houyhnhnm utopia at 40° South he sails east through the Pacific, across the same grey waters that now surrounded my boat. Gulliver enjoys a favourable wind, covering more than a league and a half each hour in a canoe of stitched Yahoo skins, before making landfall on the coast of Terra Incognita.

The wind shifted to the north-west and my voyage began to gather way. It was warmer now, and I was over-dressed. In layers of fleeces and oilskins I went on deck at night to reef the sails, only to return ten minutes later soaked in sweat. I could have done it in shirt-sleeves. The first days of the voyage were tense with this over-anticipation. I expected the worst daily. I reefed in non-existent squalls, ate often, expecting it to be my last food for some time, wore a harness and trailed a tether around the deck behind me in benign seas. But the Roaring Forties managed little more than a sigh, and the patter of rain on the coach-roof. At night I got up often to look out for ships. I saw nothing, and felt worse.

To fill the silence I turned on the radio. I carried a short-wave receiver on the boat and tuned it to the BBC. I had not listened to the World Service for the years I lived in New Zealand. The voice of London was something I associated with the sea. In the first part of the passage the radio was turned on day and night. Clinging to the boom in the darkness, reefing the wet sail, I heard from the cabin the faint monotony of football scores, familiar accents from a place I no longer called home. Boat-time was punctuated by hourly blasts of triumphal music.

Navigation in the south was very simple. For much of my last voyage I had navigated by sextant. I'd left England with a satellite navigator, but it had broken, then broken again, and I'd found I could manage without it. Taking running fixes on the sun, and occasional star sights, I usually knew my position to within ten miles. At the time I believed that by navigating celestially I was keeping old traditions alive, and that this was important. But I was wrong, and as I read more about the history of marine navigation I realised this. The true tradition of the sea is to use every scrap of technology you can get your hands on, or afford. Captain James Cook was one of the first to use Harrison's chronometer at sea, aboard HMS *Resolution* on his second voyage to the Pacific. Harrison's chronometer was, according to some landsmen, a vulgar mechanical solution to one of the great questions of the age: how to find longitude at sea. Cook, arguably the finest seaman Europe has produced, observed that Harrison's invention had been the *Resolution*'s 'faithful guide through all vicissitudes and climates'. The chronometer revolutionised navigation more profoundly than any development in the electronic age. Cook referred to it as 'our trusty friend the Watch' and 'our never failing guide, the Watch'. The irony is that keeping old traditions alive at sea is a wholly modern idea, born since sailing became recreation in the twentieth century. Once I had grasped this I bought a GPS, a device the size of a mobile phone which gives a position within metres, and stopped playing games at sea.

The only features on the chart of these waters were a number of shoals about a thousand miles to the east of New Zealand, particularly the Sophie Christensen shoal. This part of the Pacific has a higher concentration of 'vigias' than almost any other. Vigias are shoals and reefs, hazards to navigators, that have been reported at some time in the past but which are now questioned. Some charts mark each vigia PD or ED, 'position doubtful' or 'existence doubtful'. The Admiralty pilot book for this area of ocean lists ten vigias in the waters around the Sophie Christensen shoal, but notes that in 1973 HMNZS *Tui* searched the whole sector and found no signs of shoaling. The pilot gives a number of possible explanations for the erroneous reporting of reefs in otherwise very deep water: reflections from clouds, sub-oceanic volcanic activity, shoals of fish splashing, especially where currents of different temperatures meet, or discoloration caused by marine organisms on the surface of calm ocean. (The Admiralty pilot does *not* acknowledge the possibility that ships' captains fabricated the existence of shoaling in order to get their names on the chart.) If the Sophie Christensen shoal existed at all, its charted position might not be accurate.

Over the course of one squally day, when raindrops glanced through the companionway and spat in the frying pan, I sailed immediately south of the charted position of the Sophie Christensen shoal. The depth over the shoal is recorded as just nine metres, while the sea bed all around is five thousand metres down. The shoal might only be a few hundred metres across, but it took me one whole day to feel sure I had sailed past it: I prepared three meals while ducking nervously between the cockpit and the galley, watching for the curl of breakers on the horizon. These were the landmarks in the south: shoals which were drawn on the chart, but which might not actually be found in the ocean.

Before I left Auckland a relative lent me his video camera. I had never used one before, and I forgot about it for the first few days of the voyage. I already felt exposed enough, alone on this bare stage, without shoving a camera in my own face. And the thought of focusing a lens made me nauseous. The camera was kept in a watertight box, wedged into the cavity beneath the galley where you put your feet when lying on the starboard bunk. At night I slept on the opposite bunk, but I often lay on the starboard bunk during the day to read. Three days passed before I opened a book, three days before I felt strong enough to pull myself away from the sea and create a little entertainment. When I stretched my legs on the bunk my feet came up against the camera box and I pulled it out. I experimented with the video during the course of that afternoon. By nightfall it was a favoured toy.

Film provided a surreal window onto my solitary world. I set the camera up in the cockpit when the weather allowed and used it as a diary. Playing back the tape was a revelation. I saw the seas climbing and subsiding behind my shoulders. I watched the horizon lurch giddily to forty degrees. I understood now why my muscles ached and why each day was a struggle. Until then I'd had no conception of myself at sea: I believed I was a creature who stared at the ocean through startled eyes, but could not picture my own appearance. Now I saw myself shouting at the camera to make myself heard. My face was pink, my hair pulled absurdly to one side by the wind as if someone was trying to drag me away. As a character on screen my own human form was recognisable, fighting to maintain balance against the roll of the boat, making bad jokes. On film I was alive.

When the weather grew worse I stood and filmed from the hatchway. Flecks of spray were driven across the empty cockpit and mingled with raindrops on the teak coaming. A black-and-white image perfectly captured the chilling simplicity of the ocean. And always there was the roar of the wind. I was able to tune it out for most of the day, but on tape it was unending, a harsh back-note to every scene. I filmed out across the jumbled seas behind the boat, and panned the folding horizon. But when I tried to zoom in on the furthest point visible the picture dissolved, the lens unable to find any outline on which to focus.

Once, I tried to imagine what I would see if the camera could leave the boat and take off vertically through the sky, filming what was left behind. The boat disappeared within seconds, then the screen went grey.

Reality was very different. I was creeping backwards into an internal world: the rain grew heavier, I closed the hatch, and began filming in the resonant box of the cabin. I recorded the circus of cooking at sea, the ceremony of navigation, and my afternoon Spanish lesson, chanting along to a tape, ordering cold beers and tapas that never came. As the days passed I observed changes to my body. My hair, never properly dry, was sculpted by wind and sleep. There is something about the sea, the stiffening salt and perpetual damp: I had Great Hair Days in the south. But otherwise what I saw was less encouraging. My eyes grew heavy and tired. My face was grey, my chin appeared dirty, with a scrappy beard. My clothes grew salt-stained and more numerous. I looked lost. I set the camera up on a clamp in one corner of the cabin so it would always be ready. One night, after reefing the sails in the rain, I returned to the cabin and set the camera rolling. I slithered breathless across the screen, wet and greasy from the ocean. I started to pull off my sodden clothes, but got tangled in the braces of my overtrousers, tripped, and was thrown by a wave onto the bunk. I saw myself laugh at this silly mishap. It was the first time I had laughed on the trip.

Most days I filmed something, usually just a monologue. There were routine accounts of the weather, fluctuating moods, breakages, maintenance, meals, and doubts. Sometimes a *crash* cut me off in mid sentence as the boat rolled and crockery tumbled in the sink. When I spoke of the strength of the wind, the waves and the cold, I was dispassionate. But when I spoke about the distance, how far I had come and how far there still was to go, there was a different quality to my voice. Emptiness found its way onto the tape, between each syllable and every frame. Space was the one constant throughout the voyage. I tried to rationalise it, to be part of it. Most of all I wanted to feel that this place was now my home.

The ambiguous geography of Terra Incognita exploited by Swift in *Gulliver's Travels* first surfaced in ancient times. At 42° South in the Pacific, according to Theopompos of Chicos, I was sailing a thousand miles inland near Anostos, the City of No Return, which is shrouded in mist by day and fire by night. If I maintained my course I would pass through countless independent nations and city-states where the poor govern the wealthy and forests of giant orchids grow from earth rich in orichalcum, until I crossed the two great rivers, Pleasure and Grief, that divide this continent.

The Greeks believed a vast continent must exist in the southern hemisphere to counterbalance the land masses in the north and prevent the earth wobbling off its axis. They called it the Antichthon, or Counter Earth, a place ruled by laws antipodal to those of the known world. Theopompos saw Europe, Asia and Africa as mere islands, 'the only continent being that one which men place outside this inhabited earth of ours'.

Claudius Ptolemy's world map, drawn in the second century AD, includes a representation of the Antichthon. A vastly elongated African continent stretches far to the south and then east, ultimately joining Asia, making an enclosed sea of the Indian Ocean. The whole of this southern continent was named Terra Australis Incognita. Ptolemy's map exercised a powerful influence over geographical speculation in Renaissance Europe.

The maps I used to sail across the South Pacific were terribly crude. I had about a dozen, but they were all the same, called 'plotting sheets'. The chart table in which I kept them is opposite the galley, beneath the companionway hatch. But on a small boat the chart table has to do duty for other purposes, particularly as a work-bench on which to prepare food for the galley, and as a day bed, where I lie with my feet wedged in the sink because it makes a change.

Navigation with the help of a GPS was very simple but, for the focus it gave to each day, still a significant ritual. At twelve noon I got a fix with the GPS, took a chart from the table, plotted the position, and measured my day's run. For the first few days from the coast of New Zealand I used the 1:20 million Admiralty chart of the South Pacific, on which a good day's run was less than the width of my little finger. It was depressing to see that one whole day amounted to such a small impression on the ocean, and after three days I stuck the Admiralty chart under my bunk and pulled out a plotting sheet.

A plotting sheet is nothing much, a blank sheet of paper that can be used to represent any stretch of ocean. With only a little more difficulty, graph paper will serve. The Southern Ocean is so deep and empty that this is the best chart for navigation, and I transferred isolated dangers like the Sophie Christensen shoal on to one. The plotting sheet moves with you across the sea. Every few days I sailed off the edge of the page. Then I pencilled in a new longitude scale at the top of the sheet and started again from the left margin. That way the chart could keep up with my voyage.

For most of the passage east the chart table contained nothing but plotting sheets. This part of the boat is occasionally subject to flecks of spray from the hatchway, so as a precaution I kept my charts of Chile and the tropics in a watertight folio beneath my bunk. The navigation station, the hub of my proud vessel at sea, housed only a few blank sheets of paper, across which I drew a line each day. I thought navigation a dull if necessary discipline until I came to the short lesson on the use of plotting sheets. Over weeks at sea I crossed the page ten times or more. The lines of my south-east course repeated the same diagonal progress across the page, each rubbed out but its imprint remaining on the paper. Eventually, as each chart got dog-eared and torn, my courses stained with coffee rings and cigarette ash, I screwed it up and started afresh. Nothing illustrates the nature of travel over water better than the use of a plotting sheet. Even today, the most practical chart we have of the Southern Ocean is an empty page that can be anywhere.

For the first ten days of the voyage it seemed the whole ocean must be covered by a layer of thick cloud and that life here meant learning to live without anything beyond the grey disc of water surrounding the boat. This was a place with no landmarks, not even features in the sky. Time and distance were measured by the passage of light and dark, my changing moods, and the tiny structure of my daily routine: preparing meals, easing sails, answering back to a Spanish tape, turning the pages of a novel, repeatedly crossing the same chart. Everything that made my life a voyage rather than an episode of hopeless captivity was communicated through motion. I felt the sea through the corkscrew roll up my spine. The Southern Ocean was something I knew best in my muscles. I could never escape it, but I could not engage it either. By a city-dweller the skills of reading motion are little understood. The ocean was only the swing of a tea-towel on its hook.

And then one morning, after ten days at sea, I woke to find that everything had changed. The cloud had lifted. I climbed to the deck in strong sunshine. Everything was fresh and clear. Seas broke innocently around the quarters. Spray took on a soapy quality that reminded me of home. To the north-east a slab of cloud was drawing back across the sky. Elsewhere the sky was a deep blue. I ate a bowl of muesli in the cockpit, but got up between each mouthful to explore the freedom of a bright and dry world. Without oilskins or boots, everything sped up. I careered around the deck in delight. During the course of that morning I turned the boat inside-out, pulling everything I could up to dry on deck. I dozed on a pile of bedding and cushions, the trappings of my internal world all around me, chilblains tingling in the midday sun.

In the evening I mixed my usual glass of rum but now, for the first time on the passage, I was able to look out into a clear night sky. There was no moon that night to dominate the more fragile patterns of the stars and they stretched, unbroken by skyline or trees, around the dome of the sea. Space seemed so very easy in comparison with the ocean. I could see so much of it all in one go. Some stars were brighter, some lower, some looked further away. However partial, there was a sense of scale, a completeness that was fathomable. Two thousand years earlier Polynesian navigators had used knowledge of the heavens to find their way across an unknown sea. But it was not until the space missions of the 1960s that anyone had seen an ocean – all of it, at one time. Before then all we could do was take a tiny piece of water and project, extrapolate, imagine, in order to create a picture of the whole. If you wanted to know for sure, you had to set off across it. So the sea became a journey, a line of understanding. Collectively there may be a web of lines, but individually few of us have more than a handful. As I sat on deck that night drinking rum (possibly rather too much) I wondered how I would feel about space if all I could see of it at one time was a gossamer thread weaving between unseen constellations.

Two

IT WAS OBVIOUS that the weather was going to be bad. The barometer had been falling since midnight. A dry north-west gale
was howling across the sea.

The pace of the ocean world was quickening by the hour. The
wind was doing things to the water that I hadn't seen before. The
seas still weren't steep, but they were very, very long, and somehow
non-liquid, like a range of shifting dunes stretching beyond the
horizon. The swells rose up behind the boat and surged forwards
only slowly. I was running before the wind, almost as fast as the
waves. As the peaks approached, a portion to one side of the boat
sometimes burst forwards in a mass of white water. Behind the
boat I watched the green crests lurch up, false and wobbly like a
man on stilts. First the self-steering gear disappeared, then twin
lips of water, minty green, full of light and air, ran past each
quarter. It was mid morning before a sea broke right over the back
of the boat, a messy, spit-like blow that harmlessly filled the
cockpit. The surprise was to find it was wet and cold, and could
not be shaken from my clothes. Then the scene of grey desolation
behind the boat was again momentarily revealed, before the next
swell filled the skyline.

By noon the wave-crests were being torn apart by the wind.
Spume spiralled away, helpless and exhausted, into the distance.

The cloud looked sore, its surface swept painfully smooth. Somewhere to the south-west the knotted heart of a depression sank down from the sky and bit into the planet's surface. The system stamped its will on the ocean all around, as if a weather map had been stencilled onto the water: I saw the fingerprint pattern of isobars, tightly bound, squeezing new life from an indifferent ocean. The arrival of the depression was almost a relief, a punctuation mark in the timeless blur of life at sea. Even as the waves grew, the ocean shrank. It was defined now by a meteorological structure whose movements were predictable. I knew bad weather was coming and could count down the hours. The emptiness was being filled by events.

Throughout the day I made what few preparations were possible. There was a sense of fatalism about everything I did, that someone else was responsible – that other guy sitting behind the desk back home, watching the street scene outside, who thought all of this would be such a good idea. At sea I wondered if I were simply a puppet being worked by my former self. As the wind rose I took in the sails, handling the canvas roughly and lashing it tight with webbing. Work was easy. I felt strong and focused, more so than for many days. It was the waiting that had been so hard. Fear at sea is something that seeps into the boat day after day, seldom a force which bursts in with a rush and a roar.

The boat was stripped bare now, except for a scrap of headsail. The deck was clean. The empty rig was wheeling amid the waves. I loved it this way. The boat was simply a machine for ocean travel. It had no name, no character, no aesthetic: it was a function of the voyage that I had set into motion. As we careered downwind I clung to the boom, and the boat beneath me seemed to say: This is what I am, I can shrink no more – and I won't.

In the cabin I wedged cushions into the bookcases to keep my books in place. I bolted the forehatch, screw-sealed the vents, and locked cupboards. Everything was tight and pressured, like finally fastening the buckle of a leather strap around a packed suitcase. I cooked a large stew, ate some of it from the pot and put the rest in a locker. Then for some reason I put on clean clothes, almost the first since the beginning of the voyage. As I fastened the buttons and pulled up layers of zips it felt like I was dressing for a big night out.

As the light faded on that first evening I climbed back out to the cockpit. It was an exhilarating scene: everything was wind and speed, water rushing past as the boat bowled down each wave. In the cabin there had been little sense of this fairground ride. The north-west wind was hot and clammy. I began to sweat, again over-dressed. As the boat surfed down the faces of the biggest seas it cut a deep furrow, at times buried to deck level, a thick plume of water cast to either side. Too thick, really: sometimes the motion was wooden and unresponsive. The boat was going too fast. The danger when running before big seas is that the nose of the boat will be buried in the trough just as the next wave breaks behind. Then you are pitch-poled – the boat goes end-over-end. It had happened to me once before, though in a much smaller boat. This time I was better prepared, and carried a drogue anchor. A drogue is a drag device made of heavy canvas, shaped like a wind-sock but shorter. You trail it behind the boat on a long rope weighted with chain and it works like a brake, stopping you surfing too fast. When I threw the drogue over the side two hundred feet of line disappeared after it in seconds, while I slithered around in the small cockpit trying not to get tangled up. When the drogue bit into the water the nylon warp was like a rod of iron. The end of the line was attached to a harness I had made before the voyage that linked the two stern cleats to both winches in the cockpit. Even so, I was not sure that all four of these strong-points wouldn't be ripped out of the deck. Some of the ideas I'd had before the voyage seemed too complex now. I'd never been in such big seas before.

I could do no more, and bolted the hatch closed behind me. Inside the cabin at night it was a surreal world. Everything was sensation. Any sense of direction, of a voyage, even of the sea, had disappeared. The gale had bound the wind and the ocean into one. Black forces descended from everywhere. There was no pattern I could read. As I was trying to get out of my clothes, three volumes of hard-bound sight-reduction tables slid from the bookcase and fell near-vertically across the cabin towards me. I fended off the first two but the third hit me on the bridge of my nose. Now that the boat was being slowed by the drogue, more seas broke over the stern. I heard spray slosh heavily into the cockpit, and sometimes land with a bang on the closed companionway. When it did, there was a split-second pause, then a few drops of icy water surged between the washboards and fell onto the engine box.

I lay in my bunk. This was the safest place to be. I could feel the boat lifting to the seas, then the drogue biting into the water and hauling backwards. The strain was something I could feel running through the boat. It was only when I tried to resist the seas in this way that I felt their raw energy. I pictured my boat on the black ocean: the drogue anchor represented my will, digging in its heels, trying to hold back something unstoppable. The boat and everything in it was run through with tension. I could hear my teeth chattering, but it was not cold. Everything was shaking, vibration starting in the hull and being amplified as it spread through the rig.

Gales in a cruising yacht today are not like those in old-time movies, with bearded men in sou'westers battling at the wheel while the grip throws buckets of water over them. My boat was on a self-steering system: with the drogue set, there was nothing for me to do but get into bed. I have had several bad gales at sea, and slept through most of them. But as I lay there that night, shuddering in time to the vibration of the boat, I couldn't sleep. I was a victim, but not of the sea. I was the victim of that other me, the me who had sat staring at charts in Auckland and thought that the ego-trip of playing with the largest thing on earth would be worth it. That other me had calculated that the boat would be up to it. But it was the me here right now who was going to find out. And somewhere in the twelve hundred miles of ocean between then and now, those old certainties had been lost.

I must have dozed off. I woke in the small hours, shaken back to reality. There was a new noise coming from the deck. I lay on the cabin floor to pull on my jacket and overtrousers, rolling from side to side. I could feel the urgency beating overhead while I struggled with those stupid wet clothes. As I opened the hatch, the rush of the gale was blinding. I didn't want to remove the washboards for fear a sea would break right inside the boat, so I climbed over the top, slipped, and landed in a heap on the floor of the cockpit. I lay curled there for a moment, to catch my breath and waiting for my eyes to adjust to the darkness. This took some time. Then I saw the X-ray image of the sea at night. Only the wind and the seas rushing past the cockpit coaming told me the boat was moving very fast. I felt nauseous. The whole thing seemed slightly ridiculous now – the fair-ground ride had gone wrong.

Using a torch, I saw that even the tiny headsail I was using to maintain some directional stability was too much. The sail was straining up and down, buckling out of shape. Part of the leech line had pulled out and was flailing in the gale. I uncleated the furling line and started to heave. The line came in a few inches and then stuck. It wouldn't budge. I pulled again, but it was stuck.

I needed to go on deck to free the line. I was already wearing a harness, so clipped onto the jack-stay and began crawling along the side-deck. A sea broke across my back, water foamed around my knees. The water seemed to capture light: I saw my hands, strangled and blue, searching forwards for a new grip. The sail was flogging hard, cracking in spasms as if it were being electrocuted. If I didn't do something soon it would flog itself to destruction, and I couldn't afford to lose it so early in the voyage.

I followed the furling line along the stanchions and crawled up into the bows of the boat. The corkscrew motion was exaggerated here; I needed both hands just to hold on. Seas surged up over the anchor lashed in the stemhead and parted round my thighs. I traced the furling line to the drum at the base of the forestay: the line wasn't jammed, there was none left on the drum. I'd pulled the furler tight. I'd taken the sail off in Auckland to grease the bearings and had fitted a new line at the same time. But obviously not very well: there wasn't enough rope on the drum, and the line had come tight two rolls short of fully furling the sail. I pulled myself up the furler, arms and legs wrapped around the forestay, my body swinging from side to side with each roll. The clew was at head height, the steel D-ring flying around somewhere behind my head now. I had one arm wrapped around the furler and with the other hand tried to drag the sail in and untie the sheet from the D-ring. I lost count of how many attempts it took before I did it.

When I finally got back into the cabin I collapsed onto the floor. Water streamed over the greasy plywood floorboards, then chased gravity as the boat heaved, but never caught up. I pulled off my wet clothes and fell into the bunk, exhausted. The job I'd just done would only have taken a couple of minutes in calm weather. As it was, I'd been out there for over half an hour. My arms, legs and chest were stiff and sore. Even a minor, self-inflicted problem had sapped my strength. I wondered how I'd get on if I needed to go out again now to do something else. The motion on a small boat made the simplest physical things a struggle, things like pulling on a jacket, moving down the cabin, maintaining balance, controlling my own limbs. It was as if the ocean were stripping me of the things which made me human.

Mid morning on the following day the wind backed through ninety degrees and increased to fifty knots. There was a period of heavy rain, and cloud to sea level. Then, with the new wind, the rain stopped and a sheet of grey cloud again raced overhead. The south-west wind was bringing a new swell at right-angles to the first, causing the boat to roll on a difficult cross-sea. In the cockpit I hung from the steel hoop of the spray-hood, supposedly asserting my role as skipper, my legs braced out to either side so that my limbs formed a letter X. I kept it up for ten minutes, but there was nothing for me to do so I climbed back to the cabin. I wedged myself into the bunk with sail bags and cushions until I was packed in tight, but I was soon sore on my back and stomach from the pressure of each roll.

An hour later I felt the boat rise to the next wave and track down the face, but then lose its way and slew round to the port side. The tinned stores beneath the bunks crashed with the force. I heard glass jars smashing. The roll was all one way now, the weight always on my stomach. The boat was no longer sailing downwind, but sideways-on to the swells, fully exposed to the sea, most vulnerable to being knocked down. I jumped out of the bunk and stared out of the narrow cabin window. I couldn't angle my head to see the top of the next swell as it approached, but a few seconds later the boat lurched over the top. I climbed to the cockpit in oilskins and harness. The boat was wallowing in a long grey trough. I leant over the transom. The fibre-glass paddle of the self-steering gear had split off the aluminium pole, perhaps weakened by the force of the cross-swell. Hanging head first over the back of the boat, I took the pin out of the stock of the paddle. The boat pitched and the sea slopped up over my head. Once the paddle was disconnected I wriggled backwards up into the boat, then sat spluttering on the cockpit sole nursing the broken paddle. It was useless, and the self-steering wouldn't work without it. I did have a second paddle, and three times tried to fit it, but sliding the old one off was much easier than sliding a new one on, with the sea slopping into my face every few minutes. I couldn't do it. My ribs ached with bruises when I finally slid back into the cockpit. Worried about the boat lying broadside to the seas, I started to hand steer.

Self-steering was something I had long taken for granted. I use an Aries vane gear, a mechanical device that steers the boat relative to the wind in virtually all conditions. Vane steering makes a boat an almost independent entity, powered and steered by the wind, sailing over the horizon. When I was steering by hand the Southern Ocean shrank to a very simple place, with my own struggles at its centre.

I sat at the tiller all that day with my legs braced across the cockpit. They locked stiff and solid: I'd become a piece of machinery, only there to do a job of work. I lit cigarettes often, and if I was lucky smoked them down to the filter before the spray or rain destroyed them. My teeth began to chatter and chew on the filter. I didn't bother with the compass. My course was determined by the seas. I'd never seen the boat roll so far, scooping up water on each side-deck. My arms ached, my fingers went numb. Time passed. I'd now become that caricature from the movies, the figure in oilskins fighting with the helm while water is thrown across his back. But the sea is still different from the cinema image. The waves are smaller, but longer. Crests break down the faces of the same wave and reform, the whole surface lacerated by the wind into lines of white spume. Sometimes it seemed impossible that I'd ever found my way to this desolate corner of the earth, son of a chartered accountant and a lawyer from Birmingham. This was the furthest place imaginable from everything I'd been destined to know. And as I sat shivering at the tiller that afternoon, I wondered if the Southern Ocean might see it as part of its own destiny that one day we would know our planet so well that people like me would come here. I have no time for such thoughts now. I don't believe it's possible to have a relationship with the sea. But those were my thoughts at the time.

As night fell the wind eased. It was still gale-force but the seas were breaking more harmlessly, and the cross-swell had evened out. I sat blackly locked into my own small world. My role was simple and I understood everything: I either pulled or pushed on the tiller. The night was empty, but structured none the less. I knew that in the morning this would come to an end. By morning the seas could have moderated and I'd be able to leave the boat to lie ahull. I could sleep, then replace the paddle, and normality would return. In my exhaustion, dawn had become the only end in sight. The passage seemed to be all but over. Only a few more hours and I would arrive. That night was filled with time in a way that hadn't happened before on the voyage. Through the darkness and diminishing spray I watched the hands crawl around the face of my watch. The ocean was an easier place.

In the gale, time became real. The hours had purpose: I gauged the development of the depression against them, and my own failing strength. With time as my measuring-board, ocean life was quantifiable. But when the weather returned to normal the sea opened up around me. Then its true character was restored.

Time at sea is slippery. On the ocean everything shifts, it slides and mingles and becomes part of something new. The world afloat is governed by a different sort of timepiece, an ocean pendulum that sometimes stops altogether. I live in a drawn-out and dateless world, one punctuated perhaps by light and dark, but rarely by anything so concrete as night and day.

The poet Derek Walcott wrote 'The sea is history'. In the Southern Ocean I found it hard to locate myself in any meaningful concept of the present. It was the past that was often the clearest thing in view. On the ocean I feel that I am a part of history. I liken the water to a vast, unwieldy tapestry wrapped around most of the earth. The tapestry is made up of thousands of separate strands. Some strands are gold thread, some silk, some cotton, some are bold and strong, others frayed and tatty. The ocean tapestry has been woven into being by everyone who has ever been here, but also by those who have simply looked and wondered. It is an inclusive cloth. And just a few of those strands are mine, bound up with Greek cosmologers, medieval map-makers, poets, and whalers. Along the coastline the cloth is thick and heavy, in places stiff with understanding. But on the furthest oceans of the south it is threadbare, sometimes just a few lonely strands and nothing in between. There are other gaps too – holes, in fact. History at sea hasn't been continuous. There have been times when the ocean was ignored or discounted, others when speculation about what lay beyond home waters, and especially at the bottom of the world, was a dangerous activity.

Virgilius, Bishop of Salzburg, was condemned as a heretic in the eighth century for suggesting the Antipodes could be inhab-ited. Christian teaching stated that after the Flood the habitable world was divided into three continents, one for each of Noah's three sons. Shem got Asia, Japheth Africa and Ham Europe. The southern hemisphere did not exist. A medieval Spanish Benedictine abbot, Beatus of Liebana, wrote in his commentary on the Apocalypse of St John: 'The Southern zone ... is un-known to the sons of Adam. It has no links to our race. No human eye has seen it. Access is barred to men, and the sun makes it impossible to enter this region.'

An early Christian map of the world was drawn by a monk named Cosmas Indicopleustes in the sixth century. Cosmas tried to interpret the Bible physically, and portrayed the earth as a rec-tangular box representing the Tabernacle of Moses. Cosmas believed that on the underside of the earth, beyond the known oceans, there was another world where humans had lived before the Flood. This continent was now uninhabited and unreachable and the oceans surrounding it were on fire, shrouded in a mist of poisonous gas.

★

It took ten days at sea, and a gale, before I began to feel at home in the south. Those ten days were spent trying to adjust to life in the empty ocean realm. I once met a French single-handed sailor in the Marquesas who told me that the English did not understand the sea. 'For you, a seaman is someone who can tie knots and knows when to fly each flag. The sea is a place of rules and traditions. But in French a seaman, *un marin*, is someone who knows the sea and understands how to live here.' The Frenchman said these words as he served me a large gruyère and tender taro-leaf omelette in Hiva Oa. It was the first fresh food I had had in weeks. As I began to eat he took a box from a locker beneath my feet. I could see several small bottles inside. He pulled a piece of paper from between the bottles to show me. It was a hand-drawn map of the world, not a very good one as it appeared that India had originally been omitted, then squeezed onto an already crowded Indian Ocean. The map was marked with twelve prominent crosses. This box and its contents had been a *bon voyage* gift from his father: twelve half-bottles of vintage brandy, one to be drunk when each of the twelve way-points on this journey around the world was reached.

The Frenchman now took a bottle from the box and un-corked it. He poured us both a glass. I studied the map again, but although there was a cross at Tahiti, another seven hundred miles to the south-west, I could see no indication that a bottle was sup-posed to be drunk here in the Marquesas. He smiled, and showed me the contents of the box more clearly. He was not yet half-way round the world, but only three bottles remained. He said, 'But father was also *un marin*. At sea you must live completely in the present. There is nothing beyond the horizon. Learn to be content with what you have. My father would be proud of me, I think. *Salut!*' Later that evening, while he was preparing to open another of the bottles of brandy, I asked my host what he would do when they had all been finished. At this rate he would still be in the Pacific. He looked at me through watery eyes and said, 'Actually, you know, I finished all twelve bottles in the Atlantic. I bought these in Martinique. If you knew anything about brandy you would know that this stuff is not vintage. At sea, only the moment is important.'

But the French guy made it sound easy. You can learn knots and flags from books. Learning to live at sea, learning to find peace in the present moment only, is a process that must be renegotiated with each new voyage. I guess the brandy helped the French sailor.

There are two ways of looking at the routine of my daily life in the Southern Ocean. There was the superficial routine, the one I thought I followed; and there was the routine I actually kept.

I thought I had devised a detailed timetable of tasks to take care of the necessities of life and provide a minimum of variety: preparing food and numerous drinks; writing a log; navigation; Spanish lessons; reading; certain programmes on the radio. These tasks could usually be completed regardless of sea conditions (there were one or two other pastimes, like my on-going darts tournament, that were weather-dependent). I wanted to keep to this timetable strictly, not as an act of mindless regimen but as a tiny act of defiance. In the fluid ocean world precision was a luxury, and a statement of autonomy. Like finding a small flower in the desert, I cherished the arrival of each appointed hour.

But the routine I actually kept wasn't like this. When the appointed hour arrived I sometimes did not notice it, and failed to progress to the next activity.

At sea, alone, I was always sailing the boat. In reality I was focused on the wind and waves even when cooking, or writing, or drilling Spanish question forms. Certainly while sleeping. When I started sailing I might have called this 'vigilance', just the sort of stuff that good seamanship is made of, and so on. But now I don't believe 'vigilance' is the correct term. In the Southern

Ocean I saw no ships between New Zealand and Chile. Changes in the weather were rarely sudden. There was no need for me to check on the sea and wind all the time. If the weather changed or the boat went off-course, it was obvious quickly enough from the altered motion. Most times, when I abandoned my books for the cockpit there was nothing for me to *do*. I simply stared at the sea, reassured myself that the boat was moving at its best speed, that the passage ahead was getting shorter. Hours passed like this: watching the waves, keeping an eye on the ocean, oblivious of the task I was engaged in before. I cannot give a narrative account of the time I spent in the south. There is no seam of events that I can trace from dawn through to dusk each day. Time was a patchwork of experience, of tasks begun and then forgotten, hot drinks rediscovered once they'd gone cold. If I could build a collage of snapshots of my daily life it would show me reading and writing and listening and cooking; but these images would be lonely pockets of detail in an otherwise empty canvas of sea and sky. When people say, 'Yeah, yeah, but what did you actually *do* all day at sea?' I still have to reply, 'I just don't know.' The sea is a thief.

For days at a time in the Roaring Forties, the wind was in the north-west. For most of the passage my course lay sandwiched between the South Pacific high, and depressions tracking across the Southern Ocean. With the depressions further south, the high dominated, giving trade-wind-like conditions, but the sea spray was cold and the ocean sparkled beneath a deep blue sky. When the depressions tracked further north, the sky clouded over and a blustery northerly brought rain. This wind usually shifted to the north-west after a couple of days, but only occasionally backed west or south.

I kept the wind on the port quarter, so my course was mostly south-east or east. With a double-reefed mainsail and a part-furled genoa the boat would run 140 miles in twenty-four hours, making deep rolls to starboard at the bottom of each sea. My bunk was on the port side, so at night I hung in the lee cloth, which was comfortable. During the day, to read, I lay on the starboard bunk with my legs curled up, because the foot-box was stowed with gear. The companionway was always closed to keep out the spray. But when the weather was fine, wearing oilskins, I could stand in the cockpit, holding the steel handles on the spray-hood, breathing deep as the boat rolled with the seas and chased cloud shadow over the horizon. I prized these times above all others, and felt defeated when a new bank of wet cloud moved in from the north and I was driven back into the cabin by the first drops of rain.

It had been raining hard for two days when I first noticed a new sound on the boat. From somewhere indistinct I heard a *twang*. The knock of tins which had rolled loose or of other gear buried in lockers was a common interruption. But this sound had a resonant, vibrating quality I didn't recognise. I'd been reading on the starboard bunk for some time, and my legs felt cold and stiff. I guessed the noise was coming from the rigging, so got dressed and climbed to the cockpit. The sea was smothered in mist and rain. The wind was gusty and the boat's roll steep. The only noise was the rush of wind and sea, and an occasional crack from the deep reef hanging off the boom. But I could hear no *twang*, and nothing was amiss in the rig.

I climbed back into the cabin and closed the hatch. I pulled off my wet clothes and lay back down on the bunk. I'd read a page of my book before I heard the sound again. I tried to trace the source of the noise, but it was difficult. At sea the cabin becomes a sound-box, a place where noises echo inside the shell of the boat, and their significance is amplified by an unoccupied mind. The *twang* seemed to be coming from somewhere overhead, but even this was difficult to assess because when the boat rolled, the floor and ceiling became the walls. 'Up' and 'down' were not clearly defined.

I tried to read the pattern of wind and motion around the twanging noise. The sound was not regular. A minute or two might pass before it recurred. And it was a single sound: things which are rolling, like tins, knock in both directions as the boat rolls. But I only heard this sound when the boat came back upright, and only after the deepest rolls. I started searching in the toilet compartment. There were spray cans here which I thought could account for the higher pitched, hollow sound if they were rolling from side to side. But the cans were all wedged in place. I watched them quite stationary as the *twang* continued, louder now I thought. I went back to the bunk for a few minutes, and then climbed back to the deck, wondering if I'd left a winch handle at the mast-step that was sliding around.

This went on all morning, and most of the afternoon. In the cabin I could focus on nothing else. The noise seemed to get louder, drilling deeper into my head. But each time I climbed to the deck and heard the rush of wind across limitless space, the memory of the twanging sound seemed a trivial concoction of my mind. I crawled up to the stemhead to check the anchor lashings, tied back the halyards, but it was a lousy day with heavy rain and a short time on deck was usually enough to convince me that nothing serious was wrong. Over the course of the morning I emptied everything from beneath the bunks in the forepeak: the main cabin floor was wedged with storm sails, bags of parts, bags of junk, and a thousand feet of warp. I felt with my fingers all over the inside of the hull, and then of the ceiling, as the sound still seemed to be somewhere high up, but there was really nothing here that could move.

In the afternoon I started on the lockers opposite the lavatory. These had been hanging lockers, but I'd divided them up with shelves on my last voyage. I pulled everything out and stacked it on the cabin sole, except for two anchors that were lashed to the bulkheads. Then I put it all back again. Then, after another ten minutes on the bunk with a book, I decided that the sound was definitely coming from those lockers, so I pulled everything out a second time. Then I felt carefully all around the hull and bulkheads. Near the tops of the bulkheads I thought I could feel a small vibration each time I heard the *twang*. When I moved my hands beneath the side-deck it grew stronger, and when I touched the chainplate there was a clear buzzing sensation each time I heard the sound. I raced back up to the cockpit. The chainplate in question anchored the cap-shroud, the length of wire running from the side-deck to the top of the mast. I watched the shroud for some time, but nothing seemed to change. Then, on a long roll to starboard, I saw it: one of the plastic discs that sit on the shrouds to protect the sail at the spreaders rode up the wire stay about a metre, pushed by the wind; then, as the boat came upright, fell back down the stay and hit the spreader. The disc was only four centimetres in diameter, but it was thick, and though standing on the breezy deck I could hear no sound, I knew that this was what had been resonating around the cabin. I climbed up to the mast-step and flicked a spare halyard round the spreader, to keep the disc pinned down against it (the tape that had been doing this previously had fallen off). When I got back to the cabin and again lay down with a book there was little satisfaction at having finally traced the source of the *twang*. I'd spent almost a whole day searching for something quite unimportant.

This sort of wild-goose chase was repeated many times on the voyage. The sounds of the ocean were one of my guides in trying to understand my environment. Sound is a constant at sea. Silence is impossible. If only subconsciously, I was always listening.

From the deck, the sound of the north-west wind became a dull throb. It rose from somewhere beneath the horizon and swept tunelessly over the ocean. In this barren sound I found my greatest comfort in the south: the wind spoke of constant and easy progress to the east. I dreaded hearing a change in the note of its drone.

The sea itself, the water, made little noise. Waves slopped

around the transom, and heavy gobs of spray landed on the teak in the cockpit. I rarely heard the sound of the seas approaching. Individual waves just became part of that oceanic sound, the great rush that took away my breath when I pulled back the hatch at night and again felt the force of global exposure.

Inside the cabin, these sounds were lost. In fact, it never failed to surprise me that plywood washboards and a teak hatch could so effectively shut out the great roving sounds of the ocean outside the boat, and make of the cabin a separate world of noises. The sound of the wind reached in here through the whine of the wind-generator climbing and subsiding with the gusts. Sound in the cabin was strangely dislocated, an abstract reflection of the passage of a small boat under sail. With the hatch closed, the wind was almost inaudible. Instead, I could only hear progress, a long, gurgling *whoosh* as the boat rode down the face of each sea and bubbles raced upward round the wine-glass-shaped section of the hull. Sometimes, when the boat was reaching in breaking seas, a crest would shatter with a great *whump* into its side, and wherever I was, I felt my body stiffen with alarm. But these were exceptions. In most conditions, the sound of a yacht sailing off the wind in long seas is quite benign, like a child sliding backwards and forwards in the bath. My perception of the marine world was based on this sound. It varied only a little. It was a sound that conveyed limited information, a simple note on which the more subtle sounds of the ocean were built.

Some sounds heard from inside the cabin were identifiable. As the wind rose the main halyard started to bang against the mast. The other halyards were wound between the mast steps to prevent this, or occasionally tied back, but I left the main halyard free to warn of rising winds. It was a heavy rope, and the sound of it beating woke me from the deepest sleep, a warning bell from the watch-tower. The creak of the self-steering lines on their blocks was different; it rose in pitch slowly over several days, at first an anguished yelp, then desperate, until I was driven from

45

my bunk, usually barefoot in the middle of the night, with a can of oil for the blocks.

Other sounds had a less obvious source. Like the *twang* of the disc falling on the spreaders, these appeared from nowhere and stole my concentration. They were minor irritations that could grow out of all proportion. Over the first days of the passage I tried to minimise the potential for these stray intrusions into the rhythms of the sea. I found the tins that were rolling in the lockers and restacked them so they wouldn't budge. Then I found the AA-size battery that every ten seconds was knocking as the boat rolled. It was in a small plastic jar inside a plastic box beneath some engine filters, some sailcloth and a bag of toilet parts, at the bottom of the third locker I emptied. I best understood the random nature of the sea when the contents of a locker that had been bedded down and silent for three weeks suddenly started to knock. I have a friend who refuses to be annoyed by such things. When one of these stray tapping sounds begins he deliberately puts a coffee jar on its side in a locker and pulls the towel out of the cutlery drawer, so that no single sound is distinct and irritating, and together they blend into the fabric of ocean life.

I cannot do this. It's not the noise itself that obsesses me and keeps me chasing around the boat, but the need to trace its source. It is the unknown that's unnerving at sea.

Three

I WOKE EARLY one morning with a start. The wind had been dying when I'd last looked out, and the sounds in the cabin had been only slight: the rustle of water flowing around the hull and an occasional *snap* when the leech of the headsail collapsed and re-set in the westerly breeze. Otherwise, inside the cabin, it had been quite still, my troublesome stores finally at rest in the lockers all around.

But when I woke that morning I heard a number of stray sounds: a pencil was rolling on the chart table; the bowls were clanking; a CD was sliding on the floor; the cutlery was restless in its drawer. Then the boat gave a heavy jar as the mainsail crashed for want of wind. I pulled open the hatch and climbed out into the cockpit. There was no rush of air. The morning light was weak through wet cloud, the sun hidden from view. I looked at the compass. The wind was still in the west, but now very light.

Over the course of that morning the wind veered 180°, and a fifteen-knot easterly set in. A headwind. I sheeted in the sails and made the best course I could south-south-east, the boat pitching bluntly and rolling through an uneasy heel in the lumpy sea. I went back to bed. Perhaps a front would go through, and by the time I woke the old pattern of north-westerlies would have returned.

But the barometer was falling and the wind rose steadily throughout that morning. By midday it was blowing a gale from the east. I stripped the sails from the rig and ran off to the west, trailing the drogue anchor, back the way I had come.

I hate going backwards at sea. I've only been forced to run off before a gale three times, and I remember each occasion with a particular malevolence. I sat for most of that afternoon on the engine box, throwing darts. I took to my bed before it was even dark. A voyage is a fragile thing. It is only a line across the water: a line of wake which disappears seconds behind the boat, and a line of intention ahead which is as long and strong as the sailor's will to impose it. A voyage is a belief that somewhere ahead, beyond the horizon days away, the destination is a real place, with an anchorage, a bar, and people. It was difficult to put these things on hold while the boat was blown backwards. Without progress the ocean was bedlam, only noise and motion, no direction.

The gale blew for two nights. I ran a hundred and seventy miles back towards New Zealand. During that time I left my bunk only a handful of times. I drank water from a mug and ate dried fruit, but only a little of both. Each sticky meal was an effort. In my bunk I read, and listened to audio books. I gave up the Spanish lessons. Mostly I dozed. My ears grew red and sore from contact with the damp pillow.

Before light on the third day the north-easterly moderated to twenty-five knots. I slept deeply for several hours, then shipped the drogue and set a course to the south. The wind gusted to gale force several times over the next four days as the wind backed round to the north. Before this latest trough passed overhead I had spent the previous week of the passage sailing east between 45° and 48° south latitude; now I was well below the iceberg limit and still being pushed further south by the north wind.

The weather grew colder. The sky was still grey, but the sodden woolliness cracked and went still. I watched the block-like seas jumbled around the boat and wondered how drift ice would look among them. When I reefed the mainsail the fabric folded into sharp creases as it had when new. I warmed my hands on the kettle after working the sails.

After four days I was at 52° south latitude. Then the wind eased and backed into the west. When the wind and seas steadied I poled out the genoa and ran north-east. My mood was bright: I had passed the midway point between New Zealand and Chile and, as I saw it, was now sailing towards Patagonia rather than simply out to sea. As things turned out, 52° was the furthest south I would sail on the voyage. It didn't have a great significance at the time; it was just a point on the chart half-way across the ocean where I changed course and ate a panful of corned-beef hash.

My journey to this point in the Southern Ocean really began many years before I voyaged into the Pacific. In the English summer of 1984 a friend and I decided to run away to sea, as one does. We were nineteen, and none too smart. We bought a sixteen-foot open day-boat in Falmouth. The hull was fibreglass, rigged as a ketch, and the spars were pine. The rudder was hung in a well on the transom and could be replaced by a Seagull out-board. Our intention was to sail for Africa (I can't be certain, but I think this was my idea). My companion was called Bill, and our friendship was founded on a strict demarcation of roles. I was responsible for having hare-brained ideas, and for breaking things; Bill goodnaturedly repaired the things I broke, and generally tried to tame my romantic excesses. My navigation was accurate, though, and we arrived neatly off the Brest Peninsula after a thirty-six-hour passage across the English Channel. We anchored in the river at L'Aber Wrach.

Over the next six weeks we followed the French coast south, intending eventually to reach Spain and Portugal and so cross the Strait of Gibraltar. On the southern part of the French coast, between the Gironde and the Spanish border, the coastline is an empty stretch of dunes. The first section is a naval firing range, then you reach a village named Contisplage. There are holiday homes here, a few clubs, a stream enters the sea between two retaining walls, and there is a light.

It was off Contisplage that Bill and I got into trouble. We had intended to spend that night at sea, but the wind was strong from the west and we became nervous. Foolishly, we closed the shore in breaking seas, hoping to enter the stream and find shelter. The boat was pitch-poled in the surf, throwing the two of us into shallow water. Both masts were destroyed as the boat went end-over-end, and part of the foredeck was ripped from the hull as it was driven into the hard sand bottom. Rather disoriented, we dragged the swamped hull up on to the beach, then searched the waves for our belongings, as sunbathers sat up from their towels and stared blinking at us in astonishment.

We lived on the beach for five days, and received faithful help from a local man named Louic. Bill made two new masts for the boat, and we were able to replace most of the things we had lost. From Contisplage we sailed to Biarritz, then on to the Basque coast of Spain. But the summer was coming to an end now, and the weather was changeable. It rained a lot. In Santander we decided to give it up, and sold the boat to a dapper man in a sports car. I've never been able to picture him taking that battered little boat out for a sail, and suspect he just felt sorry for us. From Santander we caught the ferry back to Plymouth.

The voyage we made that summer was inspired by Edgar Allen Poe's novel *The Narrative of Arthur Gordon Pym of Nantucket*. Poe's yarn tells of two boys, Arthur and his friend Augustus, who get drunk and run away to sea in an open boat. Augustus soon falls into an alcoholic stupor, and the boat is caught in a gale. The sails are carried away. The boat is swamped by the seas. Arthur lashes his comatose friend to a ring-bolt, expecting the worst. All is well, though. The boat is run down by a passing whaleship, and the boys are resuscitated with flannels soaked in hot oil. Both make it home in time for breakfast, and their parents are none the wiser.

On a later voyage Augustus dies and is eaten by maggots, but Arthur sails on into Antarctic waters, further south than any ship previously. The sun is surprisingly strong. The ocean is calm. There is no ice in sight. The temperature rises and the current sets to the south. Close to the South Pole, Arthur discovers a temperate land peopled by black natives who speak Arabic. His crew is butchered by these Tsalalians, but Arthur manages to steal a canoe and continue towards the Pole. The sea temperature rises until it scalds his hand. The current carries him ever more quickly to the south. Finally, Arthur approaches the last white curtain and the canoe is swept over a vast cataract, inside a hollow earth.

Poe's fantasy about the South Pole was written in 1838, when the far South was the 'final frontier' of global exploration. The exact dimensions of Antarctica were unknown, although stretches of the icy coast had been encountered. Poe's story was partly inspired by real discoveries. In February 1823 a sealship had reached a latitude of 74°15′, nearly two hundred nautical miles further south than any previous voyage. The captain, James Weddell, recorded with astonishment that 'NOT A PARTICLE OF ICE OF ANY DESCRIPTION WAS TO BE SEEN. The evening was mild and serene ... our carpenter was employed in repairing the boat, and we were able to make several repairs on sails and rigging.' Weddell sailed to within 855 miles of the Pole, and saw no land. He observed a south-setting current of thirty miles within three days, and calculated that the sea temperature was probably rising. Weddell believed the South Pole to be open water.

Poe was determined that the earth should reveal one final secret before planetary exploration came to an end, so he also tapped in to the hollow-earth theory known as 'Symmes' Hole', the creation of John Cleves Symmes of Ohio, who resurrected the medieval notion that the earth was hollow, and open at both poles. Symmes supposed an opening four thousand miles wide at the North Pole and six thousand miles wide at the South Pole.

Symmes' Hole was a drawing-room joke throughout the 1820s, but widely publicised. He sent to 'institutions of learning' throughout America and Europe a letter in which he pledged his life in support of the theory that the earth was 'hollow and inhabitable within'. In 1822 he petitioned the US Congress to send an exploring expedition to test his theory. Symmes received twenty-five votes of support.

Edgar Allen Poe was not the first to speculate about polar openings. Margaret Cavendish's *Blazing World*, published in 1666, describes a journey inside the earth. The eighteenth-century *Voyage de Nicolas Klimius* is an account of a journey from the North to the South Poles, via the centre of the earth. One related piece of frippery concerns a sailor's myth. Nineteenth-century mariners believed in a paradise known as 'Fiddler's Green', only accessible to sailors with fifty years' experience at sea. When they die, these old salts are transformed into gulls and fly to the South Pole, where they enter a hatch spinning with the earth's revolutions and fly inside the planet. Fiddler's Green has pubs on every corner and free ale, tobacco, steak pie and plum duff.

The American Koreshanity sect believe we are already living inside a hollow earth. Their leader, Cyrus Reed Teed of Utica, New York State, drew inverted maps of this inside-universe. The outer world was destroyed in an apocalypse, and the few survivors made an epic voyage to the South Pole in order to gain sanctuary within. The far south is both the gateway to the new world, and our last memory of the old.

Below the fiftieth parallel I enjoyed some of the finest weather on the passage. The wind stayed in the west for many days. The sun was strong; I could wear shirt-sleeves on deck at midday when the spring wind was light. The cockpit was always dry. But

I was distrustful at first, gloomily predicting that the rain and gales would soon return, determined not to accept that the weather could be as good as it looked. I kept my hat and jacket on, and refused to wear sunglasses. But when the fine weather held through the first night and continued the following morning, I was obliged to accept my good luck.

The seas were slight, the water a bluish green, the surface a little oily in the sun: a slick of heavy, calm water seemed to surround the boat. I opened both hatches and all the locker doors, and let the cool breeze flow through the fetid confines of the cabin. I took a saltwater bath in the cockpit, changed my clothes, brushed my teeth. I counted my remaining apples, oranges and potatoes. Some of the carrots tasted of diesel. Three butternut pumpkins were dusted with a light mould on the outside of their thick skins. I placed them, and the carrots, on the cockpit bench and re-crossed the fifty-first parallel, my vegetables drying in the sun. This was an easy place to be.

The westerly breeze continued for three days and I made steady progress to the north-east, the wind on the quarter, the genoa poled out. But during that third night the wind began to fail. I was kept awake till the small hours by the crash and jar of the sails collapsing; many times I climbed to the deck to make small adjustments to the course or rig, but nothing worked. At 2 a.m. the wind died altogether. I furled the genoa, and dropped the mainsail to the deck. With the main lying all over the coach-roof I'd soon be woken by it flapping if the breeze returned. But I slept longer and deeper than I had so far on the three-week passage, and woke long after the sun had risen. The mainsail was not even twitching on the deck. There was no cloud in the sky, and not a breath of wind.

I felt drugged and stupid, unaccustomed to such a deep sleep. I sat for some time on the cockpit bench, trying to adjust to a place where the sun was now burning my neck and the sea was smooth; most of all I needed to adjust to the silence, which was complete except for the slight sounds of water moving against the hull as the boat repeatedly lifted and eased into position on the sea. My first impression that morning had been that the sea was flat, but the boat's gentle movements gave the lie to this. The sea was flat in relative terms, compared to its state over the preceding weeks: for most of that time, had I dropped the sails and so taken the balancing force out of the rig, the boat would have been thrown around with such force as to prevent me standing upright. And even today, when the breeze was imperceptible and the surface of the water without a ripple, the sea was not completely flat. It never is. As I sat in the cockpit I saw slight mounds appear in the water, gentle humps that swelled and subsided. Those that formed beside the boat caused it to lean, then flop lazily back upright. There was no pattern to the movement of the sea: the water was simply going up and down, very slowly, very slightly.

One feature of calm waters in mid ocean is that the sea suddenly becomes such a very big place; the tiny stretch of water that you can see around you at any one time is so obviously connected, a part of something vastly bigger. The wind might have failed here, but somewhere to the north there's a steady trade, and elsewhere a gale. When calm, the sea becomes a messenger from other places. You can feel these forces transmitted through the water from far away, as bulges and swellings spread over the surface and push the boat sideways; you can feel both the high-latitude gale and the tropical trade, at the same time that your own breath feels intrusive in the still sky. The sea is most powerful in a dead calm: when the water is smooth it has a global quality, a sense of there being just one planetary ocean that it is impossible for the sailor to ever truly cross.

The sea always has shape, but the shape of water is difficult to describe when it forms and reforms so quickly. I've seldom seen regular lines of swell lying uniformly across the open ocean, as one does at the beach. Sometimes, far offshore, running before strong winds, I look sideways from the cockpit and get a clear view along the bottom of the trough of a single wave for a hundred metres or more. But that's unusual. Waves don't come in neat lines. The peaks especially are hard to trace for any distance. Different sections of the peak are building at different rates; if they break, they do so at different stages, so that whenever you look there's usually one part of the wave which is bursting forwards in white water, given a strong enough wind. As the peak passes beneath the boat and you are for that fleeting moment high enough to get a view out over open water towards the horizon, the swells don't present themselves in ranks marching towards you. From the deck of a small boat the sea appears to be patterned in a series of interlinked crescents, like fish scales, each one independent and surging forwards in bursts, then falling back as its neighbour temporarily takes the lead. The wave pattern can appear random, especially from a viewpoint that rarely sees the whole picture; but when you do catch a sight of a stretch of ocean from the crest of a sea, the fish-scale waves marching forwards, autonomous but arm-in-arm, you see that there is a single, repeated pattern at sea that binds together thousands of square miles of water.

The pattern of the waves is a part of what gives shape to water, but in fact it's not what I see first when I try to capture in my mind the shape of the ocean. I look at waves from a practical point of view: the size and shape of the sea tell me the wind strength and sea state, how much sail to carry and what course to steer. The waves carry information I need, but give only a limited sense of identity to the larger world of the sea.

A more lasting image of the shape of the sea is the outline of the horizon. The horizon should be a very simple shape: it is a fixed geometrical form, and the sea from a boat should appear only as a flat disc. Perhaps the outline of the horizon is more lasting than any other image because sometimes the sea does *not* appear as a flat disc.

As I sat in the cockpit that morning, just north of the forty-ninth parallel, with the sails on deck and the boat moving only slightly on a bulging sea, the horizon on every side of the boat had sharp edges. I've seen pentagons and octagons at sea, but most often the ocean is shaped as it was today, as a rectangle, with the long sides at right-angles to the rays of the sun. The ocean has four corners, and it slopes even when calm. The rectangle is tilted along a broken axis; it's not a uniform slope, as creases swell to the surface and fluid contours shift and mingle, like the isobars of an evolving weather map. From the cockpit I looked up the slope of this oceanic meadow towards the sun, and could trace the boat's shadow downhill.

No doubt if I'd blinked once or twice and shaken my head, I could have pushed this trick of perspective from my vision and again been surrounded by a flat disc of sea. In the first days of the passage I would probably have done this: forced myself to perceive the ocean according to the rules of how it must be. But I reach a point on passage, usually when I've given up hope of ever doing so, when I cease to care if the sea does not conform and just accept it the way it appears to be.

In the calm I spent less time staring at the water. Instead, I cranked up the stereo, cleaned the toilet and scrubbed the vegetable baskets. I siphoned water from jerry-cans into the main tank, cleaned the stove and filled it with paraffin. I spent the day in housework, and the shifting, swelling water around the boat was littered with dust and rotting onion skins. After three weeks in the south I had learnt to accept that the sailor, from his boat, sees very little of the true shape of the sea. I picture myself on the ocean as a man stumbling about, holding back-to-front binoculars to his eyes, trying to see the world. I tell myself I've read the pattern, I've seen the fish-scales marching forwards across a rectangular seascape, and I hold this close as a cherished discovery. At the same time, I sail blindly over waters five thousand metres deep, of which I know nothing. The sailor is a surface-dweller, who understands surface patterns. I see the ocean in only two dimensions, and kid myself I've seen its shape and read the global forces stirring deep below my feet.

I can't remember the very first time I stepped onto a sailing-boat. It probably wasn't an event that was imbued with great significance at the time. My father was born in Jersey and lived on the island until he got married, when he came to England. There was always a dinghy in the garage at home, and every summer of my childhood we went to stay with my grandparents in the Channel Islands. Their cottage was on the beach beside the slipway at Le Bourg. There was always a dinghy in the garage there, too. We launched it from the slipway at high tide, or could bounce the trailer over the smooth, round stones beneath the slip a couple of hours either side of high water. A mile offshore there were two Martello towers, Seymour and Icho, and we sailed in the area between the towers – or the castles, as I thought of them – and the beach. It was usually a tranquil area, the sea a brownish green. On clear days the bare coast of Normandy was visible twenty miles to the east.

In their own way these were some of the more dramatic waters I've sailed in. The tidal range here is high, twenty-five feet at springs. The sea-bed shelves only very slowly and is strewn with craggy rock formations and unlikely pinnacles. At high tide only a few rocky peaks appear above the water, stained white from the gulls. But at low tide the sea-bed as far out as the Martello towers is dry, except for rock pools and a salt-water stream filled with kelp.

There was sufficient water to sail a dinghy for about four hours at the top of each tide. Taking great care to avoid the drying rocks, you could sail for a little longer than this. I never took much care, and at half tide watched rock spires and granite domes break the surface. Bouldery hillocks, covered in gulls, slid from behind the sails. If I forgot the consequences of staying out too long, which I managed to do with alarming frequency, the dinghy ran bumpily aground on some rock half a mile offshore, and I had to wade home up the salt-water stream, the ebb tide and kelp flowing round my thighs, towing the dinghy behind me. I never saw anyone else doing this but still, by some trick of a child's mind, took it to be the norm with sailing: if you stayed out on the sea long enough, a hidden landscape rose from beneath the water all around the boat.

Apparently, Christopher Columbus saw his voyage to the Caribbean in 1492 as a re-creation of the story of Jason and the Argonauts, with himself as Jason and Queen Isabella as Medea. In fact, when I read accounts of the voyages of the Age of Discovery which brought Europeans into the Pacific for the first time, I found that Columbus wasn't alone in associating sea travel with child-like fantasies.

Sixteenth-century sailors inherited a bizarre view of the world. Renaissance Europe was awash with stories about the ocean and of sea-crossings such as that of Jason and the Argonauts. Another popular collection was the *Thousand and One Nights*, which include the voyages of Sinbad the Sailor, who survives the most remarkable experiences at sea and returns home time and again with unimaginable wealth.

The cartography of preceding centuries raised the stakes: sailors might not only get rich, but were competing for the chance to fulfil human destiny and locate the terrestrial Paradise. Both the Cotton Map and the Catalan Atlas show Paradise in the south, raised up on great mountains or on a vast continent that circled the southern part of the globe. Medieval theologians believed that Paradise was somehow separate from the known world. Isodore of Seville saw the barrier as a wall of flames. The Venerable Bede believed it to be an impassable ocean: to arrive at Paradise took more than a physical journey – it required an act of baptism. The sailors of the Age of Discovery seemed best placed to fulfil the quest. They could now cross the burning seas of the equatorial doldrums and navigate the unknown Southern Ocean beyond. The baptism of sea travel would reveal the last and greatest prize to be found on earth.

Another feature on medieval maps was Ophir, the biblical land of Solomon's gold. The quest for Ophir took the Spanish sailors Mendaña and Quirós across the Pacific three times in the sixteenth and early seventeenth centuries, and gave a name to the Solomon Islands. On his final voyage in the Pacific Quirós made landfall south of the Solomons in 1606, and believed he had found part of the coastline of the mythical southern continent; he was actually in present day Vanuatu. Quirós described this place as Eden, and larger than even the wildest estimates, 'as great as all Europe and Asia ... A fifth part of the Terrestrial Globe.' The navigator summoned his crew before him, some three hundred souls from three ships, and founded the Order of Knights of the Holy Ghost, in which every one of them was included. He named the whole region, from the tropical islands to the South Pole, Austrialia del Espíritu Santo. The rivers were rich in emeralds, sapphires and chrysolites; nutmeg, pepper and cinnamon were plentiful.

The fact that Quirós drew on the idea of the Holy Spirit in his choice of name is not a coincidence. Quirós saw his Austrialia as a land of the future, a Paradise belonging to the final stage of history. Spanish explorers often had this idea. It was linked to the theologian Joachim, Abbot of Fiore in the late twelfth century. Joachim foretold a third and ultimate era on Earth, the Time of the Holy Spirit, when all races would live as one and the word of God would reach every continent and island. Christopher Columbus invoked the name of Joachim with each landfall and claimed that sea travel was his response to the influence of the Holy Spirit. Many Spanish explorers saw their voyages in the same light, as part of a Joachite push towards the last and perfect human age.

Quirós founded the city of New Jerusalem among the palm trees of the South Seas. He believed this would be humankind's final homeland. The long voyage back to Paradise had been accomplished.

When I read about the Age of Discovery, what impressed me more than the voyages themselves was the way that navigators simply imprinted their own mental geography onto the coastlines they found. For the first European sailors in the Pacific, 'place' was an ambiguous concept. The difficulties of accurately fixing their position and, I like to think, something about the very nature of sea travel and water, allowed these men to find an imaginary landscape.

I sailed north-east over the next three weeks, slowly climbing up the parallels of latitude. There were no more gales, though the north-west wind was a steady thirty knots for days at a time. There were two short calms, little more than a few hours each, but the sea was still running and the boat crashed around helplessly on the swells. Some days the sun was warm and the sky blue. Often, boiling cumulus rushed overhead from left to right. Inevitably, grey cloud surrounded the boat and the sails dripped in the drizzle. These were really the only events in the second half of the passage, and I duly entered them in the log.

Earlier in the voyage, when I'd been struggling to find my way at sea again, I had pictured this part of the Pacific in my mind and filled it with imaginary way-points. A hundred and two degrees of west longitude would mean I was three-quarters of the way across. Ninety degrees would be the start of the home run. I used longitude to calibrate a distance that was otherwise too great to conceptualise, and so divided the journey into more manageable chunks. But when I reached 102° West I completely failed to notice that an event of any importance had occurred. The sea continued unchanged, time was featureless. My notion of place was beginning to go hazy. I was simply on the sea, the global ocean, and the part I was on was no different from any other, no more significant. My world was my immediate environment: the wind, the state of the sea, the features of the sky, my books and language classes, darts, and the three remaining, now wrinkled, apples cushioned in tea-towels at the bottom of the fruit basket.

When I bought the boat and first went offshore, I had little interest in the sea itself. I saw the ocean as a road, a thing rather than a place, which would in time lead me to a new home. I had had no sense of direction on land. I was a drifter. I responded to some animal instinct to migrate but, not knowing where to go, I went to sea. Somewhere across the sea, I hoped, I would find a home.

But the further I sailed, the more I found that my attitude to the ocean changed. To drift at sea was impossible, drifting was oblivion. I've always had a course at sea: it's easy. Under sail, a sense of direction became part of the fabric of daily life. As I checked the compass, drew lines across the plotting sheet and calculated each day's run, I began to build a picture of the sea as a place, not just a road. I noticed the colours of the ocean, learned to recognise the sounds of a small hull moving through water, the texture of waves and the shape of the horizon. The sea was a place with characteristics peculiarly its own. Its colours, sounds and shapes changed over time, not distance. But wherever, and whenever, I was on the ocean, it was a place where I had a clear purpose: to sail the boat towards my chosen destination.

Going back to sea, after a long time ashore, was hard. But staying at sea was not. In the second part of the passage to Chile I found domestic bliss for the first time in my life. I nurtured my boat with almost parental concern, listening for stray sounds and passing sleepless nights in bad weather. I began a programme of housework when the weather allowed, scrubbing the bilge and the lockers beneath the bunks with salt water. Often I watched the sea, from the cockpit or through the cabin windows, and found easy reassurance that I was going somewhere. It was a quiet, largely uneventful life of books and hanging about. By the time I had climbed north-east up the chart of the South Pacific and closed the coast of Chile, I had learned that these things could be enough. I had started to feel at home on the sea.

Four

I MADE LANDFALL on the coast of Chilean Patagonia in mid December, after a six-week passage from New Zealand. Late in the morning I sighted Isla Guafo through the haze. It appeared as a mud-coloured hump, suspended above a strangely flat horizon. At sunset I passed very quietly to the south of the island, making no more than two knots in a failing southerly breeze. I sat in the cockpit, gazing at the thrashed and scrubby bush, the breakers on the rocky foreshore, and the dimly visible buildings at the lighthouse on the north point. With binoculars I explored the ridges and gullies, the way the land rose and fell, but never moved.

That night I sailed up the Golfo de Corcovado, a near-landlocked gulf that separates the mainland from Isla Chiloé. The night was pitch black, without moon or stars. In the evening I thought I'd be becalmed right here on the doorstep, but about midnight the wind freshened markedly from the south. Foam surged down the side-deck as I bore north-east up the Golfo. I didn't sleep that night, fuelled on a cocktail of caffeine, nicotine and racing excitement.

The dawn was very cold. On my left I saw the coast of Chiloé, a black strip hanging beneath wet cloud. In the cockpit I gulped breakfast between shivers. Finally the sun climbed over the Andean foothills and burned the cloud off the Golfo, and on my right I saw its rays shining on the snowy cone of Volcán Corcovado.

I spent that morning running up the coast of Chiloé in a thirty-knot southerly and strong sunshine. Early in the afternoon I entered the canal that leads up to the town of Castro, and worked slowly inland through green water, surrounded by rolling farmland.

After three hours I approached the final bend in the canal, Punta Peuque. The water was deep close to the point and I motored about ten metres from the shore. Large slabs of weathered rock jutted out over the water, shaded by pines. At the sound of my engine a dog ran out from the shadows and stood perched on the nearest bit of rock, barking at the boat. With each bark its tail dipped and its head jutted. I cut the engine revs right back, so that on the ebb tide the boat was almost stationary, ten metres from the dog's nose. I stayed here for some time, just listening to the dog's bark resonate under the trees and carry over the canal, both pitch and frequency perfectly regular. And it was only now, when I saw this dog's commonplace reaction to someone passing by, that I properly realised I'd made landfall at last.

I have a friend who believes that landfall is the defining moment of sea travel. She has sailed more than forty thousand miles in the Pacific, and likens landfall to rebirth. She believes that the emotional forces released by the act of making landfall can, with practice, be harnessed as agents of personal development. So with each landfall she strives to be reincarnated as herself, but minus some aspect of her personality which she has decided to ditch.

If this is true, and landfall is akin to rebirth, then in Chile I was born again as a Zombie. I don't even like dogs. In fact, I dislike them very much indeed. But I kept the boat in the same position for several minutes, the engine idling, the mast just clear of the pine branches, captivated by the sight and sound of the first land mammal I'd seen for a month and a half. I believe I even said something like, 'Hello, boy! Hello there! Where's home, then?' Normally I throw stones at dogs that bark at me.

This was how it continued for much of that afternoon and evening. Landfall found me stripped of any ability to discriminate, and each wonderful, inconsequential detail of life on land left me dumbstruck, with delight and gratitude, but also like a fool.

Once I got over my fascination with the barking dog I rounded Punta Peuque and got my first sight of the town of Castro at the head of the channel. The road south of the town was busy with traffic at the end of the working day. Horns peeped in the distance. A truck gunned its engine. I found the deepest satisfaction in listening to each one. A traffic jam snaked down the hill past some excavations: workmen waved the traffic through in clouds of dust. I waved back happily. Corrugated iron roofs were stacked chaotically up the hillside, ablaze in the low sun. On the wharf a handful of figures first stared, then smiled, as I motored past. I was grinning absurdly by this stage.

I anchored just beyond the wharf. There was that first perfect moment of complete calm. The air was thick, I could feel it not moving. I heard birds and insects all around me. I idled about the boat, coiling ropes and clearing up, aware for the first time in weeks that I was actually floating. At sea there's little sensation of being afloat; such delicacies are lost in the greater motion. Sometimes now, when I took a step, I compensated for a wave that never came, and moved about the boat in a series of clumsy lurches. I decided to sit down.

Along the shoreline rows of *palafito* houses extended over the water on stilts, their cypress timbers burning a rich red in the evening sun. Yellow skiffs were tied to railings outside the front doors. The tide was low and fishing boats were scattered along the silty beaches, lying heavily on their sides. Buff-necked ibis wandered through the shallows, wood smoke hung over the water like mist. On the far side of the canal, pastures and wood-land spread over gentle hills.

I took the dinghy in to the Armada compound and knocked on the office door with my passport and papers. Trim men with moustaches looked at my documents while I stood giggling in the courtyard. The land was humming, vibrating. I kept stamping on it. The officers occasionally lifted their eyes and smiled.

By this time I hadn't slept for thirty-six hours. I felt stiff, with aches and pains sunk deep in my body. There's a peculiar glamour to the tiredness that comes after the sea. The lack of sleep just serves to disguise something else. When you first step on land after a long passage, you realise that your body has changed. There's a swagger to your stride when you walk on land. At sea you've given a workout to muscles of balance and co-ordination that are employed nowhere else. You can stand upright in a world that heaves, and sleep while your muscles are still working against the roll. You have an agility, a set of physical skills, that aren't needed here on land. You have become, in some small way, a different kind of animal.

So I swaggered through the Armada compound and, with a loping, ungainly stride, arrived in the street. A steep hill led in to town. The wooden board-walk was worn smooth by the passage of feet. I wandered past dusty shop windows and into a *ferretería*, a hardware store full of farm implements, eight-inch copper nails and ranks of wood-burning stoves. I stood in the centre of the shop, scanning this wealth of information, then roamed down the aisles, running my fingers through the dust on the shelves. I'd forgotten about anything as dry as dust.

A stairway led to an upstairs bar with convex floor and ceilings. The windows bulged outwards and the empty room looked ready to pop. I sat on a stool at the bar. Later some back-packers came in.

It was an evening of flux. I knew that I could not be two people at the same time, both Jekyll and Hyde, and that the sea creature in me would not survive. So I sat on my bar stool, talking to someone else who had drunk too much beer, reciting a silent eulogy to the dying sailor, his sea muscles atrophying, his powers of balance fading away. I longed for sleep, but I dreaded sleep also, because I knew that with each night's sleep I'd walk a little more like everybody else, and the only true thing I'd brought back from the sea would have gone.

Landfall is always a mess. It is inevitable. At sea I dream obsessively about those first days ashore, picturing fresh citrus, beer and seafood, chance encounters that blossom into friendship, conversations lasting deep into the night. But it never works out that way. In Castro I ate quickly, had conversations quickly, got drunk quickly, left everywhere quickly, and then slept quickly – just so I could go and do it all again. I've come to the conclusion that my landfalls are a mess because I like them that way: it's the mess that makes them real. Land is a place where you can blunder around like an ox, bouncing off each new sensation, following any whim, and still stay alive.

Castro is a major port of call on the back-packer trail through South America, and I attracted little attention in the town. At the top of the hill, in front of the church, there is a windswept plaza. People like me were sitting around on many of the benches, picking grit from ice-creams and examining guide-books. One day I chatted to a young woman from Baton Rouge, Louisiana. She was blonde and frail, her lips cracked by the sun. She'd just spent two years in Bolivia with the Peace Corps, teaching nutrition. She didn't look like she practised what she preached. She said, 'I thought I couldn't do it at first, I was that lonesome. My village is a four-hour walk from the nearest road. Then you have to catch a ride in to town, where there's a telephone. It's an overnight journey just to call home. The villagers watched everything I did – you know, a *gringa*, they were fascinated. At night I saw faces staring in at the window. I thought, I can't do this for two years, I gotta get out. But it passed. I think given time human beings can learn to live anyplace.' She was on a short break now before going back to the village for another two years. I told her my flight from Auckland had been very slow, delays in Papeete. After the spotlight of life alone on the ocean, this kind of anonymity among the crowd of travellers was the best rest of all.

I spent the first few days after landfall hanging around in the plaza, eating bowls of greasy seafood stew from stalls nearby and taking long walks through the countryside to neighbouring villages. I had no firm idea of where I would go in Patagonia. I only knew that I had two months available. By the middle of February I needed to head north and begin the long passage back to New Zealand through the tropics. Two months didn't seem a very long time, given the scale of this coastline. Southern Chile boasts one of the most complex systems of waterways in the world. A maze of canals, fjords and *esteros* or inlets stretches one thousand miles from Isla Chiloé in the north to Cape Horn in the south. I'd occasionally studied charts of the coast on the passage over, but from seaward the land had seemed abstract, a distraction from my life at sea. Even in Castro I made few plans. I assumed I'd rest in the town for a couple more days, then sail as far south as I could in one month, before turning round and coming back.

But as things turned out, I was very lucky in Castro. Anchored off the *palafitos* was a forty-five-foot steel yacht called *Teokita*, belonging to Maggy and Ian Staples. They'd been in Chile for over a year, and planned to spend the summer sailing slowly south, drawing charts of each anchorage they visited. The charts would be included in a pilot book they were writing for yachts visiting Chilean Patagonia, to be published by the Royal Cruising Club Pilotage Foundation.

They often invited me over to look at information they'd already gathered on the canals, and to warm up by their stove.

Maggy was an earth-mother figure, always in an oiled woollen pullover knitted by craftswomen here on Chiloé. Her straw-coloured hair was perpetually blown wild, and sometimes actually had a piece of straw sticking out of it, from a bird's nest or a thicket of *quila* grass she'd been investigating. Ian was fond of strutting around the deck in fluorescent tights and sea-boots.

After a few days they suggested I sail south with them and help with the survey work. Having two boats would make it easier, and possibly safer. I was nervous of this idea at first. Maggy and Ian were from Henley-in-Arden: they would be slow and cautious. On the other hand, they had a diesel heater on their boat. As Christmas approached, a south-westerly gale brought heavy rain and cold temperatures in from the ocean. I told them I would be delighted to tag along.

We made our first survey in Estero Pailad, a day's sail from Castro. The entrance channel was two miles long, between tumbling cliffs of red clay. Then the channel opened into a wide inland lagoon, which split in the middle distance and disappeared up two velvet-smooth valleys. Olive-green grasses climbed from water meadows to the skyline, dotted with copses of cypress and rambling homesteads. We anchored off a hamlet on one side of the lagoon. In the morning Maggy and Ian re-checked the entrance canal. We could see that the head of the *estero* was shoal, so I went that way as my boat drew less water. Ian said he'd come looking for me with a tow rope if I didn't show in a couple of hours. That afternoon we climbed the ridge to the east and Maggy sketched the outline of the whole bay, and in the evening on *Teokita* we married the various surveys with the plan drawn from the ridge. When it was done, Ian snapped it up: 'One more for the file.'

They had stockpiled a huge collection of information on the coastline of Chilean Patagonia over the year they had been here. This was now kept in six bulging folders above the chart table. Some of it came from their own experience, most from talking to fishermen and other sailors. The pages were crammed with often messy sketch-charts and written descriptions of anchorages in English, Spanish, French and Italian. Sometimes two different sources had provided two very different drawings of the same bay. When we arrived at the place in question, we often found that the most basic drawing was the most useful. We then made our own surveys, and Maggy drew a new chart, so that the cartography in the finished pilot would be standardised. When possible she made a tracing of the bay from the radar screen on *Teokita*. Otherwise she drew an outline by hand. Her drawings were bold, in black ink, simple representations of often complicated topography. Any depth over ten metres was simply indicated as 'deep'.

We spent the next two days surveying the southern part of the coast of Chiloé, especially the area around Quellón. The main channels on the coast were already well-charted, but even on the largest-scale Chilean Navy sheets most of the little inlets and coves are either not surveyed, or the cartographer has filled them with kelp and rocks. We found that these bays were usually clear of obstruction, and made perfect anchorages for small boats. But there was almost no visibility beneath the surface in these waters, and we entered each new place nervously, dead slow. Sometimes we checked it out by dinghy first.

A few days before Christmas Ian gave me a list of places to survey, and I set out for a cruise among the islands alone. I sailed north-east through archipelagos of undulating farmland and misty sand-spits. In the afternoon I reached Isla Buta Chauques. The island was about five miles square. In its hills lay a large lagoon with fingers of salt water cutting deep into the bush. Getting into the lagoon looked difficult. The published chart showed kelp and shoal water across most of the entrance. I inched my way forwards up the canal, but saw no dangers. Open fishing boats were pulled up along the shore. The tree-line was scattered with crayfish pots, buoys, and skiffs. In the distance a man was casting a net into the water from the prow of a punt. On the opposite bank a woman, stooped, barely moving, was gathering shellfish, tossing them into a wicker basket on her back. Along the ridges smoke rose from several houses hidden in the bush.

It was a peaceful place, and I decided to make my survey under sail. A tender breeze was blowing from the south and I reached silently to the east through rich pastures. Cattle, hock-deep in the water, were lowing close on either side. A dozen or more Peale dolphins plunged beneath the boat, driving the depth-sounder crazy. After the Southern Ocean it was like a balm. I held a sketch-pad cradled in one arm and drew in a rough outline of the bay. After a mile I passed a turquoise church tucked at the head of a cove. Then the lagoon divided. I furled the genoa and ran to the north. The water was shoal, the channel no more than forty feet wide. Beyond this, a hook-shaped fissure curled gently behind a low hill and ended at a mud beach. I anchored here for the night.

From the masthead I sketched a more accurate outline of this inner branch of the lagoon. Then, as the sun fell behind the ridge to the west, I sat in the cockpit and worked up a finished chart. The pilot book required a written description of each anchorage. I put the chart to one side now, and began to write.

Isla Buta Chauques: 42° 17′S 73° 08′W

Approach

Chile chart #609 shows two kelp patches (Boca del Medio and Boca Pajaros) in the western entrance from Canal Chauques. No kelp was seen in 1998 although the area may be shoal. The approach should be made with caution from the northern part of the Canal Chauques using the bearings shown in the diagram. The lagoon itself is relatively free of dangers.

Anchorage

The eastern part of the lagoon divides in two. The northern branch is entered through a narrow channel formed by a sand spit. The channel is clear of obstructions and has a minimum depth of 3m. Anchor at the eastern end of this bay in perfect shelter. 10m. Mud.

The wind fell silent after dark. As the tide dropped the drying mud-flats along the foreshore sucked and popped in the stillness. The sounds of children and dogs drifted across the water. Cattle moved heavily through the grass nearby. The moon sent silver light through copses of manioc on the west shore. Beneath the weak glow of the lamp, as I formed each clipped sentence in the dry language of pilotage notes, I understood how I wanted to spend the two months that I had in these waters: drawing charts of places that had not been surveyed before. Without Maggy and Ian I don't believe I would ever have put the rush of the ocean behind me. Alone, I would have just bolted south through the canals, as if still surrounded by monotonous seas.

We left Isla Chiloé in two boats early on the morning of New Year's Eve, and set a course south-east to cross the Golfo de Corcovado. In the afternoon waterfalls and bare slabs of scarred rock appeared out of the haze. This was my first close-up sight of the mainland. Scrub climbed steeply behind low cliffs to a line of black, boulder-shaped mountains that nearly filled a charred sky. Hours passed as we sailed down the coast, but nothing changed in the landscape. That night we anchored in a group of islets and reefs just west of Bahía de Tictoc. In the morning, before we left, we drew a chart.

On the shores of the Canal Refugio we came across a settlement belonging to the family of Juan Carlos Schydlowski. Juan

Carlos was a Chilean aristocrat and junk bond dealer. He told us that he'd been Forbes Salesman of the year 1986. Two years later he was arrested and sued by the Internal Revenue Service for $28 million in unpaid taxes. Juan Carlos spent three years in jail, before being released and ordered to pay fifty dollars in costs. At this point the family sold the ranch in New Mexico and fled to the forests of Patagonia, where they now lived in stylish beach houses, adorned with tapestries and contemporary art but built from driftwood, without electricity or water. It was a two-day journey by sea to get out. The son, Allen, was twenty-one. He had spent the last eight years living in the forest. Allen was building an underwater temple for dolphin worship, formed of upright floating totem poles chained to the seabed.

On the wall of one of the beach houses there was an aerial photograph of this part of the coast. Maggy took a tracing from the photograph and we used this as the basis for our chart from Bahía de Tictoc and Bahía Mala. We made surveys in the Schydlowskis' Zodiac, and in our boats. The whole area was marked as shoal on the largest published chart, but much of it was navigable. At the centre, in Bahía Anihue, there is a perfect, all-weather anchorage.

We followed the Canal Refugio south through the mountains, then crossed the brown waters of the Canal Moraleda to reach the islands in the west. We spent two weeks here in the Archipiélago de los Chonos, making surveys and drawing charts. There were more than one hundred islands forming a broken jigsaw pattern, the last outcrops between the continent and the ocean. They rose dome-like and mellow on every side and stretched unchanged beyond the skyline. Occasionally we saw evidence of a nomad fishing camp in the trees, otherwise the area was uninhabited. Many of the islands were not named.

We made our most satisfying discovery in the Archipiélago: a new island. Isla Valverde is in fact two islands, divided by canals and an inland lagoon. On the published chart the lagoon is shown as a lake. We named the two islands Valverde Este and Valverde Oeste.

Among these low islands the wind was clean and the sailing easy. But still there was a sense of unease here. The world we saw around us was familiar from the Chilean naval charts, but in a thousand tiny ways also very different. Headlands were more prominent, islets more numerous, reefs non-existent, anchorages better protected and more open by turns. The discrepancy between the charts and reality lent this landscape a fluid quality. Occasionally I wondered if we weren't in some ways still at sea. The charts we made formed a trail that could be followed by others, a twisting line of knowledge through a far wider stretch of geography that we never saw.

We re-crossed the Canal Moraleda in fine weather. The wind was so light it barely filled the sails. The boats were side by side, heeling imperceptibly, tiny white rigs picked out as specks in the empty bowl of the Patagonian skyline. We were heading for the village of Puerto Aguirre, which according to the most detailed Chilean chart does not exist. The village lay at the centre of a network of craggy channels and bays. Small islands guarded every approach, their sloping rocky shores worn smooth and glowing yellow in the afternoon sun. Children were gathering shellfish and jumping from rocks into the sea.

A lane of crushed shells wound up the hillside between creaking wooden cottages, their pastel paintwork heavily weather-worn. Fuchsias drooped from window boxes and bushes of red *estrellita* spilled from gardens out into the road. On the beach I saw a grey-haired man who was walking slowly towards me, wearing a light cotton jacket and carrying a camera. I asked him if he came from the island. He said he lived in Puerto Montt, but came here every summer for three weeks to run a dental clinic, giving the islanders their annual check-up. When I told him that we were leaving tomorrow for the mainland, he said, 'Old people here call it the "Continent". The ladies pretend never to have seen it. When young people leave for the city, they give them up for dead.'

Two days later we motored up Seno Aisén, and anchored in a lagoon behind the deep-water port at Chacabuco. The entrance channel was narrow, with barely enough water to stay afloat.

I caught a mini-bus up the valley to Aisén to buy supplies. Maggy and Ian were waiting for a friend who was flying out from London: they thought they would be here two weeks. It was time to move on. As a leaving present Maggy gave me a drawing of the 'Chacabuco Monster', her name for the williwaws, the violent squalls of wind that swooped from the mountains and made you wake with gritted teeth in the middle of the night. As if to emphasise what a sobering influence they had been on me, I left the anchorage too early in the tide and went aground in the entrance to the lagoon. Maggy looked up from her drawing on deck and gave me a characteristic wave, as if nothing had happened. I'd float off in half an hour when the tide rose.

I spent five days making surveys around the Estuarios Quitralco, Elefantes and Cupquelan. Ian had given me a list of places to chart that they would not have time to visit. I kept the list close, so close I could recite it, a catechism to make sense of voyaging through this maze of land and sea.

The defining feature of these waters was the San Rafael glacier, which swept between the mountains, then crashed into an all but landlocked lagoon. The only entrance to the lagoon was up the eight-mile-long Rio Tempanos, which formed a fracture-line through the surrounding marshland.

I made a chart of Bahía Quesahuén, the key anchorage when visiting the glacier, then entered the river at the start of the flood tide, an hour before dark. It could have been a muddy creek in Africa, except for the icebergs floating in the stream: blue bergs, in brown water, surrounded by green bush. I had to weave a course and shoot small rapids between larger bergs that had grounded in the river. As darkness fell a cool glow of light seeped around the rocky buttress that obscured the glacier. When I entered the lagoon the whole basin was filled with moonlight reflected from the brilliant white sheet of ice that fell from unseen mountains and seemed to continue across the water. I picked my way between glowing bergs to find an anchorage on the west shore.

In the morning I made a survey of the lagoon. It was full of floating icebergs, but otherwise free of obstructions. A boat could anchor off any shore, depending on the wind direction.

Before beginning the passage back north I made a detour, thirty miles out west into the mountains of the Península de Taitao. I ran down the long and lovely Estero Puelma in a light northerly. The last fifteen miles were uncharted. At the head of the *estero*, on the northern side, a narrow bay pushed up to the feet of a circle of dark brown hills. I tacked gently inland between two islands, steering with my butt and drawing a pretty bad chart along the way. Behind the second island a reef protected an anchorage, and I dropped the sails for the night.

This was half-way. Tomorrow I would begin the passage north through the canals to Chiloé, then up the continental coastline towards the turquoise waters and wet horizons of the South Seas. I celebrated this turning-point with a subdued party. Land is lonelier, and this place seemed more distant, than anywhere I'd been at sea.

I made a late start the following morning. Much too late, in fact, as I was to find out. The sky was heavily overcast and it was now blowing thirty knots from the north. I hoped to find an anchorage that night somewhere in the Estero Barros Arana. It was forty-five miles, with little prospect of finding shelter along the way.

As the light faded I was in the Barros Arana, beating into a steep sea. I was cold and tired, fingers clenched around the steel hoop of the spray-hood. I carried too much sail, still hoping to find an anchorage before nightfall. In the distance a long bay cut up into Isla McPherson. At its head there was the prospect of finding shelter. But I wasn't going to make it. The bay was uncharted. It would be dark before I even reached the entrance.

The wind moderated after dark. The rain grew heavier. I reefed the sails right down and plugged over towards the far shore of the canal. When I saw the darker black of cliffs in the moonless night sky, I went about and headed north-east. I worked to the north like this for an hour, then turned and ran back south. Then I did it again. I imagined I would have to do this all night. It was much too deep to anchor in the canal. But at the southern end of the second circuit I saw a dim light close by in the rain. Soon there was a guy standing just next to me, his head cowled in a blue hood, his brown cheeks wet and shiny. He was standing on the gunwale of an open fishing boat, holding the rail of mine. There was a heavy crunch as the two boats met on a wave. Another figure sat at the engine. They told me to follow them towards the shore.

The water grew calm and the wind eased completely in the lee of the land. I dropped the sails and fired up the engine. Then I saw rock and bush very close on either side. We were in a channel. I followed a bit further, both boats crawling, trees moving heavily in the wind all around, but the water was smooth. A voice floated out of the darkness, but I couldn't catch it. The fishing boat came back and the man in the hood rattled my anchor chain on the foredeck to make the point very clear. I dropped anchor and heard their engine fade, then be cut.

I woke early the next morning to the *chok-chok* sound of an axe in the forest nearby. Men were shouting and laughing ashore. I climbed to the deck. The cloud still hung low, but the rain had stopped. I was anchored in the middle of a small bay on Isla McPherson. The entrance was so narrow that on the chart the two sides touched. To the east, forest climbed steeply to the ridge line. In the west the land rolled away in thickets of coarse *quila* grass and scrub towards the shores of the main canal. Small, stony cays broke the surface in several places. Herons pecked among the stones. Anchored nearby was a fishing boat of forty feet, and scattered around the shores of the bay were the small open boats I'd seen from time to time in the canals. I was in the middle of a nomad fishing camp.

I rowed towards the shore. Half a dozen boats were stacked along the pebble beaches, lying at awkward angles. They were identical, painted yellow above the waterline, red below, double-ended, with very strong sheer. A number was painted on each flared bow, and a name on the stern: *Mariana, Río Amarillo, Águila Negro, Darwin, Patagonia, Pacífico.*

Several men were repairing nets, sitting cross-legged on the wet shingle. All around were heaps of crab pots, coils of warp, bundles of float flags. 'Hoy!' shouted one of the men, and I went and sat down beside them. I asked if any of them had been the men in the boat the night before. One of them waved towards the camp. Another shrugged. The third asked where I had come from. I told him and said, rather obviously, 'Bad weather last night. I couldn't find an anchorage.'

'*Saco de huevas* [dickhead],' said the third man, and thumped me on the back.

'I started too late.'

'*Belotudo* [dickhead].'

I spent that evening in the camp. A torn tarpaulin had been stretched between trees and posts. The rain had set in again and dripped down almost everywhere. About fifteen men sat around on crates and piles of fishing gear, sucking on *maté* pipes or tending kettles over a fire. Many had wet hair and clothes; everything was damp. They didn't seem to care. Today had been a rest day – Sunday – and their spirits were high. Someone had made a makeshift hammock out of a net and was swinging back and forth, pushing himself with a pole. The men spoke in energetic bursts, their language riddled with slang I couldn't understand. They were from Aisén. They came out to camp in the summer, for six weeks at a time.

I didn't draw a chart of the anchorage on Isla McPherson. This mass of fishing boats all around made my charts of the 'unknown' seem absurd. These waters were very well known, but the fishermen navigated without charts.

Several times that night I looked among the faces of the fishers to find the two who had helped me the night before. When I asked, four different people claimed it had been them, including an old woman. Then the camp shook with belly-laughs. The latrine area was over a shallow rise behind the camp, among boulders that led down to the canal. Presumably my rescuer had been taking a leak, and seen my lights. It could have been any one of them.

On 24 February I saw the ocean skyline for the first time in over two months. It was three hours after sunrise. The water in the Canal Tuamapu was an oily green, the wind was light. Granite islets flanked the canal, burning amber in the morning sun. It was a perfectly clear day. To the east the snowy cones of Mt Melimoyu and Volcán Corcovado were visible sixty miles distant, both wrapped in a deep blue sky. But to the west, beyond the cliffs of Isla Tuamapu, the view stretched unobstructed over the Pacific, my first view of the open sea since I'd sailed into the canals in mid December.

Through binoculars the Pacific looked distressed, driven by a strong southerly from which I was sheltered in the canal. I watched the slot of ocean across the entrance to the canal, its surface rolling but the waves inseparable from this distance. The sea looked to be twisted, lifted up and sloping towards the sky.

As I sailed beneath the cliffs of Isla Tuamapu a long, easy swell crept around the buttress of rock ahead. Once clear of Islas Bajas the sea cut up all around and a heavy, dirty wind fell from the cliff tops. I sailed for three miles across troubled waters, the boom occasionally crashing as the boat both pitched and rolled. Then I found the cleaner flow blowing up the coast and set a course north-west, reaching in thirty knots of wind and foaming seas.

Behind me the skyline was a jumble of blue peaks and ridges. I tried to find Isla Anita, the place where I'd made my final survey in Patagonia the night before. Anita was just another small island in the Archipiélago de Los Chonos, its single deep bay entered through a rocky channel. The anchorage was sheltered by low hills and scrub – it wasn't a particularly attractive place. But as I'd drawn the chart the night before, this bay had meant something to me: the last anchorage, the final survey ... It was one of those peculiarly sentimental bonds with a foreign landscape that travellers take the liberty of making. I tried to find Isla Anita now among the peaks and ridges, a final farewell. But the islands of the archipelago had melded with the mountains of the mainland. The land was a monolithic barrier, and the waterways sunk within it were impossible to trace. From five miles offshore, Isla Anita had disappeared.

It was a wild ride to the north-west. I gained some fleeting protection in the lee of Isla Guafo, but otherwise my course lay exposed to the wind and swell coming up from the Southern Ocean. I'd forgotten – so quickly – what open water was like. After the short, kicking seas of the canals, the roll and plunge here seemed everlasting. I'd already forgotten how the boat submerged to deck level in a seaway, wave crests foaming at head height. I stood for all that first day in the cockpit, watching the ocean landscape gather and subside. In the afternoon the south coast of Chiloé sometimes faded into view through the haze. At sunset I was fifteen miles off Cabo Quilán. I poled out the genoa and altered course to run before the wind, parallel to the coast. I cooked dinner and drank beer, beginning to readjust to the wayward symmetries of deep, open water.

I slept infrequently that night. The coast of Chiloé lay twenty miles to the east, unlit and unseen in the darkness. The wind was strong at my back. I felt keyed-up, breathless. Everything was fresh and unfettered, the freedom of an all-night sea lay ahead. When I thought of the canals now, I remembered only the twists and turns, the shifty winds, the pressure of finding an anchorage before dark. Sailing back onto the ocean seemed like escaping from a warren of underground caves. The night sky was vast and clear, borne through the hatch and down inside the boat. From my bunk I could see the stars wheeling across the companion-way. I moved constantly between the cabin and the cockpit, unable to keep still. It was a sensation that I remembered from passages long before: a sort of paranoid restlessness, a reaction to the soft winds and star-studded nights of tropical waters. As I surfed northwards towards the tropical latitudes, I knew that everything was about to change, and the boat was going to become a very different place.

I saw shipping that night, coastal vessels working between Puerto Montt and the Pacific ports further north. Their lights rolled heavily on the swells, and those coming from the south crawled past so slowly. After midnight I saw more lights dead ahead, coming straight towards me. I pulled the self-steering chain from the tiller and pushed the helm hard over, sailing off at 90° to get out of the way. The headsail cracked as I furled it, the boat rolling and seas slopping over the beam. Within minutes the ship was beside me, a cruise liner gliding past at twenty knots. Each cabin had a terrace: I saw tables and sun beds run by in a blur of lights and railings.

Dawn broke sticky and bitter-sweet. The stickiness was on my face, around my eyes, on my lips and in my mouth. It was February: high summer in the south. I'd packed away the heavy sleeping-bag I'd used since leaving Auckland and the previous night had wrapped myself in a blanket on the bunk. On deck a jacket had been enough. The stickiness was something else I'd forgotten about living at sea in warm waters. It's a feeling on your skin and under your clothes, a human cocktail of sweat and salt, and that boat grime that's generated even thousands of miles offshore. In this sense the sea isn't a clean or cleansing place at all; you wear it all day, and over time you learn to pull it closer around you to hasten sleep.

The sweetness was in the air all around: the distant scent of land. Far to the east, as the sun rose, headlands appeared in the granular light. The land looked dusty, arid plains falling to shallow valleys that merged with the sea. Throughout that morning the land ebbed and flowed without conviction. Sometimes it faded from view. Later a ridge line appeared, or the rounded crest of a hill. But the smell of the land was constant throughout those first days of the passage. I made long, downwind tacks offshore, taking the southerly on the quarter, usually gybing at sunset and dawn. At the end of each offshore tack the coast was thirty to forty miles distant. No land was visible, but the smell was still present, just, that light but unmistakable tang of land that hits the back of the nose. I wondered if it was a desert smell, or savannah, hot earth and baked grasses. Then I thought I smelt pine needles, and later a spicy cinnamon.

Poets write of the smell of the sea, but really the ocean has no smell. Far offshore, on a long passage under sail, the sea is just the sea, salt is bland, and the only thing that smells is you. Offshore, the single-hander sails across an ocean of his own BO and bad breath. What people mean when they talk about the smell of the sea is actually the smell of the coastline. On the coast, the sea smells of kelp, dunes, mangroves, forest and farmland. But boats are machines, so the sea also smells of grease and bilge oil, diesel, burning meths and kerosene. The smell on petrol station forecourts reminds me of the sea. And of course, as I've mostly sailed alone, the sea also reminds me of me.

The most lasting impressions I have of the smell of the sea are all tinged with dirtiness. In the Southern Ocean, when I curled up to sleep I wanted to fill my head with comfort thoughts. The sea smells I conjured up then were always the same: the great, stinking port cities of the South Seas. Papeete, where fragrant copra wafts over the filthy lagoon from the warehouses at Fare-Ute; Apia after cyclone Val, when the harbour was thick with rotting vegetation and dead horses floated past the anchored boat; and most of all Suva, the angry melting-pot of the Pacific, where the concrete floors of the market drain into the lagoon and the air is laden with the stench of the landfill at Navesi. Long after I left the tropics, when I'd forgotten many other things about the sea, I still remembered clearly the steaming, tropical stew of harbour life in the islands.

Off the coast of Chile the smell of the coastline was bigger than this, big in a global sense, a wider, weaker smell, the stink of humanity sanitised by the surrounding aroma of continental land. Twenty miles offshore, the sea smelt of forests and grasslands, perhaps alpine flowers from the Andean foothills.

The waters off the coast of Chile are a scream for a sailing boat heading north. Ocean forces power up from the south. A thousand miles out to sea, the South Pacific high pressure system generates southerly winds which funnel up the coast, trapped between the anticyclone and the Andes, while beneath the keel the cold waters of the Peru current flow towards the equator, adding fifteen miles to a day's run. An ocean conveyor-belt sweeps up the coast of South America towards the tropics. For a sailing boat, these must be some of the easiest waters in the world.

The route that I was now following had served as a gateway for European shipping entering the Pacific after the Age of Discovery. Magellan's battered crew in the *Victoria*, having found a strait through the Patagonian peninsula from the Atlantic, sailed these same waters. The Pacific got its name because of the impression this stretch of sea made on the Admiral-General – a name many of us have had cause to dispute while sailing else-where in the ocean, but off the coast of Chile 'pacific' is a suit-able term. When Bougainville finally escaped from the canals and followed this coast north, his crew sang the *Te Deum*.

These waters are thickly embroidered with European fantasies. In the sixteenth and seventeenth centuries there were numerous reported sightings of the mythical Southern Continent. Theo-dore Gerrards was sailing off the Chilean coast in 1599. A gale blew his ship off course, and he was unsure of his position when he saw a mountainous land covered in snow, 'looking like Norway', which appeared to extend north-west towards the Solomon Islands. Twenty-five years later, the ship *Orange* re-ported sighting the Continent twice in the same waters while on passage from Cape Horn to the Juan Fernández group. So wide-spread was the belief in a huge land mass in the South Pacific that when Tasman sighted New Zealand in 1642 he named it Staten Land, believing it to be connected to the island of the same name south-east of Argentina.

The Spaniard Juan Fernández sailed a course between west and south-west from the coast of Chile in *Our Lady of Remedy* in 1576. After one month at sea Fernández made landfall on what he described as a 'fertile and agreeable continent ... inhab-ited by white people ... very well disposed and cloathed in fine cloths'. This report was made in secret, and was contained in the Arias Memorial, a highly confidential sixteenth-century list of Spanish discoveries in the South Seas which was lost until the late eighteenth century, when Alexander Dalrymple discovered a printed copy of the manuscript, supposedly while browsing in a London bookseller's. Fernández was generally a reliable observer, but this landfall on an 'agreeable continent' is usually greeted with scepticism, of course, as an exaggeration, if not a straightforward fabrication. One possibility is that Fernández reached Easter Island, almost a hundred and fifty years before the first recognised European visit. His reference to 'white people' is not as far-fetched as it sounds. Many of the first Europeans in the Pacific commented on how pale-skinned they observed the Polynesians to be. George Robertson, master of the first ship at Tahiti, remarked of the islanders that 'This race of white-skinned people has a great resemblance to the Jews.' It has also been suggested that Fernández in fact made landfall in New Zealand, while yet others insist he reached the shores of the lost continent of Mu, the Pacific's equivalent of Atlantis, once home to sixty-four million inhabitants descended from Celtic wizards.

Even the normally starchy Admiralty pilot book lapses into a note of ambiguity when describing the waters west of Chile. In a caution to navigators it states: 'Several outlying dangers in the area, from the coast to longitude 100° W, have been reported from time to time. Where the seabed is uneven, the effect of seismic disturbances, frequent in the area, may be to submerge an existing islet or rock, or to thrust a hitherto submerged peak almost to, or above, the surface of the ocean. Subsequent examination has revealed no uncharted dangers, but the reports are mentioned as a warning that dangers may be found in this area.'

My passage up the coast of Chile was the first stage of a much longer voyage back to New Zealand. I hoped to carry the southerly wind and Peru current six hundred miles north to the Juan Fernández Archipelago, then follow the outer edge of the South Pacific high north-west up into the tropics. It was now late in February. By early April the risk of cyclones should have lifted in the tropics, giving me two months to take the trade winds through the islands and get down to New Zealand before the onset of winter.

The Juan Fernández group is three hundred miles offshore in a south latitude of 34°. For the first few days out of the canals I stuck close to the coast. Sailing along a coastline is different from sailing elsewhere. Regardless of sea conditions, there is a quality to inshore passage-making that is constant. It was only possible to see occasional glimpses of the coast of Chile, at the end of each inshore tack, or when I strained my eyes to penetrate the coastal haze. At night the coastline was easier to define. I saw the flash of the lighthouses at Punta Corona and Isla Mocha, but more clearly I saw the loom of towns and cities hanging in the night sky. The twin settlements of Corral and Niebla presented a wide, watery streak of light to the east, a false dawn. Later I saw the loom of Lebu and Concepción, simple reflected images of street lamps, headlights, house lights and neon, thousands of component parts spread across the sky as one mass reflection of human life.

But really the loom of the land was always there as I sailed up the coastline, even by day; not the visible loom of lights, but something similar, a physical loom, a 'presence'. Even when I couldn't see any evidence of land, it was always there. Land has an invasive quality that creeps over the waters beyond the coast-line. A passage along any coast is similar in this respect: it is lop-sided, bordered by a force that's present even when unseen. From ten or fifteen miles offshore, land is a conundrum: it should be a comfort to have it so close, my home and habitat; but land has its dangers, coastal shipping, inshore fishing craft, the doomsday scenario that in your comfort you oversleep and sail yourself onto the rocks.

While sailing in the canals, I'd felt the traveller's guilt about family and friends back home. In Castro, Puerto Aguirre and Aisén I'd queued to make phone calls in airless boxes to people who had been waiting for weeks. I felt selfish and irresponsible when I heard their voices. But something happens to the land as I leave shoal water, perhaps about five miles offshore: I cannot see the faces of loved ones any more; land loses the power to really touch me. It becomes a featureless barrier in the sea. It smells of air-freshener, and is best seen in the lifeless loom of cities in the night sky. I can picture the land from offshore, but feel little for it. Leaving land the first time on the voyage, from Auckland, was difficult; but after that I sailed offshore with few regrets.

On the fourth evening out from the Canal Tuamapu I did not gybe at sunset, which had been my habit over the preceding days. Instead of putting in a long tack back towards the coast I continued to sail north-east, on a course that should take me to the Juan Fernández group within a further two to three days, a course that was now slowly taking me further from the coast. I saw the loom of no settlements that night, no shipping. By dawn the next day the land was well below the horizon, and when I looked at the ocean I only ever looked ahead. I'd already been at sea for three days, but it seemed that the passage had only now properly begun.

Five

Waking up at sea is like a distant wave rolling towards, then into, your body. It is very weak at first, somewhere on the limit of consciousness: a slight sense of activity that might come no further. But soon it's swelling up all around, unstoppable, a rush of noise and movement and first light.

I sit up in the bunk and stare down the cabin. It looks cold and dirty before the sun is up, its surfaces slippery with the damp of night-time. It is a plain scene: chipped white paintwork and once-varnished trim. A grubby tea-towel is swinging from the grab rail, a wooden spoon has fallen onto the bench and is sliding around. I take in these details without interest. First thing in the morning I'm focused on something bigger: the oblong sky visible through the companionway hatch.

Dawn twilight is barely established, the sky is an even, dark grey. I can see the top of the wind generator, its tail fin dipping as the boat rolls, the blades spinning just fast enough in the southeast wind to form a white disc in the sky. In strong winds the generator begins to whine and the pole vibrates in the gusts. Today, I can only hear a fluttering hum: the wind is a steady fifteen knots, a little lighter than before. It has eased over the last twenty-four hours, and the outlook for the day ahead is so far good.

This preliminary observation completed, I need some more

concrete reassurance that all is well, so I look to the right, at the compass. It is mounted in the bulkhead beside the companion-way. From inside the cabin I can see through the back of the plastic compass bowl. But only just. There's little light, it's three metres away, the dial is small, the bowl is smeared, I really need my glasses. The other problem is that I've forgotten the course, the three numbers of the course being steered, the sacred code that defines my whole purpose here. There have been so many numbers over the last months, so many combinations of three, that for a moment I'm stymied. Figures are swirling in my head as the blurred numbers on the compass card swirl in their pool of oil. I might have steered a hundred different courses over the voyage to date, perhaps a thousand: I had no idea. Some of these courses lasted only a few minutes, others for days on end without alteration. But on passage no course seemed less significant than the one before. In hindsight it's easy to round all the numbers out and just remember that I was sailing south-east, or north-west. But at sea I seldom generalised like this; I couldn't stand back and see that larger picture of the ocean where multiple wind-shifts, tacks and gybes have merged to form a single rhumb line. Precision is something I cling to, a life-belt, and I won't let go. A ten-degree change in course might be all that separates three days ago and today. My course was not south-east or north-west: it had three hard digits, a bar-code that governed each tiny section of the voyage. I recorded each one pedantically in the log book. I believed I'd imprinted it in my mind.

This is the process of waking up at sea. You sit upright in the near darkness and try to remember where you are going. Exactly. The course is the only rationale, here. Remembering it after sleep means again learning to care about ten-degree differences; it means re-establishing the pedantry that has got you where you are, and will some day get you home again.

From where I was lying on the bunk I was facing the compass from the wrong side, looking towards the back of the boat. So the numbers I had to remember were not the course itself, but its exact inverse on the opposite side of the compass rose. I squinted, and pulled myself up on my haunches to get a little closer. From the figures swirling in the bowl, three slowly separated themselves in my mind and fell into sequence: 120°. This was the course I had been steering when I last turned out the light in the small hours. With the boat on self-steering the compass swung around, but it was an even swing to either side of the course. Nothing had changed: the boat was still sailing in the desired direction. And in the same moment that I realised this, the wave of anxiety I had felt since before I opened my eyes began to subside.

I watched the compass for a short time, then collapsed backwards onto the bunk. It had been a quiet night. The wind had eased a little, but was still steady in the south-east. The seas were shallow and long. I lay still for a few moments, feeling smug. The passage was going well. Another day had begun.

At night, with a lee-cloth tied up to keep me in place, the bunk becomes a cot. I climbed over the cloth. The cabin floor was slippery, a film of moist dust sticky beneath my toes. The sun would need to be above the horizon for a couple of hours before the surfaces dried out. In warmer latitudes this pattern was repeated almost daily on the boat, a micro-climate of dew and dampness at night, evaporation in the early morning, and baking heat through the rest of the day. By evening this sliminess under my feet would have caked hard, the timber floor-boards greying through broken varnish.

I walked to the galley. My lips were sticky, too, my mouth dry. But it was too soon to drink. The first thing was to go on deck and stare down the empty length of the ocean.

I stepped onto the engine box and through the companion-way. As I pulled myself from under the spray-hood I saw that the sky was still mostly grey, but yellowing in the east. Then I lowered my eyes to the sea.

The first reaction was how cold the water looked, and how strangely-shaped. Small swells formed, seldom for long, then collapsed sideways, or back the way they'd come. In places the surface was smooth and raised, like scar tissue, never broken by a wave. At dawn the ocean often looked pocked, distorted, not the same place where I'd spent the night. Through the hours of darkness I'd felt the simple rhythm of sailing down-wind in small seas, a cycle of motions and sounds that was largely predictable. I built up a mental image of the sea that conformed to this rhythm, of waves and troughs in sequence. But at dawn I was often surprised when I looked out and saw this: a place where there seemed to be no pattern, where waves rose apparently at random.

It was still only half-light. The upper limb of the sun had not yet broken the horizon. I could only see about a hundred metres. Beyond that, both sea and sky were equally impenetrable. So what I saw of the sea at dawn was greatly foreshortened: I was sailing over a circular sheet of black water, two hundred metres across. In these conditions the ocean was very hard to read. It didn't tally with what my body had been feeling all night. Once the sun rose and the horizon receded far into the distance, then the patterns of the ocean would again be visible. But I needed this broad canvas to properly understand the state of the sea. The endless horizon is full of easy reassurance. It is the small area of water around the boat that's unknown.

There is sometimes a period of lighter wind at dawn, lasting about an hour, through the transition from darkness to daylight. On the preceding days of the passage this hadn't come about, but on this morning a lighter breeze did establish itself. During the night I'd sailed with the wind on the quarter, a light number one headsail downwind, fed by the half-furled genoa poled out to

windward. The first thing I did on deck that morning was roll
out the rest of the genoa. It would make only a small difference
to the speed of the boat, but I liked to make such alterations at
dawn, to assert my command at the start of the day. I stood in
the cockpit for a short time, adjusted the wind vane steering a
couple of clicks, and watched the headsails wobble in the uncertain breeze. Then I set the fishing line, went down into the cabin
and put the kettle on.

I know little about fishing, but it doesn't seem to matter on
the ocean. I used small lures in the hope of only catching small
fish. There was no refrigeration on the boat, so I wanted no
more than could be eaten before it went bad.

The fishing line is kept on a heavy plastic hand reel. Once the
line is set I wind its end the wrong way round a winch many
times. When a fish takes the lure the winch turns on its ratchet,
making a loud clicking sound. I can hear this noise from anywhere on the boat, and it carries sufficient importance to wake
me from sleep.

While I waited for the kettle to boil I ate dates. Immediately
after setting the fishing line there was a sense of anticipation.
Dawn was a good time for fish: I sat expectantly on the engine
box, listening for the winch to click as the line ran out. When
the kettle boiled I made coffee. When I had any bread I made
toast, otherwise I ate a breakfast of biscuits and jam. The radio
was always playing. Sometimes it was turned on most of the day,
an endless cycle of news and analysis. I've never been so well-
informed on world events as when alone on a small boat in mid
ocean. By the second round of news I had forgotten about listening for fish, so that, if and when a strike came, it nearly always
took me by surprise.

I mostly caught fish like bonito or yellow-fin tuna, and sometimes mahi mahi. I might catch one fish a day for a week, then
for the same period of time catch nothing. Dusk, like dawn, was
a good time, but a fish could take the lure at any time of day.

Occasionally the line went screaming out and the winch roared. This meant something large was on the other end: usually the line broke, or the hook came free. But a smaller fish, say a bonito, might only be heavy enough to turn the winch a few clicks, or sometimes just the one. So it wasn't a deafening sound by any means, but in its context it was quite unmistakable: the greased clunk of engineered metal slotting into place. Whenever I heard that sound I froze on reflex. And my very first reaction was always the same: who's that? Despite the obvious logic that it was a fish, my mind momentarily followed the same dead-end chain of thought: the winch is operated by hand . . . whose hand is it? ... how did they ...?

The thought was over almost before it had started, and I scrambled into the cockpit to haul in the line. Later, as I cleaned the catch, I had to acknowledge that even after four months at sea, on an instinctual level I still hadn't acknowledged the reality of my solitude on the ocean, since my most immediate conclusion was to assume the impossible: there's another person on the boat.

The lighter air didn't last through sunrise. By mid morning it was again blowing twenty-five knots. I refurled the half-genoa I had rolled out a few hours earlier, as the rig strained and the wake spread loudly behind the boat. I spent most of the morning sitting on the engine box, my head in the companionway. There was partial shade here, when the boat rolled and the spray-hood shielded the sun. As beams of sunlight flashed across the page, I read the pilot book regarding the group of islands I would sight tomorrow morning. On some level, I suppose, I was just holding out for the single click of the winch that would announce a visitor.

At the very beginning of the voyage, for the first days out of Auckland, I sometimes imagined what it would be like to have another person on the boat. I pictured where they would sit, how I could rearrange the stowage behind the bunks to make room for their stuff. Mostly I imagined the things we could talk about – practising Spanish, and, later in the voyage, French (even talking to the video camera had helped ease the loneliness). I thought that if I could talk to a real person about the sea and how far there was to sail across it, the passage would become easier. I remember I even entertained the idea that in Chile I could look for crew. It wouldn't have been difficult, among the back-packers in Castro. But after the first week of the voyage I never considered this idea again. And now, as I surfed north-west across the Chile Trench towards the Juan Fernández group, it was the furthest thing from my mind.

With a friend I once went on a very long walk which required us to carry everything we needed in rucksacks. We started off with packs full of items we regarded as essential, but over the first few days of the walk we both lightened our loads by up to a third, discarding things that on reconsideration we didn't truly need. I suspect that when I go to sea alone something very similar happens, except that what I'm discarding over that first part of a trip is emotions. If I thought about having another person on the boat now, I did so in purely logistical terms: all the water they would drink; the food they would eat; the space they would take up. Sea travel reduces people to the things they consume. The sea makes me a ruthlessly practical machine of self-repression. On the ocean I can simply blank out whole categories of feel-ings, because they contribute nothing to the ongoing voyage. I'm a survivor: I travel light.

The navigator Juan Fernández was summoned before the In-quisition in Lima in 1570, on charges of sorcery. Fernández ran a small trading vessel, *Our Lady of Remedy*, between the ports of Concepción and Callao with such speed and daring that his crew named him 'el Brujo' – the wizard of the Pacific. The inquisitors believed this nickname was too close to the truth, and that the navigator's fast passages were not possible by natural means alone. Juan Fernández persuaded them otherwise.

Three years later, running the same route down the coast, he stood offshore in the vicinity of 33° latitude in search of a fairer wind to fetch Concepción. Four hundred miles beyond the Pacific coastline of Chile Fernández did find a lighter south wind, and also a small group of uninhabited islands, to which he gave his name.

That same year Fernández obtained a grant from Spain to establish a colony on the islands, and took possession. He stocked the bush–clad hillsides with goats and rabbits, and stuck it out for two years before the isolation drove him back to sea. Thereafter the islands became a favoured port of call for European ships bound north into the Pacific after rounding Cape Horn. Provided the wind was in the south, ships could anchor in a sheltered bay on the main island. Ashore there was fresh water, meat (thanks to Fernández's rabbits and goats), and plentiful timber. The climate was temperate and the sea a steely blue. Better still, the Spaniards were four hundred miles away on the mainland. The Juan Fernández group became a favoured watering-hole for English buccaneers, who came here to careen and carouse, and to dream of meeting a Manila galleon in the waters further north.

In the spring of 1704, as the *Cinque-Ports* was making final preparations to depart the Juan Fernández group, one crewman flatly refused to continue with the voyage and demanded to be put ashore. He was landed, with difficulty, on the boulder beach, with a gun, powder, shot, tobacco, a hatchet, knife and kettle, and a bible. Alexander Selkirk was picked up four years and four months later, when the story of his solitary life on the island fascinated Europe and inspired Daniel Defoe's novel *Robinson Crusoe*. So was the castaway myth born in the popular imagination, of a sailor, all alone, surrounded by the ocean, learning to survive.

The following morning I made landfall on Isla Robinson Crusoe, the main island in the Archipiélago de Juan Fernández. From ten miles offshore the island hung like an inverted exclamation mark over the ocean. Towering rock fangs and door-shaped mountains bit so boldly into the sky they seemed divorced from their foundations beneath. I sailed closer across a birdless sea. The breeze was dying and the boat shuddered as the sails flogged. The lower slopes of the island were a moonscape of eroded red earth and perched boulders. At the summit, the hillsides climbed near vertically to a crown of silver-green bush.

Cumberland Bay was the only anchorage, a scoop in the island's lee. Groundswell crept around the bay's shallow flanks, sending a heavy surf crashing onto the boulder beach. A ribbon of houses was just visible through the spray, at the feet of a string of mountains and ridges. To the north the ocean stretched empty for tens of thousands of miles. At anchor the boat rolled, sometimes heavily, on the long oceanic swells. Once or twice during the day a sea-breeze set in, and the boat swung round to face the heat-haze of the tropical Pacific to the north. At night I rolled in my bunk, as if still under way. Throughout the days I spent here at the village of San Juan Bautista, I could never properly relax. The surf never stopped. Ashore, I worried constantly about the boat. On the boat, I was impatient to explore the island. This place was fraught with raw energy, the boat at anchor pinned somewhere nameless between the land and the sea.

I rowed towards the concrete wharf through a fleet of open fishing boats moored in the bay. They were painted white, the woodwork torn and scarred. The boat nearest my own was *Crustáceo*, dedicated to the lobster fishery which was the island's only industry. I landed at steps where the fishermen unloaded their catch. Swells rose and fell five feet or more. I jumped onto the slimy concrete landing, threw the inflatable dinghy onto my back and scampered up the steps, water chasing my heels and swirling around my thighs.

The harbourmaster was trim and neat – they always were. 'If you see them pulling the fishing boats up the ramps,' he told me, 'you should leave within one hour. There's a north wind coming.'

It was early evening. I strolled down the winding lane that led through the village. The island had just got its first public telephone booths, ultra-modern aluminium cowls beside the earthen road. There were few people about. In places the road was paved with worn bricks, but mostly it was mud dried into deep runnels. Pretty cottages stood back in gardens laid out with shells and flower beds. Beyond this the hillsides were scorched and bare from erosion. At the western end of the village a small path led down towards the water. There was a bar here, predictably called the Robinson Crusoe. I followed a path down to a rickety deck built on stilts overlooking the bay. Surf crashed continually into the boulders below. The air was thick and bitter with salt. I drank a beer, then went inside.

The beamed ceiling was too low to stand upright. The windows were small and high. Light filtered through cracks in the walls. Even indoors I had to shout to be heard above the surf. A woman ran through the menu for me. 'There's lobster,' she said. I waited for the other items. She prompted me: 'You have to choose.'

'Choose?'

'Are you going to eat or not?'

I sat down while I waited for my food. The furniture was made from old pallets. I looked around the small room. The walls were hung with rusty buoys, harpoons, oil-lamps, a yellowing piece of scrimshaw-work, fish nets, a canvas hammock, decayed wooden blocks, a ship's wheel, frayed rope-ends, fish jaws, shells, a straw hat, model ships, wooden anchors with iron-bound stocks, a torn and undistinguishable flag, worn lengths of chain, a turtle shell, a binnacle, a painted figure-head.

So here it all was again: the assorted maritime paraphernalia found in pirate pubs and Chinese junk restaurants from Plymouth to the South Seas. But there was a difference here. The Robinson Crusoe was obviously authentic, a living museum of the island's past as the most important staging-post for European shipping heading north into the unknown Pacific. Here was that elusive quality the fake places cannot reproduce: the sense that one good push would be enough to send the whole structure toppling forward on its stilts and smashing into the boulders below in a heap of splintered timbers and scuttling cockroaches.

During the course of the evening the bar filled. Mostly they were young runaways from Santiago who had come to the island for the summer, filling a makeshift campsite on the hillside above the village. They were here to live free and have a good time. Even entering the bar was hilarious fun. Wearing white T-shirts and jeans, with red or blue handkerchiefs around their heads, necks, arms and thighs, they bounced through the door in noisy groups of three or four, laughing and clapping, tousling each other's hair. Then they shared a beer. Jovito had deserted from the army. Esteban worked as a stevedore in Concepción. Gloria Inés was having a telepathic relationship with Michael Jackson. Guillermo just wore handkerchiefs and did drugs. I drank too much beer, and spent a long time talking to Gloria Inés. She had written a book about her 'relationship' and gave me a copy. She told me I had the ocean in my blue eyes, and that the spirit of the waves and stars was with me. I shudder to think what I told her. Gloria Inés said that on my voyage home through the constellations of the South Pacific, I shouldn't be surprised when I heard her voice calling through the gale.

★

I dragged the dinghy up onto the wharf shortly after dawn the following morning. It had been an uncomfortable night, hot, with little air coming down the hatches and persistent ground-swell in the anchorage. The village was silent, save for the odd throat clearance behind a curtained window.

I climbed the lane, past the campsite and up above the village. It was still much too early. My brother-in-law had made a film here at Juan Fernández and I was on my way to see one of his contacts, Ivan Laeva, the head of the forestry and parks service in the islands, CONAF. To kill time I strolled down the network of paths that followed the contours through the outskirts of the village.

An hour later I was shown into Ivan's office in a prefabricated building overlooking the CONAF nursery and compound. Ivan shook my hand warmly when I explained who I was, and showed me a chair. It was a small room, very hot and airless. I began telling Ivan about my trip so far. He was a tidy man in a crisp, snow-white linen shirt. Although I'd been in Chile more than two months, Ivan was the first cosmopolitan Chilean I had met. The islands were a UNESCO biosphere reserve, and he headed a team of international scientists on a big budget. He wore round, wire-rimmed glasses. His hair was razor-cut, and he used plenty of product.

After a couple of minutes I realised something was wrong. Ivan wasn't listening to me. In fact, he stood up, walked round his desk, and opened the window on the north side of the room. Then he returned to his seat, and I continued with my story as best I could. But I began to feel uncomfortable, so close to another person, in such a small room. I became conscious of myself. When I pictured myself in Ivan's office I saw, almost for the first time, where I had come from and what the sea had done to me. I sat on a maroon swivel chair, my hair and beard uncut for four months. I'd worn the same T-shirt and shorts since the start of the passage from Patagonia nearly a week before, day and night. Salt had dried in spirals on my forearms. Clearly, opening the window hadn't been quite enough to clear the air. Ivan soon suggested that we go outside, and he would show me round the nursery.

We walked down the hillside and entered one of several large netting cages where seedlings were growing in raised beds. Juan Fernández is a unique environment. Most of the species of flora and fauna are endemic, and many are now endangered. Ivan told me that more than forty per cent of the original forest had been destroyed by goats and rabbits introduced as a source of meat by passing sailors, and the area was now severely eroded. The seedlings would be planted out to stop further damage.

I listened to Ivan as carefully as I could as I followed him between the netting cages, then down onto terraces where larger plants were growing. I nodded gravely, and looked knowing, but I was beginning to realise how much knowledge I'd lost at sea. I'd woken up that morning and climbed into the cockpit, as I did every morning on passage. Only this time I kept going, into the dinghy and onto the wharf. I did nothing differently, and found myself in a place where I'd forgotten the rules. It hadn't crossed my mind that this morning I could wash my face and put on a clean shirt.

I spent four days at Juan Fernández, mostly in the company of the island's fix-it-man, Ernesto Melgarejo, his wife and two young sons. The anchorage was uncomfortable so I spent the days ashore, being shown around by Ernesto, or at his house. We climbed up to Selkirk's lookout on a high ridge, then took the arid track across the southern flank of the island to the airstrip at the point. All the goats on this island had been eradicated, but the hillsides were running with rabbits. At one point I asked Ernesto about the Robinson Crusoe, the bar I'd gone to on my first night. He said it was a tourist place. That night I went to the bar he recommended, the one the locals preferred. It was quite empty.

I hadn't intended to stay on the island for long, and would probably have left on the third day, but it dawned windless and flat calm. An hour later I was seated on a zebra-striped sofa eating an enormous lobster for breakfast, presented to me by Ernesto's wife in consolation for the delay. It became something of a joke in the family that I couldn't leave the island until the wind blew. Once or twice as I ate they checked outside to see if the cloud was changing shape, or the leaves were moving on the trees. By lunchtime the children were blowing raspberries every time they saw me, then falling about in hysterics.

I took a path above the church and climbed steeply through the bush to the west of the village. After thirty minutes' hot climb I came out above the tree line and began ascending a scree slope which stretched up to the ridge. A perpetual slide of stones fell beneath my feet. The ridge was very narrow, with a giddy-making drop of a thousand feet on the other side. In places a cornice of rock folded away into the emptiness, pebbles rolling quietly over the crest and out of sight. Further along the ridge, where the slope on the village side was gentler, two twisted pines clung to the knife-edge. I reached them about mid afternoon, and sat down in the shade with a water bottle.

There wasn't a breath of wind. When I lay down, the whole island seemed to throb slightly beneath my back. From this height it appeared as if the surf was breaking right over the houses in the village. I looked to the north-west, the way I would sail once the wind returned. The ocean was a rich blue, and rigid. About ten miles distant the view disappeared into the heat haze, and the sea lost its colour, becoming grey and grainy where it met the sky. This was the place I would reach within two hours of leaving the anchorage.

I looked directly down from the ridge into Puerto Inglés, the bay to the west. The ruins of the fort were barely distinguishable from the boulders that had tumbled down the eroded hillsides around the bay. The Englishman Gerald Kingsland had landed here in the 1970s and set up camp. Kingsland had heard the story of Alexander Selkirk, and came to Isla Robinson Crusoe to live out his own fantasy of life on a desert island. His camp must have been a wretched place. There wasn't a tree in sight, and the desert bay was a heat-trap for the northerly sun. Kingsland soon quit Juan Fernández, but was later cast away on Tuin Island in the Torres Strait, with a head full of erotic fantasies, and Lucy Irvine.

The first known fictional account of marooning is an Egyptian papyrus fragment, *Le Naufrage*, the tale of a solitary castaway on a beautiful island, learning to survive. *Le Naufrage* has been described as the earliest written story of any kind: the first European fantasy was being cast away on the ocean in a place beyond everything you have ever experienced before.

When I stared across the sea to the north-west, towards the tropical haze of islands, reefs, and blue lagoons, I saw my rhumb-line tangled with the courses steered by most of the first European ships in the Pacific. Some of these vessels simply disappeared in the South Seas, foundering in cyclones or on reefs and islands that weren't on any chart. The tropical South Pacific has the highest concentration of islands of any ocean; many are atolls, only a few metres above sea-level, and very hard to see at night. Sailing through these waters without a reliable chart was like playing Russian roulette. But it is now believed that some, perhaps many, of the sailors whose ships were wrecked in the Pacific did not drown, and that Alexander Selkirk's marooning was not in itself unusual; what made Selkirk different as a castaway was that he was later picked up again.

The *San Lesmes* was part of a squadron under Loaysa, instructed to follow Magellan's route to the Spice Islands. Of the original seven ships that left the Basque region of Spain in 1525, only four made it into the Pacific the following year. These four sailed north up the coast of Chile until they reached a temperate latitude, then set a course north-west into the tropics. In mid ocean the *San Lesmes* became separated from the other ships in a gale, and was never seen again. It was assumed she had been lost at sea. But various discoveries over the years have suggested that the *San Lesmes* was actually wrecked on Amanu in the Tuamotu archipelago, a line of eighty coral atolls strung like a net across the South Pacific. It appears that after striking the reef at Amanu Atoll the captain of the *San Lesmes*, Hiro, tried to lighten the ship and so float her off by dumping cannon and stone ballast into the lagoon, where they were found in 1929. Unable to free the ship, Hiro then took the boat and sailed with the crew to the neighbouring and larger atoll of Hao. Quirós, landing at Hao eighty years later, found Spanish-speaking Polynesians and a man with red curly hair, gold jewellery, and spaniels, the breed of dog typically carried on Spanish ships in the Age of Discovery. Later a cross was found in the same area, made of cedar, seemingly from ship's spars.

The probable fate of the *San Lesmes* exposes another way in which Alexander Selkirk's story (and Robinson Crusoe's) is untypical: the myth of the 'desert', or deserted, island. The Pacific peoples were too good as navigators to leave many places untouched. During the centuries of the Pacific migrations the Melanesians, Micronesians and Polynesians found, and inhabited, virtually every island and coral reef in the tropical Pacific, north and south of the equator. An alternative image to that of the solitary castaway cutting a daily notch into a coconut tree might go like this. The ship is wrecked on a coral reef unseen on a moonless night. Those crew members who aren't drowned in the surf or torn to shreds on the coral stagger at dawn onto one of the coarse sand beaches of an islet in the atoll. As they look around the exhausted faces of their surviving shipmates, they know they will probably spend the rest of their lives here. That might not be very long: they've arrived on an overpopulated atoll, where competition for space, food and water is often fierce, and where no white man has ever been seen before. Survival will require great diplomacy.

Before dawn the following morning I saw the navigation lights of a large ship standing off Cumberland Bay. At the same time I could see figures scurrying about beneath the arc lights on the wharf. As dawn broke, a naval vessel dropped anchor in the outer soundings of the bay, and a group of uniformed Armada officers embarked in a lighter at the wharf and motored out towards the ship.

I paid a measure of attention to these comings and goings, but was distracted by something else: the wind had returned. In the bay itself the water was still, but I could see an occasional small white-cap half a mile offshore. There were patches of low cloud scudding across the sky and, seen through binoculars, the trees on the central ridge-line were moving.

I rowed to the wharf with my papers. The previous day a smaller, rusting supply ship had arrived at the island. It had been tied to the wharf all night, crashing heavily into the timber piles on the long swell. The water swirling around the piles was now littered with splinters. The work of unloading the ship had begun the day before. Crates were now stacked all over the wharf, to-gether with fridges, televisions, furniture, mattresses, and another new phone-box. A small crowd of people had already gathered on the wharf, looking for their new possessions or inspecting the grey naval ship anchored in the distance. The arrival of this ship marked an important day in the island's calendar. It was the end of summer: the ship would take all the back-packers home to the continent, and also some of the islanders, who would spend the winter months with relatives in Santiago and Concepción.

The cargo ship at the wharf was still half-full. Every few minutes the derrick hoisted another net onto the quay, amid much shouting of directions and advice. Ernesto was standing in the centre of the hold directing operations. When he saw me he put his foot into the hook of the derrick and was lifted up onto the quay. Ernesto and I always conversed in Spanish, which was a limitation because my skills in it were even now underdeveloped. He did, however, know one word of English, which he repeated quite often, as a couplet. This word was 'very'. As we'd climbed up to Selkirk's lookout two days earlier, toiling through the bush, Ernesto had panted, 'Oh, very ..., very ...' The adjective was always missing, but could usually be guessed from the context. In this instance, the missing word was presumably 'exhausted'. When we reached the lookout he'd sat beside me and, gazing at the view over the island and ocean, uttered a wistful, 'Ah, very ..., very ...', the missing adjective surely 'beautiful'. Now, on the wharf, I told him what he could see for himself: the wind had returned. I would be leaving the island within an hour. He asked where I was going. I said I was heading for French Polynesia, but hoped to make some stops along the way. But I could see that naming my destination didn't really answer his question. Ernesto didn't know what sailing to French Polynesia in a small boat meant. Was I talking a week? A year? I explained that it was about three thousand miles to Gambier, the most south-easterly of the French islands. It should take about a month to get there. Ernesto gave me a sweaty bear-hug, and the Chilean handshake, which has three distinct moves. He looked at my boat in the anchorage, then out to the open sea, and said slowly, 'Ooh, very ..., very ...' Normally I could guess what Ernesto was trying to say. It was obvious, from a shared knowledge or perception of the world, despite the linguistic gap. But this time I didn't know how he would have finished his sentence. I had absolutely no idea what adjective he might use to describe an ocean voyage.

I made my way back through the crowd to the base of the wharf where the Armada office was located. There no answer to my knock and, as the door was unlocked, I walked inside. The office was empty. Presumably the Armada staff were out at the naval vessel. I went back onto the wharf but couldn't see any of them, so sat down on a bollard outside the office to wait. To clear out of Juan Fernández, I needed to see the harbourmaster. Boats have to get a 'clearance', in Chile a *zarpe*, from each country, sometimes from each port. When you arrive at a new place you hand in the old clearance, and when you leave you are given a new one. The exact nature of these formalities depends on the country and its attitude to, or familiarity with, visiting yachts. In some places, officials demand to see your clearance as soon as you arrive, and there are supposedly severe penalties for those unable to produce one; elsewhere, especially in the Caribbean, it can be hard to find an official who has the remotest interest in your clearance. Generally speaking, the Chileans had belonged in the first category, but in this case, because of Juan Fernández's status as something of an annexe to the mainland, the harbourmaster hadn't actually taken my old clearance from me when I first came ashore, though he did register my arrival in a large book.

I waited for ten minutes outside the office. I was impatient to get started now that I'd made the decision to leave. No one I asked had seen the harbourmaster, or knew when he might be back. As I still had my clearance from my last port, I could show that at the next island, and not mention having stopped at Juan Fernández. It just meant there would be no entry in the harbourmaster's book recording my departure.

I hung about for a couple more minutes, then carried the dinghy down the steps at the wharf and rowed briskly back out to the boat. So in one sense, I've never actually left Juan Fernández: in bureaucratic terms at least, I'll spend the rest of my life on the island.

There was a light breeze blowing across the bay by the time I got to the boat. I sailed off the anchor, then under the western headland of Bahía Cumberland. Directly in the island's lee the wind was dirty and progress slow. I sailed north for half an hour. Then, as I came out from the island's wind shadow, the breeze settled in the south-west, and I was able to set my chosen course.

I was bound for Yosemite Rock, which lies two hundred and fifty miles north-west of Juan Fernández. Yosemite was reported in 1903, and the Admiralty pilot describes it as a white rock of some length with pointed heads three to four metres high. Ships searching for Yosemite in 1904 and 1909 found nothing; other vessels have reported a feature in the charted latitude, but up to ten miles further west. Yosemite is a classic vigia, an island, reef or rock which has been reported but whose position, or existence, is now doubted.

I made good progress that morning, reaching in easy seas. There was little sun, the sky being mostly filled with banks of cloud, which made it cool to sit on deck and watch the sea. In the afternoon the wind freshened and I retreated to the cockpit. The cloud darkened and sank lower in the sky. As night fell, I thought it would rain.

I found it difficult to sleep that night, and was surprised how much even a short stopover at anchor could affect my routine. The wind had risen to twenty-five knots, now forward of the beam, and my passage to the north-west was becoming bumpy in a rising sea. I lay on my bunk for long periods, and must have dozed off at times, but never so deeply that I couldn't hear the water rushing round the skin of the boat, and I woke feeling more tense than when I'd closed my eyes.

In the cockpit time passed more easily, so I spent much of the night there. I expected the rain to start at any moment. The air was hot, thick with tension. As the boat pitched on the swells a small window of ocean separated from the blackness all around and raced beneath the leeward rail, occasionally pouring round the stanchions. In the cockpit I could stand comfortably, my feet on either bench, holding the steel handles in the spray-hood frame. I could see almost nothing of the ocean around the boat. I read the state of the sea by the combination of effort it took my spread-eagled arms and legs to remain connected to the boat. That night it was an almost restful series of gyrations, as a hot wind swept sideways over the boat, soothing my nerves.

In the small hours lightning set in, bursting in sheets, sometimes on two sides at once. But there was no thunder: it was absolutely silent, and still not a drop of rain. In the flashes of light I saw that the horizon was very close, the sea like polished black metal, the sky a pale grey, layered and complex. Throughout the night I stayed in the cockpit for half an hour or so at a time, allowing myself to unwind. When I thought I was ready I climbed back down to the cabin and again began the exhausting process of trying to get to sleep. This went on till 4 a.m. Then I started on the chocolate.

Before I went to sea I didn't understand what people meant by 'bingeing'. As I remember, it was off the coast of Portugal on my voyage out to New Zealand that I first discovered the joys of eating four bars of chocolate in an hour. These days, in these deserted waters, my technique had evolved. That first night out of Juan Fernández I chased the chocolate with a mug of brandy, and slept through till well after dawn.

The beam wind had risen to thirty knots when I woke, and the boat was over-pressed. I reefed the sails slowly, my mouth very dry. Then I sat on the engine box, drank a little water and ate a breakfast of prunes. Soon there was further lightning along the horizon to the south-west, and I decided to alter course. I furled the genoa completely and ran off to the north with the wind behind the boat, the line of least resistance. This new course would pass Yosemite by. The weather was too dirty to be playing around with vigias. I acknowledged this change of plan very simply in the log and then forgot about it. I change plans quickly at sea, give up long-held hopes and intentions without regret.

In this case the process of moving on was sweetened: there was a second vigia, and arguably a more interesting one, another two hundred and sixty miles further on. Hopefully the weather would be more settled by the time I arrived.

Emily Rock was first reported in 1869, when it was described as 37 metres long and 4.5 metres high. The vigia was seen again in 1873 by two vessels, but this time reported as nearly fourteen hundred metres long, consisting of sand and volcanic stone. Later, the Chilean corvette *O'Higgins* searched for Emily Rock but saw nothing. Another attempt to find the vigia in 1903 proved unsuccessful. Since then several ships have passed near the reported position but seen no sign, either of land or of shoaling.

The Admiralty pilot records the two lengths given to Emily Rock by navigators, while Yosemite Rock, the first vigia I'd hoped to visit, is simply described as a 'white rock of some length'. Exactly what 'some length' means is unclear. Both are described as 'rocks', rather than 'islands' or 'cays'. Maritime terminology is surprisingly unclear when it comes to defining these things. The *Mariner's Handbook*, also published by the Admiralty, is intended to complement pilot books by giving background information for navigators, with a particular emphasis on definition of terms. The *Handbook* defines 'island' as 'A piece of land of less than *continental* size which, under normal conditions, is completely surrounded by water.' An 'islet' is 'A comparatively small insular mass, i.e., smaller than an *island* and bigger than a *cay*.' A 'cay' is 'A small insular feature usually with scant vegetation; usually *sand* or *coral*. Often applied to the smaller coral *shoals*.' 'Rock' is defined as 'An extensive geological term, but limited in hydrography to hard, solid masses of the Earth's surface rising from the bottom of the sea, either completely submerged or projecting permanently, or at times, above the water.' There is nothing in these definitions relating to absolute size.

This stands in marked contrast to the exhaustive detail given in the *Mariner's Handbook* on the subject of ice. It carefully defines

174 different varieties of ice, and related ice events. Different types of iceberg are categorised with precision: 'growlers' are less than 6 metres long, 'small bergs' are 6–60 metres, 'medium bergs' are 61–122 metres, and so on. No fewer than forty-one photographs are provided so that mariners should be left in absolutely no doubt about what sort of ice they are looking at.

But when it comes to defining the land, hydrographic terminology is vague. What is the difference between an 'island' and a 'rock'? There are other vigias in this sector of the ocean: to the south the chart shows two more, Podesta Island and Sefton Reef. Podesta is actually smaller than Emily Rock, but Podesta is given the title of 'island'. Do the words 'island', 'islet', 'cay' and 'rock' conjure a slightly different mental image for each of us? Perhaps the larger land masses are universally understood, but the land's peripheral features, those that only just rise above the surface of the ocean, allow an individual interpretation. For me the difference might be this: an island or islet has sufficient vegetation to support life; if my boat sank and I swam ashore at an island or islet, I would be saved. But if I were cast away on a rock or cay, I'd die in any case.

In 1540 a Spanish ship was wrecked off the coast of Peru, well to the north-east of my present position. The only surviving crewman, Pedro Serrano, spent two nights in the water. On the third day he sighted land above the sea and swam ashore. There was no vegetation at all, and no fresh water: the surface consisted entirely of sand and rock a few metres above the waves. The castaway ate shellfish and turtles, and collected rainwater in the turtles' shells. He survived here for seven years, and so adapted to his environment that thick hair grew all over his upper body, protecting him from exposure. A ship sighted Serrano in 1547, and eventually he returned to Spain. He became something of a novelty, a freak, in the courts of northern Europe, where he still wore his hair long, as proof of his hardships. A German prince gave him a pension.

I ran under a double-reefed mainsail for the rest of that day. The wind was a barrelling warm force, still in the south-west. In the evening a light rain finally began to fall in a stronger gust of wind. I slept better that night. On this downwind tack the motion was again that long diagonal roll down the face of waves that had been my home for many of the last months. Overnight the wind backed to the south. I set more sail and altered course a little to the west. By the time the sun was up the wind was in the south-east. I laid a course direct for Emily Rock.

The pilot book gives two reported heights for Emily Rock, the first of 4.5 metres and the second of 6. One remote possibility to explain why subsequent navigators have been unable to locate this vigia is that it was formed by volcanic activity, and that a subsequent eruption caused it to subside. If this were so, the old rock might now be an area of shoaling, with no visible feature above the sea. To find this vigia I might be dependent on finding an area of lighter-coloured water, and on the depth sounder.

Six years earlier, in western Polynesia, I had sailed over an area of mid-ocean shoaling. It was an unnerving experience. On passage from Wallis to Funafuti I clipped the edge of the Macaw Bank one evening at sunset. The shoal is a well-charted feature, but the thought of the sea-bed so close beneath the keel, so far offshore, left me both anxious and alert. The minimum charted depth is just 18 metres. With the sun so low the sea was a monotone blue-black: I could detect no alteration in its colour above the shoal. Instead I was dependent on the echo-sounder, an old-fashioned model, a dial with a flashing light to denote different depths of water. It isn't a powerful device, but can generally be relied on to find a sounding up to 40 metres down. As darkness fell that night I watched the dial closely for any echo, a flash of red light to show I was sailing over the summit of a mountain range as high as the Alps. First I got a weak signal at about 40 metres, then the depth rose rapidly, first to 25 metres, then to 20. I stood tensely in the cockpit, the sky and sea around me black, my one fragile link with the planet's surface dependent on the flickering red lights of the dial. I ran downwind for five miles, the sea very slight, a mere joggle on the surface of the ocean. An hour passed during which I never fully relaxed. Then the sea-bed began to fall away, the last lights on the sounder went out as no bottom was found. The sun had set, there was no moon: the water and sky were inseparable. I sailed, breathless, beyond the peak of the sub-oceanic mountain, over the cliff's edge and on across distant plains and valleys more than four thousand metres below the boat.

Now, I made good time towards Emily Rock. By dawn two days later the breeze had fallen to fifteen knots. The sky was almost clear. I hoped that I had found the trade winds, the engine that would drive the boat for several months to come. Conditions were perfect: in the strong sunshine any rock or area of shoaling should be clearly visible.

Five miles before I reached the charted position of Emily Rock I turned on the echo-sounder. There was no bottom. The sea was an orderly sheet of glinting blue, little troubled by white-caps. There seemed to be no remarkable feature. I walked up to the bow to look behind the headsail, then climbed to the spreaders to gain the advantage of height. I saw no breakers, nor any indent on the horizon. In the cockpit I set my gaze on the echo-sounder repeater, the paint on the needle now flaky because condensation had got into the dial. The needle stayed firmly at its upper limit, denoting that no bottom could be found. I spent an hour alternating between watching the depth sounder and scanning the horizon and the sea for something, I didn't know exactly what. Then I began to feel absurd, and ate lunch.

The most recent sighting of any of the four vigias in this area was in 1908. Several unsuccessful searches have since been made for each one. The Admiralty pilot book acknowledges that the four vigias are probably non-existent – but all four still feature on Admiralty charts as cartographic facts.

Six

On either side of the equator, in every ocean, trade winds blow from east to west. Stable areas of high pressure generate these continuous and dependable streams of wind. At least, this is the general picture described by every tome on meteorology. The reality, for a small boat dependent on its sails, isn't always so perfect, but the trades are still some of the most reliable of winds, and sailors have been taking advantage of them for centuries.

Columbus took the trade winds across the Atlantic. Magellan and all the early Europeans who followed him into the Pacific sailed north from the coast of Patagonia in search of an easterly flow. The trade winds mark a broad thoroughfare across the ocean. They form a geographical narrative, like the Silk Road.

In the trades, the way ahead is clearly signposted. Puff-ball cloud forms in parallel lines which arc the sky from horizon to horizon. The cloud is low, full of bright, white light. Sometimes, to windward, sheets of grey squall cloud hang above a darkening sea. The squalls slide effortlessly closer; they may pass by on either side, but just as often the horizon all around the boat slips imperceptibly behind a veil of cloud, the sky goes a deep blue, then grey, before the boat is buried in a tumult of wind and rain. Elsewhere, in pockets of hopelessness I'd rather forget, the wind may fail for days at a time. Here, mirages gather on the skyline and the sea feels shallow and full of spite.

In the South Pacific, the trade winds are formed by anti-cyclones in temperate latitudes. From my position at Emily Rock the trade blew strong and steady for the first days of the passage as I sailed north-west, deeper into the tropics. In this wind the cabin was a cool and breezy place, mostly in shade, but slashes of sunlight would come through ports and hatches when the boat rolled. In the morning the chart table was too hot, fully exposed to the climbing sun, so if necessary I lay on the bunk with a book to cool off, or listened to the radio. By lunchtime the sun had travelled round to beat on the side of the boat, and I could move back and sit on the engine box to write at the chart table.

On deck the trade was fresh, between twenty and twenty-five knots, always warm and woolly: in these latitudes the wind is a light angora that surrounds your whole body, tugging in the direction of the flow. I ran between a hundred and forty and a hundred and fifty miles a day, and was sure it could get no better than this. At 27° south latitude I altered course and sailed due west for Easter Island, some thousand miles beyond the horizon.

Over those days the sea took on a quality I hadn't experienced so far on the voyage. I plotted each day's run as a routine, measuring out the miles as if progress was a certainty. The swells were a metre high, sometimes a metre and a half, perfectly suited to a boat of this length. As each one passed around the keel I felt my home perform a cycle of predictable motions, lifting at the stern, dipping to leeward, always stiff and reasoned. After breakfast each morning I faced the prospect of a whole day of easy progress. In the cabin I had time on my hands, surrounded by an ocean world of wind and seas that appeared almost mechanical.

I cut my hair and trimmed my beard. I sat with charts and

books of the islands ahead and dreamed that this might be my best passage: I could reach Gambier in eighteen days. It was light and warm: for many days this alone was sufficient to guarantee contentment. I drank lime juice from a glass placed day and night on the gimballed cooker. I found pleasure in simply looking at that glass. It was a heavy, round tumbler, a little taller than the width of my hand. I had never used a glass in the Southern Ocean for fear of breakages; instead, I drank everything from the one stainless-steel tankard. But in the trades I came to accept that glassware could again be part of the fabric of my life. I looked proudly at the glass sometimes, as sunlight flashed through the airy cabin. I saw it as a trophy of the peaceful times I had won for myself. As the trade winds settled into place over the ocean, I all too quickly became accustomed to this genteel world of sipped drinks and mahi mahi steaks poached in Chilean chardonnay. It was easy to forget how quickly it could all fall apart.

Many of the things that I remember about the passage through the tropics happened at night. Even when nothing happened at all, I still remember the nights. Daylight can be a corrosive force on the tropical seas. It is an anomaly of the marine landscape: by day, there is often nothing to see. The sky is hard and burnt, the water a bulge of silver reflections. When the wind is light, the heat is desperate. During the day I often hid in the shade, seldom venturing out for long. There are events hidden among the shadows and languor, of course, but they are indistinct. Critically, in my memory, all lack a clear starting-point at which any one event can be said to begin. And because most things that happen at sea are so routine and inconsequential, without a starting-point, they disappear.

At night it is different. In the night-time any event, even a binge on chocolate and booze, is bounded by sleep, and so begins at the point of waking. The night has this clarity, like a frame around each scene, which has the effect of making it seem the most eventful time at sea.

I woke one night early in the passage and knew that something was wrong. My first clear memory is of standing in the cockpit, almost numb from inertia. I couldn't think, or even focus my eyes at first. There was liquid everywhere. Then I began to feel the rain, heavy pellets biting into my bare back. After that I was fully awake.

The sky was yellow, cloud was layered at different heights, tearing overhead. Sheet lightning flashed in several places around the horizon, a gold circle revealing wet, black cloud. The sea looked thick and warm, like boiling broth.

Sound came from no one direction but was all around, a mix of wind, waves, and rain beating on canvas. The boat was run through with energy, its roll urgent. The waves were steep and close, and the bow was being buried in the troughs, green water coming over the stemhead, white furrows cast to either side. When I'd left the deck two hours earlier the wind had been a steady trade, the boat carrying full sail.

The squall had struck hard. Now the boat was over-pressed, the sails wrinkled and misshapen, straining to get free. The pole holding the genoa to windward was pinched tight, trembling when the boat surfed. The backstays were rods. The whole rig looked out of place: a paper-and-dowelling kite caught in a gale.

I hesitated. I was already beginning to feel cold, dressed only in shorts. I pulled the harness out from beneath the spray-hood. I preferred to wear it under, not over, a jacket: it was quicker to put on against bare skin.

Running along the deck are wire ropes called jackstays, attached to a strong point at either end. The harness is connected to the jackstay with a webbing tether. This way I can walk up and down the deck trailing the tether behind me, always attached to the jackstay. Otherwise, with the boat on self-steering, if I fell overboard I would be left to drown. Jackstays are standard even on crewed yachts.

I was still cold. My jacket was also stuffed beneath the spray-hood. Now it was sodden with rain from the squall. As I pushed my hands through the wet sleeves they kept catching on the lining. I shoved harder, growing impatient. I needed to get the wind out of the sails quickly. The boat was careering downwind and I was worried it might broach. With the jacket finally on I did up the zip. The tether came up underneath the jacket, onto the harness at my chest.

The sheet for the furling genoa was coiled in a pocket in the cockpit coaming. I pulled it out and flicked two turns off the winch, then the rope was snapped from my grip, the sail rushing forwards, spilling its wind. But the sheet fouled. I'd let the rope run too quickly: it had tangled at the block midway down the side-deck, three metres short of its full extent. The sail was flog-ging heavily, being pulled up hard by the jammed rope. I needed to free the jammed rope.

I moved to climb out of the cockpit, but stopped. I'd forgot-ten the tether. It was hanging down between my legs. I clipped the other end onto the jackstay, then set off down the side-deck.

I don't know exactly what happened next. I've climbed around the deck at night hundreds of times, sometimes without a harness. It was a bad squall that night, but not exceptional, the rain hard, the wind at forty knots. The problem was that I was carrying too much sail. Now, half-released, the genoa was crash-ing in the air overhead, sending tremors through the boat. One minute I was moving down the narrow side-deck as I had so often done before. It is a tight squeeze around the spray-hood, awkward on a rolling boat. I was looking at the tangled rope in the block just ahead. Then it all changed.

The first thing I remember was a crushing blow to my chest.

It felt like being broken in half. The jerk was unforgiving, spinning me round in the water like a rag doll. My body felt numb and dead. But I knew exactly what had happened: I'd fallen over the side of the boat and was being dragged through the water. The strong-point on the jackstay had held. The tether was stretched like a bar over the rail, then down to the harness on my chest. I was somewhere against the boat's quarter.

I couldn't breathe. Water seemed to be everywhere. I'd been stunned by the initial blow, and now didn't know up from down. I could find no window through which to break out into clear air. And for a moment there seemed little point in trying. I had thought I would struggle and fight, keep going to the end, but actually those first moments in the water were a time of resignation and defeat, of sulking at the self-inflicted mishap. The sea was hard and unyielding: it seemed I was being dragged across gravel.

When I lay on my front and arched my back I found I could get my head clear of the water. My right shoulder was hard against the side of the boat. At anchor in flat water, it's just possible, when you are swimming, to reach the toe-rail on deck and, if you are fit, pull yourself out of the water. But with the sails still set, the boat was heeling over downwind and this distance was increased. In the big swell I kept slamming into the side of the hull. Here it was slimy with weed, the underwater sections exposed as the boat heeled.

I pulled myself up on the tether and made a lunge for the rail. Nothing happened: I couldn't lunge against the force of the water. The sea was pouring in through the cuffs of my oilskin jacket, which was ballooning out around my shoulders, dragging me back. The bottom of the jacket was pulled up around my chest by the tether attached from underneath. I could feel the jacket biting into the small of my back. I had to get it off.

When I lowered my head to look for the zip, my body dived back under the water. My hands were torn from the collar. I rolled onto my back and dropped my chin. This way I could breathe, and the collar-opening was protected from the seas. I found the zip with my fingers and undid the first half easily, but the bottom part of the jacket was bunched around my chest by the tether, which was now stretched hard over my shoulder. The fabric of the coat was torn all around the zip, and the zip itself was so buckled that the slider had jammed. I started trying to tear the zip open. As I struggled, the loosened jacket came off my shoulders. I put my arms behind my back and the water did the rest, pulling the jacket down around my waist like a skirt. It was still caught around the tether. I tore at it some more, now from the bottom of the zip. The material finally parted, perhaps the zip broke. The jacket was gone in an instant. I must have lost my boxer shorts as soon as I hit the water: now I was naked in the harness.

I pulled up on the tether, waited for the boat to roll back towards me, then grabbed for the toe-rail with my right hand. My fingers closed around the worn teak. But when I let go of the tether with my left hand to get it on the rail, the force of the water broke my grip. I fell into the sea, and was again slammed up hard against the tether. I didn't wait now. It was impossible to rest in the water: every second left me more tired. I pulled up on the tether again and got one hand on the rail. Just then the boat gave a long roll downwind, lifting me almost clear of the water. Without its weight around me I was able to pull my shoulders up onto the rail, then hook my feet up one at a time. It was a horrible tangle: there's no side-deck here because the cockpit coaming comes almost to the edge of the deck, and as I wriggled under the life-lines the tether got caught on the stanchion. I unclipped it and slid into the cockpit.

The first thing was to get the bloody sails in. I was thankful I had this task, some urgent work to focus my racing mind. I crawled along the side-deck and freed the tangled sheet in the block. From the cockpit I furled the genoa. The second headsail was hanked onto a separate forestay. This time I released the sheet more slowly, to spill the wind from the sail, then walked to the mast and took the halyard off the winch. Standing in the bow, I pulled the cracking sail to the deck. The power had now drained from the boat's rush downwind, and as the body of the sail came onto the deck the noise overhead was hushed. The motion began to ease. Lightning strikes revealed a luminous green world folding and reforming beneath driving rain. Between times it was pitch black: I couldn't see my hand. I pulled the last of the genoa down slowly, feeling from hank to hank. Even blind, there was a growing sense of control. I lashed the headsail to the jack-stay, then worked my way back down the deck.

In the cabin I dried myself, put on a dry jacket, and went out-side again. I wondered for a time if I would need to reef the mainsail as well. I waited five minutes. Then the boom of the thunder became more distant, and the boat began to stall as the wind died away.

I sat beneath the spray-hood in the cockpit and smoked a cig-arette as the lightning receded to the north-west and patches of starry sky emerged to windward. The seas were shapeless. Heavy strands of spray occasionally slopped out of the darkness. It took me a long time to warm up, though the wind was softer now and my hair began to dry. My legs were still stained slightly red where they had rubbed against the red anti-fouling paint. I felt empty, and thought I might drift off to sleep. But I was dragged back to the present. The front of my jacket and my legs were wet and sticky. I realised that I was being sick. A thin, salty bile was trick-ling from the corner of my mouth and down my neck.

I woke feeling stiff, as if I'd been struggling while asleep. From my bunk I looked through the companionway. I could see a few faint stars in the dawn twilight. I focused my eyes on the compass. The wind had shifted, and the boat was sailing twenty degrees off-course. I needed to get up and put this right.

I looked at the short journey necessary to reach the cockpit. It was only a few metres, no more than ten movements: over the lee-cloth, three short steps down the cabin, two steps onto the engine box, through the companionway, a stoop, and into the cockpit. Perhaps half-a-dozen of these micro-journeys together made up the total distance I would travel in one day, between the bunks, the galley, the chart-table and the deck. My feet and hands fell on the same places exactly: on the engine box the timber had become hollowed out where my right foot always turned on descent. Sometimes I resented the limits of my cycle. I could anticipate each tiny part of the way ahead, which muscle I'd flex and how hard. Just for a moment, when I first woke up and looked at the way to the deck, I saw a treadmill I'd be walking for weeks to come.

I stood upright in the cockpit. The sky was absolutely clear. The sun was just breaking the horizon to the east, from where a twelve-knot breeze was buffing the ocean. The boat was rolling slowly downwind in a slight sea. It already felt hot. On a day like this dawn can seem the hottest time, with twelve hours ahead and the sun not even fully risen. The trade was warm, and stale. I learned to discount the convention of 'fresh sea air'.

Sailing west at 27° south latitude, I was on the limit of the south-east trade winds. For the first days of the passage from Emily Rock the wind had been fresh, pushing the boat hard and sending a cooling breeze down the companionway. But then the trade began to ease. A lighter south-easterly kept the passage moving, but sometimes I covered less than a hundred miles in one day. At night, and in the hours before dawn especially, the wind often dropped to ten knots, and the leech of the genoa gave a periodic slap – not the great belly-crash of a sail when the wind is truly dying but a tight, light *phud* sound, which seemed almost harmless but was enough to keep the possibility of a calm at the forefront of my mind.

In these lighter conditions the breeze didn't have the strength to carry down the companionway into the cabin. Below-decks it was unbearably still. As an alternative to the shade of the cabin I stretched a small piece of canvas across the cockpit, from the spray-hood to the backstays. The only piece of cloth I had was rather narrow, more an overhead strip than an awning, but by moving about beneath it I could usually find some shade while sitting directly in whatever breeze there was.

I spent some time in the cockpit that morning, rigging the awning and adjusting the sheets and self-steering. The ocean in this early light was the colour of cedar, and looked almost as hard, with just a few inexplicable folds and dimples that must have been a trick of the eye. By the time I'd finished establishing a course my face was damp with sweat. It was 7 a.m. I needed a drink.

I sat on the engine box and pumped a glass of water at the sink. It was a foot pump. I had heard and felt something crunch in it two days earlier; now the lever came back up only very slowly. It took a minute to pump a glassful of water, one feeble squirt at a time.

I knew I wouldn't try to fix the pump today. It was hot in the cabin. The rising sun was shining directly down the companion-way, already tingling on my shoulders and head as I filled the glass and then gulped the contents. The pump was slow, but still working. Why bother to fix it yet? As the passage went on and the sun got higher, and hotter, I cared less about these small problem-solving tasks about the boat. No doubt tropical heat often has this effect on Europeans, this torpor, but I believe it is stronger at sea.

Temperature has a disproportionate effect on the ocean: it can make two separate stretches of water that are otherwise very similar appear wholly different. On my passage to Chile in November, at the furthest point south, the mean sea surface temperature was 8°C. In my present position, in late March, it is 24°C. But only the first of these statistics, the low figure in the south, was truly apparent at the time.

In the Southern Ocean, although the wind was sometimes bitter, it was the sea itself that froze the heart of the boat. I remember lying on the bunk reading during the day, in thick socks, feeling the numbness spread from my feet and into my ankles. I believed I could feel the cold creeping through the skin of the hull from the ocean. The cold was in the sea, and the true nature of my journey, as one across water, could never be denied. In high latitudes the ocean was inescapable, a current of cold anxiety flowing round the boat. In the south I would have looked at the damaged water pump straight away. I was made uneasy by any form of malfunction.

The effect of temperature in the tropics is very different. Though the sea was certainly much warmer, I couldn't feel it inside the boat; instead, the dominant temperature came always from above, from the sun. I spent the days seeking shade, always focused upwards from the boat at the empty, simple sky, never downwards, at the unknown ocean. For days at a time in the tropics I had little sense of a journey across deep water. Instead, my boat was travelling somewhere beneath the sky, near the very bottom of the world. There seemed to be nothing below me. The sun was hot, but harmless. I could worry about the pump when it produced no water at all. There was a spare one somewhere.

The ancient Greeks observed that the temperature rose as a traveller ventured south from the Mediterranean. They also knew of the frigid Arctic wastes in the north, a land where in winter the sun never shone, and they associated it with Cimmerian darkness. Early Greek thought speculated that if a traveller continued on a journey southward, the temperature would continue to rise until a burning southern land was reached, the ant-arctic.

This view of a cold dark north and a hot south satisfied the

Greek fascination with symmetry up to a point, but by the fifth century BC had been replaced by a more complex map of the global climate. Parmenides drew an equatorial axis onto the sphere, and the world was divided into distinct climatic bands. At both poles there was a Frigid Zone. The Temperate Zone stretched across the centre of each hemisphere. And along the equator was the Torrid Zone, or Tropic Sea. Some suggested that the Tropic Sea could never be navigated, and thus began no end of superstition regarding the crossing of equatorial waters.

In the Christian world view the Tropic Sea was hell-fire itself, and any ship that attempted the passage was damned. In the Dark Ages, travel from Europe was mostly restricted to pilgrimage. Even in the following centuries, those others who did venture forth, such as Marco Polo, mostly travelled in an east–west direction, ignoring the southern hemisphere.

The idea of the equator as an impassable barrier blocking access to the south continued to be influential in medieval Europe. The Hereford *mappa mundi* does not extend as far as the Torrid Zone; the south, even if habitable, is unreachable. One reason that Christopher Columbus's proposed voyage to the Spice Islands found favour in Spain might have been that he chose the 'Christian route' to the east, avoiding a crossing of the equator.

This, of course, was to ignore the experience of other mariners. It is possible that the Phoenicians made a voyage across the equator as early as 600 BC. Herodotus tells how a Phoenician *bireme* with two rows of oars left the Red Sea and sailed down the African coast. As the ship rounded the southern point of the African continent the crew saw the sun on their right-hand side, to the north. According to the story, the Phoenicians returned to the Mediterranean by way of the Pillars of Hercules, the Strait of Gibraltar.

The first authenticated European voyages to the south were

ordered by the Portuguese Prince Henry the Navigator, who sought a sea route to the east. Cao returned in 1484, having reached 13° south latitude on the coast of present-day Angola. Diaz made landfall on the Cape of Good Hope four years before Columbus's first voyage.

In fact, the problem for a sailing boat crossing the equatorial seas is not so much the heat, though that can be oppressive, as the lack of wind. Although reliable trade winds are found both north and south of the equator, along the axis itself there is a band of doldrums up to several hundred miles wide, the exact extent of the calms depending on season and longitude.

I had approached the equator from the north while on passage from the UK to New Zealand in 1991, having recently transited the Panama Canal, then been boarded by the US Coastguard some days after that. After that, progress had been very slow.

In the Gulf of Panama, the waters enclosed by the coastline of the isthmus, there is often a fine northerly breeze, and I covered the first two hundred miles from Balboa without problem. But soon the northerly died, and the Pacific has seldom seemed so big. When it came, the breeze was only light, a southerly at five to ten knots. It would pick up for a couple of hours in the morning, just long enough to raise the expectation that this time it would hold. Once or twice it blew all night, even at fifteen knots, and I got up for breakfast thinking I might finally spend a whole day under way. This aspiration fell apart, even before the coffee was made, when the sails again began to crash and the boat to nod helplessly on the small seas. I limped midway between Isla de Malpelo and the Colombian coast, a hundred and fifty miles offshore. I had etched Isla de Malpelo into my mind as a landmark after which things would begin to improve; I saw the island as marking the entry to the Pacific. But after the island it got much worse.

The first calm lasted seven days. At 3° north of the equator, the sun was merciless. I had no furler system for the headsail in those days, so the genoa lay in a lifeless pile on deck. The mainsail was draped over the boom, providing a little shade in the cockpit. It took five days for me to become so numb with disappointment that I could no longer even scream at the sea. When the wind returned there was no pleasure in hoisting the sails: it seemed to be much too late now to ever find pleasure at sea again.

I sailed south for forty-eight hours into an uncertain headwind. Twice it got up sufficiently to lift white-caps from the surface of the sea; but between times it all but failed. In those two days of halting progress I covered a further hundred and twenty miles, leaving me at 1° north of the equator – another sixty miles to go. Then the wind died again.

The second calm lasted three days. I had seldom seen the ocean so flat before. I played a game with a hard-boiled egg, the last surviving egg from Panama, which I didn't care to open for fear it would be rotten. I placed the egg in the centre of the chart table, and let go. Then I timed how long it took to roll to one of the sides of the table, subject only to the shifting gravitational pull on a calm ocean. The longest interval was sixteen seconds, the average about eight, and the shortest only two. For a significant number of those sixteen seconds the egg hardly moved at all; then it began to turn slightly in a clockwise direction; finally it carved out ever deeper arcing rolls before coming up against the half-bulkhead forward. After a short time even this slight activity was too exhausting, and I crashed out on the bunk, hot and sad.

On the third afternoon of this second calm I heard an unusual noise coming from somewhere outside the boat. I climbed to the cockpit. I could clearly hear the sound of an engine now. There was a yacht, about a quarter of a mile distant, heading this way. It was a Swan, sixty feet long, rigged as a ketch. They were motoring slowly, presumably to save fuel. The genoa was furled, the stay-sail lying on deck, the mizzen in a cover, and the mainsail hanging loosely from the boom. The boat was mostly steady in the water, moving with understated ease, but now and again it rolled to either side, from the combination of swell and its own momentum. When it did this the wire halyards, which had about a metre of slack, slapped against the main mast, making a sharp and resonant cracking sound. It was this I had heard from inside the cabin, not the sound of the engine. It seemed strange that they didn't tie the halyards back. The cracking noise must have penetrated every corner of their own boat.

I could see no one on deck at first. Presumably the boat was on autopilot and the crew were below-decks in the shade and, perhaps, air-conditioning. But then it altered course, slowed further, and came towards me. They pulled up parallel to my own boat, just far enough away to prevent the masts clashing. There were four men on deck now, all dark-haired and bearded. An Italian flag was hanging from a radar stand on the transom. They shouted a greeting and we established that they spoke no English and I no Italian. The helmsman shrugged and smiled. We communicated that we were both bound for the Marquesas. We stood looking at each other a little while longer. One guy put his two hands together in front of him, then pointed to the sky, presumably praying for wind. I made an enthusiastic praying gesture in reply, then tried to suggest that my heart was being torn out by this calm – an over-ambitious mime, as he appeared baffled.

The helmsman shrugged again, gave a final wave, and put the boat back into gear. There was a muffled roar from the engine and the Swan continued slowly towards the horizon, the wire halyards still cracking against the mast as the crew slowly filed down the companionway.

I watched the boat on its way, and was about to go below myself, when I stopped and reached for the glasses. The ketch was about a hundred metres away, but it was turning. I watched as it completed a broad turn to starboard until it was facing me again, coming directly towards me. I could make out the helmsman behind the large wheel, and some of the other crew now coming back up the companionway and standing on the side-deck. I felt then a different kind of vulnerability from that normally experienced at sea. I believed I had learned to live with the dangers posed by the water itself, but the chance of a human threat on the ocean was something for which I was unprepared. There were stories about pirate attacks, but these were mostly confined to cargo shipping: a small yacht has little of value. And pirate attacks are generally restricted to specific areas of ocean and coastline; most sailors in the South Pacific pay them little attention. Nothing similar has happened to me at sea since then, and I remember that day because I have never felt more aware of being alone at sea, if only for a few moments. They had a more powerful boat, I had nothing with which to defend myself, and they were four to one.

The ketch motored back past me, went behind my boat, then cut the revs on the port side. Three crewmen were lined up along the rail, smiling through thick, curly beards. One was holding a bundle, and indicated that he was going to throw it. The helmsman motored in a bit closer and, standing on the cockpit coaming, I caught a hard little package, a plastic bag bound up with a length of duct tape. They clapped and cheered as I pulled at the plastic. Inside were two cold beers and a chilled jar of cockles. The four crewmen on the Italian ketch were now holding cans too. They gave me a toast, then motored away, the halyards still clanking.

This was on my first voyage, and I didn't drink a lot in those days. There was no alcohol on the boat: I thought of myself as a social drinker. But that afternoon I sat in the cockpit, under the draped mainsail for shade, a beer in each hand. I was just north of the equator. Between swigs I held the two cans against either side of my burning face.

★

The first description of baptism at the line was written by the Parmentier brothers aboard a French ship in 1529. But similar sea baptisms had long been practised in the Mediterranean and Europe. The Greeks sacrificed at headlands, the Phoenicians at the Pillars of Hercules, the Vikings at parallels of latitude. There have also been ceremonies for crossing the tropics of Capricorn and Cancer. But it is the King Neptune ceremony observed when a ship crosses the equator from north to south that has endured to the present day, if perhaps most commonly in the form of a cabaret show on a cruise ship. Even in the Age of Sail baptism at the line was seen as light relief for the crew. The passage of the equatorial doldrums could be long and hard. One Dutch ship spent five months becalmed on the line in 1672. Only twenty of the ship's company survived. Of these, a seventeen-year-old cabin boy took command, and eventually brought the ship to the Cape of Good Hope.

Sea baptism was an important rite of passage, signifying the beginning of a new stage of the voyage. The ceremony on the equator has taken various forms, but usually involves one of the crew dressing up as Neptune, God of the Sea, then shaving, daubing in tar or dunking in bilge-water all those on the ship who haven't crossed the line before. The ceremony as performed aboard English ships is commonly thought to have been the most harsh. One consequence of the ritual was the routine humiliation of young officers in front of the seamen. In one variation the captain himself was dunked in a barrel. Other versions of the ceremony had a dig at clerical authority, a drunken sailor giving a sermon on vice in a parody of a church service. The whole ship's company might well be drunk for days on end as the vessel laboured through equatorial calms. The Dutch East India Company eventually banned the practice of baptism at the line, believing it to be potentially subversive.

★

I had set 100° west longitude as the first staging-post on the return voyage to New Zealand. To my mind this imaginary line on the ocean marked the gateway to the South Seas. Up to this point, my voyage from Chile had taken me through empty waters. But now I was only five hundred miles from Easter Island, and after that the chart of the tropical Pacific begins to get busy. There are the great archipelagos of eastern Polynesia, the Tuamotus, Marquesas, Austral and Society Islands. Volcanic formations fan out to the north and west: the Cooks, Samoa, and Tonga. In equatorial waters the muddy mountains of Melanesia give way to coral atolls. These pin-prick territories of the Micronesian archipelagos stretch far to the north and all but merge with islands in the East China Sea.

I had made the decision to celebrate crossing the hundredth meridian several months earlier. In late November of the previous year, fifteen hundred miles south of my present position, I had crossed the same meridian from west to east. I had looked to the north then, and warmed myself with the thought of tropical breezes, and celebratory meals prepared on calm seas.

I create milestones like this on all my passages, some ritual, usually a meal, to acknowledge progress, and the fact that one ocean has many separate identities. In this case the meal had a special significance: it would use up the last of the fresh produce I had brought from South America, and it was my birthday. That dawn I caught a yellowfin tuna. I'd anticipated this evening for the whole of that day, and went to some lengths with my preparations, taking a salt-water bath in the cockpit, choosing an island shirt and selecting a CD.

I ate one fillet of the fish raw. Then I put the last of the potatoes into the frying pan. While they cooked in butter, I sat back on the engine box. I told myself to enjoy the beer, turn up the stereo. But although the passage had reached an important milestone, I was beginning to fear that there was little to celebrate.

The wind had been light for several days, no more than twelve knots. There was none of the distinctive puff-ball cloud that is often present in the trades. As I waited for my food to cook I had a sense of dread that the wind would die to coincide with these festivities. I moved gingerly around the boat, as if the shift in weight could alter the precarious balance of the sails. I found myself on tip-toes, hoping I wouldn't be noticed, now uneasy in this easy world where drinks stayed upright and chopped garlic stayed in a pile, missing those stiff rolls to either side that told of a good night's progress ahead.

When the potatoes were cooked I fried the fish, and took a clean white plate from the rack in readiness. Just then both head-sails gave a shuddering crash. Moments later the boom wrenched against its preventer as the mainsail also collapsed and refilled. I put my cutlery back into the drawer and climbed up into the cockpit. It was very light, seven knots of breeze from the south-east. Luckily the wind had been dying slowly, over many days, so the sea was slight and even; a swell would have thrown what little wind there was from the sails.

It was a broken night. I ate my meal interrupted by periods when the sails fell about helplessly and the boat shook with the strain. Each time I climbed to the cockpit, but there was little that could be done. Over the next few hours the boat would make way for ten or fifteen minutes at a time, then stumble as the sails crashed. Sometimes it was just a single bang, and the boat maintained its momentum; other times the boat came to a halt altogether, then painfully re-gathered way. I suppose I slept through some of the commotion, but it seemed that I was con-stantly woken by the blocks wrenching, then the bang of canvas, followed by multiple shudders through the hull. Occasionally I climbed to the cockpit, as if this might do some good. There are few more depressing sights than white sails falling about in the green darkness of a tropical night. I kept this up until 3 a.m., then dropped the sails and lay ahull, drifting on the Pacific swells.

My twenty-four-hour run to noon the following day was

sixty-five miles. The next day I covered thirty nautical miles. The trade had died. In my experience, this happens more often than meteorological texts acknowledge. But in this instance it was possible that I was slightly in the wrong position, too far south. It had been something of a toss-up exactly which route to take through this part of the Pacific. Some sailors chose the direct route from South America to Easter Island and enjoyed a fair wind the whole way; others thought it better to sail north of the rhumb-line in the expectation of a more consistent trade. I had gone somewhere between the two. Perhaps this was a mistake: if the high pressure was further north, then at 27° South I was too close to the centre of the anticyclone.

On the third day the wind was in the east, still light. I decided to head north in search of a stronger flow. I covered fifty-five miles in the following twenty-four hours, and spent four hours drifting. The hundredth meridian west of Greenwich had turned out to be an inauspicious milestone. My celebratory meal had heralded not the gateway to Polynesia but entry onto a forlorn, placeless stretch of ocean, seemingly without end. The boat limped slowly to the north. The sun grew hotter each day.

The Pacific coastline of the mythical Southland was assumed to lie somewhere between 20° and 30° south latitude, in the same waters I was now traversing on the passage west from Chile. Part of its coastline was supposedly sighted near my own position, by a buccaneer named Edward Davis. Davis was a friend of fellow-buccaneer and travel-writer William Dampier, who refers to him in *A New Voyage Round the World*. In 1687 Davis sailed south from Central America in the *Batchelor's Delight*, bound for the Horn. Dampier wrote:

> Captain Davis told me lately, That after his Departure from us at the Haven off Rio Lexa [Realego,

Nicaragua] he went after several Traverses, to the Galapagos, and that standing thence Southward for Wind to bring him about Tierra del Fuego, in the Lat. of 27° South, about 500 leagues from Copayapo, off the coast of Chili, he saw a small sandy Island just by him; and that they saw to Windward of it a long tract of pretty high Land, tending away towards the North West out of sight. This might probably be the coast of Terra Australis Incognita.

A second report is found in a volume published by the Hakluyt Society. Lionel Wafer, who sailed with Davis on this voyage as surgeon's mate, records finding a 'small flat Island, without the guard of any Rocks. We stood in within a quarter of a Mile from the Shore, and could see it plainly; for 'twas a clear Morning, not foggy or hazy. To the Westward, about 12 leagues by Judgement, we saw a range of high Land … And there came thence great Flocks of Fowls.'

The reported finding of Davis Land attracted attention in several European capitals. Davis's discovery lay on the same latitude as large deposits of gold in South America. Jacob Roggeveen sailed up the coast of Chile in 1722 with secret instructions to find Terra Australis. His employers, the Dutch West India Company, believed Davis Land to be the key. Roggeveen voyaged north-west from the Juan Fernández archipelago towards the position given by Davis. As Roggeveen states in his log, by 2 April *The African Galley* was in the right place but 'had not come in sight of the unknown Southland, for the discovery of which our Expedition and Voyage is specifically undertaken'. Roggeveen sailed on to the west, and on 5 April sighted a small island, which he named Easter Island because it was Easter Day. Easter Island was high and green, not the sand island described by Davis. In a reference to the three buccaneers Davis, Wafer and Dampier, Roggeveen remarked in his journal: 'Nothing more remains to be said than that these three (who were Englishmen) must have been rovers from truth, as well as rovers after the goods of the Spaniards.'

Many of those who searched for Davis Land commented on the unreliability of the winds in the latitude of his reported discovery, namely 27° South. Early European sailors believed there was a message in these Pacific calms. They reasoned that only land of continental proportions, somewhere beyond the horizon, could thus interrupt the otherwise reliable trade winds.

Commodore John Byron sailed into the Pacific in 1765 to search for Davis Land. Byron reprovisioned the *Dolphin* at Juan Fernández, then sailed north-west towards the position indicated by Captain Davis. He saw no land, but believed he was close to something very big. He recorded 'vast flocks of birds' over the ocean, and that he lost the great swell and accompanying trade winds which had pushed the *Dolphin* for the last thousand miles. 'Had not the winds failed me,' Byron wrote, 'I make no doubt but I should have fell in with it, and in all probability made the discovery of the Southern Continent.'

One of those convinced that the coastline of Terra Australis would be found near the 27th parallel in the South Seas was a Scot named Alexander Dalrymple. A cartographer and geographical theorist of some eminence, Dalrymple combined the reports of navigators like Davis with evidence from the Dieppe Maps to compile in 1767 a volume of everything that was known about the area, *An Account of the Discoveries Made in the South Pacific*. It is more than wild speculation; Dalrymple makes a scholarly theoretical argument in favour of the existence of a southern continent, supported by the evidence of sightings by the likes of Juan Fernández, Gerrards, Quirós, and others. Like Byron, Dalrymple believed that the proportion of calms near the 27th parallel was significant. He wrote: 'If there is no continent, or extensive range of land in the South Pacifick Ocean, there can be no variability of wind, but a constant SE or ESE trade wind must prevail the whole year. If this trade wind is not constant, there must undoubtedly be land.' Dalrymple's very great enthusiasm for his subject is evident. He states that 'The number of inhabitants in the Southern Continent is probably more than fifty millions.' The Southland filled the whole area from Juan Fernández to New Zealand, and from the Tropic of Capricorn to 50° South. It was of 'greater extent than the whole civilised part of Asia, from Turkey to the eastern extremity of China. There is at present no trade there, though the scraps from this table would be sufficient to maintain the power, dominion and sovereignty of Britain.'

Carteret, Wallis, Bougainville and de Surville all searched for Davis Land in the vicinity of the 27th parallel. All were plagued by calms, but there was no further sighting of the Continent.

Fourteen hundred miles off the coast of Chile, I was drifting over the mythical Davis Land. From the deck of a small boat my world, as ever, was an empty horizon. There was nothing to see, just like yesterday. Yesterday was all around me. So was last week. And tomorrow was sloshing around out there somewhere, too. Nothing changed.

The wind had died early the previous afternoon. It had been calm all night. The sails lay in dispirited heaps upon the deck. They looked soiled and worn, though in reality they were only a few months old. The sky was a watery blue wash, without a wisp of cloud. In the whole sector around the sun the colour had been destroyed: the air was white.

The sea moved heavily, like engine oil. There wasn't a ripple on the surface. Domed swellings rose around the boat in no discernible pattern, as if someone were blowing into the surface of the water from below. The boat rolled slowly, very stiff. It seemed that at any moment the ocean might set hard.

There was nothing to do. Or perhaps, I could do nothing. I

turned on the radio, but its talk was of a world I no longer knew. A book was hopeless: I could seldom read a sentence before my concentration dissolved. I felt the ocean like a magnet trying to pull me from myself, as if it resented any demonstration of will other than its own. Again and again I found myself climbing to the deck, only to stare pointlessly into the void. Each time I hoped that finally there might be something there: the first stirrings of a breeze, a bank of cloud marching over the horizon, a new swell, birds or fish. But each time there was nothing. I clung to the rigging, staring at the sea. The emptiness seemed so intense I could feel it, like standing at the mouth of a great cave. I wondered if I would start hallucinating soon, and rather hoped I would. At least it would make a change.

Desperate for a sight of something new, I leant over the side of the boat. The water-line was thick with goose-neck barnacles. I watched them for a long time. Their rubbery stems were almost flesh-like, human. Each time the boat moved they were dunked beneath the surface, lost somewhere in the blandness I couldn't see. The ocean gave no sign of its depths. It could have been a pond, lost at sea. There was no sense of scale here. Distance was measured in time, time in speed, and size became meaningless. Today the boat was everything, the ocean a convex mirror beneath the towering mast. But tomorrow – perhaps – when the trades howl and the boat squats harried beneath spitting seas, then I will again feel small and little-noticed, free to read a whole page of my book in peace.

So the surface was there as a barrier to my eye, one more device to keep me in my place. All I knew was that when the boat rolled back on the swells and the barnacles I'd been watching on the water-line again came into view, they appeared glistening and refreshed, writhing about like scores of babies' fingers in the sun.

I decided I would run the engine for a few hours. I rarely did this in calms. The wind-vane steering would not work without wind and I had no autopilot, so motoring meant sitting at the tiller, plodding towards the featureless horizon at four knots. Normally I found it easier to drift around waiting for the wind to come back. Today, though, I couldn't face it, and felt that even the noise of the diesel hammering away might offer some relief.

I climbed down into the cabin and opened the engine box. Back to familiarity. I turned on the fuel in the usual way, opened the sea-cock in the usual way – and then stopped. I looked again at the sea-cock. There's a hole in the hull here to pipe sea water for engine cooling. The sea-cock works like a tap: it sits on top of the hole to seal it off when not in use. The hole in the hull is small, no bigger than a coin, so it could easily be obstructed. Once the water has passed through the sea-cock it enters a short tube which has a screw-down cap at its outer end. Inside the tube is a filter. With the boat out of the water, it's possible to unscrew the cap on top of the tube and, if the sea-cock is open, see straight through the hull to the world beyond.

I stopped because I was thinking about the barnacles I'd seen growing along the water-line. Presumably there were more, out of sight beneath the surface. If a few of them were anchored around the engine-water intake, then the flow of water through the sea-cock might be restricted.

I closed the engine box without starting the engine and sat down. I was rather pleased with this. I had dreamt up a problem, a little worry of my own, something clear and logical to think about. I was going to drag this out.

I lit the stove and put the kettle on. I smoked a cigarette. Then another one. Worriers like to smoke. I drank tea and ate lunch, feeling better than I had for a long time. I didn't fidget about, I wasn't pulled back on deck to stare at the empty sea. After lunch I had a long sleep, and woke feeling wonderfully worried and relaxed. Then I went back to the engine box. I opened the lid in the usual way. Now it was a place of intrigue. I checked that the sea-cock was shut, then unscrewed the cap on the end of the filter tube. There was no debris in the filter, but that didn't prove much. The only real test was to open the sea-cock. Then I'd be able to see right through the hull into the ocean.

I reached down and rotated the lever handle through ninety degrees. It seemed that nothing happened for a long time. It's like that when something is coming upwards and straight at you: it takes a while to realise there's any movement at all. Then it's right there before your eyes, like a snake striking, and you wonder why it's taken so long to focus.

This was blue, a liquid blue light bubbling and frothing from the tube towards me, shockingly formless. But at its centre I could see its source so clearly: a burning circle of blue – the size of a coin – from which a column of water burst upwards. There had been nothing like this in my life for a thousand miles. Just a sullen sun arcing the sky, and a relentless sea. But here, in the oily engine box of all places, was a slot of purity.

The water streamed in, lying in pools on my legs and shorts, staining my filthy body, swirling round the engine mounts, assaulting my senses. I had to turn it off. There was nothing wrong with the water intake. My little worry was over. But it didn't matter now. I'd seen the light burning up through the bottom of the boat.

I grabbed a couple of things, then climbed onto the deck and pulled off my shorts. I went in head first, holding the mask tight with my hands so it wouldn't be knocked off, my eyes open all the way. And in one wet, noisy moment, everything from before was gone.

There is only blue, and silence. Blue to America, blue to Asia, blue to both poles. I roll on to my back. The surface is a blinding, golden blue.

It's the same thing down here, you can't see through to the other side. The boat appears as a milky blur. Only the keel is with me, the deep red paint dwarfed by blue. But from neither world can you see beyond the surface. Are they really two sides of the same coin? Must I go back to that other place? It's so close now, the abyss of the calm. As I float up towards the surface I'm falling in towards it. But not yet. I roll back for more of the blue drug, down towards the darker, cloudier blue. The light comes from three sides, in shafts. This place is limitless. Endless. But so short. Just one breath.

Seven

IT IS SOMETIMES difficult to identify the moment when the wind returns after a calm. In retrospect it seems like a process, not a single point in time. The process is hazy, with an uncertain number of moves.

There are many false starts during a calm. You try to be unimpressed by the first appearance of wind. Don't get your hopes up that it will last: that's the intention, at least. But still the boat is set like a trap to detect the first puff of a breeze.

Any boat, drifting at sea, will lie side-on to the wind. So, in a small yacht, one thing you hear when the wind rises after a calm is ripples or wavelets lapping against the side of the hull. But this is a coarse signal: I've probably been asleep if this is the first I know of a returning wind. At about the same time I hear the mainsail, hanging off the boom, begin to move in the wind, a slow, heavy flog sufficient to send a slight vibration through the boat.

If I am awake, though, I know about the return of wind before one of these coarser measures makes itself heard. Awake, the first clear indication of a breeze is usually the wind generator beginning to spin. It is mounted on a steel pole at the back of the boat and generates electricity for the battery. From almost anywhere in the cabin my view through the companionway is of empty sky, with the wind generator planted firmly in the centre. If the fins are just turning, but then stopping, then turning a little more, it's pretty hopeless and the sails, if I hoisted them, would barely get the chance to draw. If the fins of the generator are spinning at a constant speed, but not very fast, so it's still possible to distinguish each one individually, then it's a little more promising: sailing close-hauled will work so long as the sea is slight, but down-wind will be messy, with the sails collapsing and rolling around. But if the generator is spinning so fast that it has become a white blur against the sky or a flickering wheel in the moonlight, then it's definitely worth getting out of bed.

When becalmed I look at the wind generator often. All too often, perhaps: it becomes a reflex, a nervous tic, that interrupts my writing or cooking or reading. It sometimes even wakes me from sleep. Each time I raise my eyes to the companionway and see the six fins of the generator absolutely still, there's a slight deflation, the thump of bad news. I avert my eyes, unimpressed, and vow not to look back until I hear some movement in the water – a sure sign of wind. A few minutes later I look back at the generator again.

Just occasionally the wind does come back with a whoosh and a roar. Becalmed one time on an earlier voyage, five hundred miles east of Tonga, I saw a bank of thick cloud approaching from the south, much bigger than any squall. The cloud closed all around. I felt it cold and wet as first the sun disappeared overhead, then the last of the horizon was pinched out in the north. I had the mainsail up while the sea was still flat calm. Then a southerly set in at twenty-five knots, and I started to reef down before I'd even finished coiling the halyard. The wind rose to thirty knots during the night and stayed fresh for the remainder of that passage.

But mostly it is hard to identify one point in time when the wind returns. On this passage, sailing into the tropics from Emily Rock, the calm was complete for three days, the boat adrift.

Then the breeze again began to toy with the ocean. Early in the afternoon the wind generator maintained its spin through several repeat glances over a five-minute period. I sailed north during the rest of that day, a light east wind on the beam. At sunset the breeze failed and I dropped the sails, but was woken at 10 p.m. by the sound of the mainsail battens tapping the coach-roof, so set the sails again. The easterly was stronger now, and I poled out the genoa and sailed downwind. Within an hour the sails were slatting and the blocks kicking on the side-deck. I drifted for the next two hours. Occasionally the wind generator would spin, but never for more than a few moments without stopping. In the early hours of the morning it seemed steadier, so I put up the canvas once more. I can't remember how many times this happened during the night, or how many times I was woken by the hated sound of the sails collapsing.

Usually on nights like this I reach a threshold. By two or three o'clock in the morning I've ceased to care whether the boat is sailing or not, and crave only the peace of sleep, far from flogging sails. I furl the headsail and drop the main in disgust, then sleep as the boat drifts.

But that night I never reached such a threshold. On one of the occasions that I reset the sails, perhaps the third or fourth, the wind held. This time I wasn't woken up after half an hour by the sails crashing. I fell into a deep sleep. When I woke it was to look out on a different world: the calm was over. The sun had risen more than two hours earlier. In the cabin it seemed utterly silent, save for the almost forgotten rustle of ocean passing around the hull and the occasional creak from the steering lines. The boat was sailing steadily into the west, across a sea flecked with white-caps.

I climbed out of bed and stood a while in the cockpit, feeling the wind on my body and making a few adjustments to the sails. At dawn, after a night like that, it can seem that the wind's return isn't a coherent event at all, but something bound up with the turmoil of broken sleep. In this way the wind enters the sailor's subconscious. Looking back, the calm appears to have the quality of a dream: it ends at the moment of waking. I can only recall a few disturbing events, but they are receding fast, beyond the power of memory. Once, I wrote a diary of a calm, to have a record. Otherwise, time spent becalmed appears as a series of black holes in my recollection of the voyage.

Periods of complete calm are the most foreign experience I have had afloat. I suspect they have defined my perception of the ocean more sharply than any other event at sea. But still I know little about them. When the wind dies I am left with a feeling of powerlessness, of total redundancy, my purpose, the course, taken away. Perhaps something in me dies, too: the belief that I have a will here, and can control my own fate. Becalmed I am in limbo, a figure at the centre of kaleidoscopic images of heat, frustration and mind games. Calms have that unmanageable quality of a dream: they are too weird, too difficult to process. In the morning light it's easiest just to forget it ever happened.

March 20th dawned dry and clear. Soon, in the distance, I saw the rounded green haunch of the Península Poike, the most easterly point on Easter Island. The wind was light, the sea even. By midday I was sailing slowly along the north shore of the island. I passed Hana Hoonu and continued towards the tussled dome of Maunga Terevaka, the highest point. The grassy hillsides were a deep, silvery green. The summits were flat and bleak, melancholy in the strong sun. Low cliffs fell to the water. A string of breakers reappeared beneath each successive headland to the west.

Easter Island is the centre of Polynesian civilisation in this part of the Pacific, and I had long wanted to come here. Dotted over the hillsides are the gaunt stone *moai*, Polynesian statues on terraced altars. The *moai* had stared inland – their backs to the sea

– for more than a thousand years, in recognition of what the people believed to be the only inhabited land in the world.

The anchorage at the island is poor, only an open roadstead in the lee. Some yachts arrive at Easter Island after a long passage and are unable to anchor because of the conditions. Others are forced by a change in the weather to leave at short notice. So I was lucky, because in this light easterly trade the anchorage would be tenable.

In the afternoon I sailed past the small settlement at Anakena. Behind the few houses at the head of the bay I saw a minibus climbing slowly up a dirt track, a plume of dust hovering obstinately in its wake. I watched the bus for some time. Even more than breakers, cliffs and hillsides, it was these everyday scenes of human activity that made the strongest impression after a long passage. I tried to imagine myself inside the bus, somebody else at the helm.

It is easy to describe what happened next, not easy to explain it. When I reached the western end of the island, instead of turning south for the anchorage I left the tiller on the wind-vane steering and continued on the same course, sailing west, away from the island. By nightfall I could just see the lights of Hanga Roa twinkling in the distance. Within an hour the skyline behind the boat was bare.

I put a little north in the course over the next days, to reach the 25th parallel. The wind was fresher now from the south-east so I gybed morning and night, re-poling the genoa to windward each time. This was perfect trade-wind sailing. The boat ran steadily for a hundred and forty miles a day, the roll urgent but never intrusive. The sun was strong, the wind warm but cooling.

At 25° south latitude I continued to follow the coast of the unknown Southland as it was depicted by Renaissance cartographers. The world map made by Giacomo Gastaldi in 1550 shows

a Southland named 'Tierra de Fuego Incognita' with a continuous coastline in the Pacific stretching from Mexico to China.
Gerhardus Mercator's world map includes a southern continent
which fills the whole of the South Pacific, thought to have been
influenced by the Inca legend of a Pacific land mass. The first
conquistadors heard the story that the Inca Tupac Yupanqui had
voyaged west for six hundred leagues and made a fabulous landfall on the coastline of a tropical continent. The Inca supposedly
returned after one year with piles of gold and silver, a copper
throne, black slaves, and the skin of an animal resembling a horse.
The conquistadors assumed the Inca had reached the Southland.

Mercator's friend and rival was Abraham Ortelius. In 1570
Ortelius gathered together more than seventy maps and published one of the first modern atlases, *Theatrum Orbis Terrarum*.
Ortelius's southern continent extends as far north as the equator
in the Pacific. He made up names for some of the more out-
standing features: the Cape of Good Signal, the River of Islands,
the Sweetest River. He labelled the southern continent the
'Southern Land not *yet* known', as if it could simply be willed
into existence.

Despite the lack of any real evidence from sailors navigating
these waters, or possibly because of it, a steady stream of theor-
ists petitioned their respective governments for help in being
first to make contact with the new southern land. Roger Barlow
had sailed with Cabot in search of new spice islands in the
Pacific. He told Henry VIII that in the ocean to the south-east
of China would be found 'the most richest londes and ilondes
in the worlde, for ... gold, spices, aromatikes and pretiose
stones'. The Elizabethan geographer Dr John Dee wrote of a
great empire that could be built in Terra Australis. In 1657 Peter
Heylyn argued in his *Cosmography* for a new voyage to be made
in search of Terra Australis. Eighty years later, in his revised
edition of Harris's collection of voyages, John Campbell wrote
that 'It is impossible to conceive a country that promises fairer

Bill Peers aboard the sixteen-foot day boat we tried to sail from Cornwall to Africa

After the wreck at Contisplage. The boat turned upside down and was dismasted. Most of our gear was later washed ashore

Our castaway camp on the beach at Contisplage: Bill is tapering the end of the new main mast. The new mizzen mast is already stepped in the boat behind him

In 1570 Abraham Ortelius produced the most detailed atlas of the world since Ptolemy, *Theatrum Orbis Terrarum*. Gerhardus Mercator praised Ortelius' determination 'to bring out the geographical truth, which is so corrupted by mapmakers'. None the less, Ortelius' world map is dominated by a typical sixteenth-century portrayal of the mythical Great Southern Continent

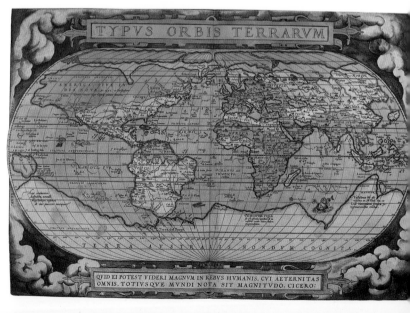

Palafito houses along the waterfront at Castro, Isla Chiloé

Approaching the Canal Refugio

Icebergs in the
Rio Tempanos

Recrossing the
Canal Moraleda

...an Fernández, birthplace of the ...astaway myth

...he church at Akamaru, the ...rst built by the Picpus Fathers at ...ambier

Mother-of-pearl inlay on the altar at the cathedral at Rikitea: the remains of the 'Mad Priest' Honoré Laval lie in a crypt nearby

Taravai, Gambier: the first Europeans in the Pacific often commented on how pale-skinned they observed the Polynesians to be, leading to no end of speculation about the origins of the South Sea islanders. William Dampier suggested that the Pacific peoples might be descended from the lost tribe of Israel

Tahiti

Tied to the wharf, Papeete

Wreck of the *Nicky Lou*, Beveridge Reef

Pete Atkinson with his homemade underwater camera housing. The circular contraption behind him is a shark cage, made from chain link garden fencing and a length of irrigation pipe. It was designed to 'concertina' for ease of stowage on a 36-foot yacht, and used to photograph tiger sharks at Minerva Reef than this Terra Australis.' Campbell believed that Tasmania, New Holland, New Zealand, and Quirós's Austrialia were all part of the same land mass. He said of the British, 'We want not Capacity, we want not Power, but we want Will ... let us deserve, and we shall succeed ... If we search, we shall find; if we knock, it will be opened.'

Most days on the passage west I had a sleep after lunch. With the sun so high and my night's rest so often broken, an afternoon nap became an inevitability. When I woke I spent an hour or two quietly until four o'clock, which was the time I took my daily bath in the cockpit.

My bath became one of those rituals around which a certain part of each tropical day revolved. Four o'clock was, I decided after some trial and error, the best time. In the late afternoon the sun was still hot enough for sea water to feel refreshingly cool, while with only a couple of hours to go before sunset there was little chance of getting uncomfortably hot again before the cool of nightfall. Throughout the heat of each day, 4 p.m. was the target I set myself. After that, the long wind-down into night could begin.

My bath was a simple routine. I sat on the cockpit bench and slowly tipped half a dozen buckets of sea water over my head and shoulders. I didn't use any soap. So-called 'salt water soaps' don't work. On my previous voyage through the islands I had discovered Joy, the local washing-up liquid, which lathers well in salt water. But I wouldn't be able to get any Joy until I reached the French islands, and didn't regret the absence of soap. At the beginning of the passage I used to towel myself dry after the last bucket to remove the salt. But by now I didn't have a clean towel, and anyway, I liked the salt.

It takes a certain period of time at sea to become sensitised to how the ocean feels on your skin, and the variations that are possible. In the first days of the voyage away from the coast of New Zealand I was aware only that the sea was wet and cold. Temperature appeared to be the sole variable. In the Southern Ocean the spray felt bitter and hard, and when I dipped a pan over the side to scrub it the water numbed my hands. In those high latitudes, as I knelt on the cockpit bench washing the dishes, my shoulders were perpetually hunched in defence, waiting for the next sting of spray on the back of my head and the cold creep of water down my neck. In the far south I battled to keep the ocean out: outside heavy jackets with strapped collars, behind washboards and bolted hatches. I had little direct engagement with the water, except for a slight but constant slipperiness on my face and in my hair, which never properly dried.

Sailing in tropical waters allows a different type of exposure to the ocean. Washing in salt water changes the way your skin feels, and so changes your perception of the environment. In the short tropical evenings, after my bath, I'd watch the salt hardening into streaks on my arms and legs. My skin felt dry, a slight prickling sensation that I learned first to accept and later find comfort in, as a simple sign of connection between the sailor and his sea. When I rubbed my forearm, white powder sprinkled to the deck. In heavy rain squalls I stood in the cockpit feeling fresh water stream down my body. When I licked my lips, the water running down my face tasted salty from my hair. When the rain stopped, the wind dried my body in minutes. I felt light and silky, my hair separated from a salty mass into individuals strands. But I felt no cleaner after such a soak in fresh water. No doubt it's an illusion of the lone sailor, but I never felt dirty, far offshore. The baths I took in the tropics were not about getting clean so much as staying cool and fresh, and feeling at home on the sea.

At 24° south latitude, the trade was again fickle. One afternoon there was a light westerly – a headwind – an ominous sign. Then several short calms left the boat spinning beneath the meridian sun. A thousand miles from Easter Island I made landfall. Even from a distance, Henderson looked uninviting. It is a raised coral island, about six miles by three, with bare cliffs and a mop of green bush on the central plateau. Quirós sighted the island in 1606, and it was named after Captain John Henderson in the 1800s. But Henderson is best known for the part it has played in the story of Pacific castaways.

It began with the whaler *Essex*, an old ship by 1819, 87 feet long, 238 tons, square-sterned with no gallery and no figure-head. The first mate, Owen Chase, recorded how the ship had recently been thoroughly refitted in her home port of Nantucket and was now, 'in all respects, a sound, substantial vessel'. The *Essex* had been victualled and provisioned for a whaling voyage to last two and a half years. She sailed in August 1819.

The *Essex* encountered heavy westerly gales in the Southern Ocean and took five weeks to round Cape Horn. The following year she arrived in the Juan Fernández islands and took on wood, water and fresh meat. Then her twenty-eight-year-old captain, George Pollard, set a course for the whaling grounds at the Galápagos Islands.

At eight o'clock on the morning of 20 November a pod of whales was sighted near the Galápagos. The captain and most of the crew gave chase in the boats (at least three whales were taken), leaving the mate, Owen Chase, on board the ship. Chase's account of the events that followed was later published. He saw a large sperm whale about eighty-five feet long leave the pod, blow several times, and swim straight at the ship. The whale struck the ship on the bow with its head, giving the crewmen onboard 'such an appalling and tremendous jar as nearly threw us on our faces'. The ship trembled like a leaf. The whale passed beneath the ship, grazing the keel with its back. The whale was then seen again, apparently in convulsions, 'enveloped in the foam of the sea that his continual and violent thrashing about in the water had created around him, and I could distinctly see him smite his jaws together, as if distracted with rage and fury'. The whale then charged the ship again, struck it for a second time, and disappeared. Chase records that though whales had sometimes been known to attack the small open boats from which the harpoons were actually thrown, and even to clamp these boats in their jaws, no whale had ever rammed a ship before.

The *Essex* rolled onto its side and began to sink. The masts were cut away, which righted the ship, but she was awash at deck level. The crew were now all in the open boats. They spent the first night tied to the half-submerged hulk of the *Essex*. In the morning a hole was cut in the deck and salt-bread and casks of fresh water retrieved. Then the *Essex* was given up for lost. The wind was in the wrong quarter to sail to the nearby Galápagos Islands. There was no other land close to hand. Thirteen hundred miles to the south-west lay the Marquesas – the most obvious islands to head for – but they were not even considered: they were thought to be inhabited by cannibals, and nineteenth-century sailors regarded the prospect of cannibalism with horror. Captain Pollard made the decision to sail south to about 25° in the hope of then picking up a westerly wind which might carry them to the coast of Chile or Peru. Twenty men embarked in three boats. These whale boats were light and fragile, designed to be rowed fast in pursuit of whales. Now overloaded, they were quite unsuitable for such an ocean crossing.

The boats sailed south-south-west across the Pacific for nearly a month. They were frequently becalmed. Chase wrote, 'Our sufferings during these calm days almost exceeded human belief. The hot rays of the sun beat down upon us to such a degree as to oblige us to hang over the gunwale of the boat, into the sea, to cool our weak and fainting bodies.' Food and water were strictly rationed. 'The privation of water', says Chase, 'is justly ranked among the most dreadful of the miseries in our life; the violence of raving thirst has no parallel in the catalogue of human calamities.' Owen Chase guarded the provisions with a loaded pistol.

On 20 December 1820 the crew of the *Essex* sighted unknown land. Chase wrote, 'It is not within the scope of human calculation ... to divine what the feelings of our hearts were on this occasion. Alternate expectation, fear, gratitude, surprise and exultation each swayed our minds and quickened our exertions.' We now know that this landfall was Henderson Island.

Henderson didn't offer much in the way of sustenance. The castaways found a few crabs and small fish, then ate peppergrass and birds' eggs. After two days they found a spring of fresh water in a cave that was exposed only at low tide. The men were still in terrible condition. 'Our bodies had wasted away to almost skin and bone, and possessed so little strength as often to require each other's assistance in performing some of its weakest functions. Relief, we now felt, must come soon, or nature would sink.'

Reluctantly, Captain Pollard decided they must again put to sea. The plan was to sail for the coast of South America, perhaps falling in with Easter Island en route. On 27 December the three boats set sail to the east with seventeen men on board. Three men chose to stay on Henderson and take their chances.

Two weeks into the voyage Matthew Joy, the second mate, died of starvation and exposure. Shortly afterwards Owen Chase's boat became separated from the other two. Of the calms which followed, he wrote, 'We began to think that Divine Providence had abandoned us at last; and it was but an unavailing effort to endeavour to prolong a now tedious existence.' Occasionally whales spouted around the boat. 'We could distinctly hear the furious thrashing of their tails in the water, and our weak minds pictured their appalling and hideous aspects.' Another man died, and his body was committed to the sea. But then another died; after a night's deliberation, of which Chase says, 'I have no language to paint the anguish of our souls in this dreadful dilemma', the survivors ate his heart.

By the middle of February the men were desperate. 'Our cadaverous countenances, sunken eyes and bones just starting through the skin, with the ragged remnants of clothes stuck about our sun-burnt bodies, must have produced an appearance ... affecting and revolting in the highest degree.' Finally, on the 17th, a sail was sighted. She turned out to be the *Indian*, Captain Crozier, 'to whom we are indebted for every polite, friendly and attentive disposition'. The *Indian* had been northbound up the coast of Chile. Captain Crozier took Owen Chase and his men to Valparaíso. They had made one of the most remarkable open-boat voyages of all time, sailing more than five thousand miles across deep ocean. Chase's boat was at sea for twice as long as Captain Bligh's, whose own open-boat voyage to safety became the stuff of legend after the mutiny on the *Bounty*.

Of the two other boats that had left Henderson with Owen Chase, Captain Pollard's had already been picked up by a ship south of the Juan Fernández islands. Three men had died. The first perished early in the voyage, and was eaten. The four remaining men then cast lots. A crewman named Coffin drew the short straw. He was shot by Charles Ramsdale and eaten. Ten days later another crewman died and his body was in its turn devoured. The third boat was separated from the Captain's on 28 January. No survivors were picked up, and the boat was never found. The three men left on Henderson Island were eventually rescued by the ship *Surry*. They had been cast away on Henderson for 111 days.

The sun was setting when I passed south of Henderson Island. There is no bay or recognised anchorage of any sort. The crew of the *Essex* had had difficulty landing their open boats through the surf. I once met a couple in Tahiti who had managed to anchor their yacht precariously on a narrow ledge on the western side and swim ashore, though they couldn't climb the cliffs.

I looked up the west coastline through binoculars. The conditions were very light, the trade steady in the south-east: ideal for trying to find an anchorage and get ashore, if only for a short time. But though I watched the west coast for many minutes, I didn't take the tiller off the self-steering chain. I wasn't tempted to step foot ashore. With the wind in the south-east, I continued sailing west, away from the land, at four knots.

The tropical night fell quickly. Henderson disappeared from view before it sank beneath the horizon. I moved into the cabin and began to prepare an evening meal. Owen Chase's journal is believed to have been one source for both Melville's *Moby-Dick*, and Edgar Allen Poe's *Narrative of Arthur Gordon Pym of Nantucket*. One more recent newsworthy event regarding Henderson happened in 1957. An American named Robert Tomarchin was landed on the island from a yacht, along with his chimpanzee Moko, to recreate the castaway experiences of the three *Essex* whalemen who had survived for nearly four months on the island. The yachtsman and the chimp spent three weeks marooned together before the call came to take them off.

Two days later I sighted Pitcairn Island. In the midday sun Pitcairn was a bright green dome on the south-western horizon. It was on uninhabited Pitcairn that Fletcher Christian and his fellow-mutineers from the *Bounty,* together with a number of Tahitians, established a castaway society beyond the reach of British justice. Forty-six of their descendants still live on the island today.

I approached Bounty Bay from the north. There was a tiny breakwater here which protected the island's only landing. The anchorage at Pitcairn is notoriously poor but, again, conditions were very light: the anchorage would never be more tenable than on a day like today. Over the VHF radio I heard a burst of local chatter. My radio reception has never been good, but something else was distorted about the voices I listened to: I thought I heard the tones of archaic Somerset, transported to the South Seas.

It seems that Pitcairn's story as the most remote island hide-away is not yet at an end. Six wealthy timber merchants and a tax judge based in Wellington have put forward an offer to buy the island and turn it, effectively, into a corporate country. The proposal is for two airstrips, one on Pitcairn and one on nearby Oeno, a $50-million investment in tourist accommodation, exclusive rights to the 200-miles fishing zone, independence within five years, and Pitcairn citizenship for thirty company shareholders and directors. The spirit of Fletcher Christian lives on.

The deputy governor of Pitcairn, Karen Wolstenholme, is part of the British High Commission in Wellington: Pitcairn is the last British colony in the South Pacific. Wolstenholme vetoed the independence, citizenship and fisheries parts of the deal, but said the islanders had encouraged her to pursue the airstrips and tourist lodges.

I hove-to off Bounty Bay for ten minutes. The island is beautiful and dramatic: dark cliffs rising to a craggy green plateau, partly shaded by cloud. The sea was the colour of the sky. But I didn't anchor the boat. The wind was holding, and I set a course to the north-west. It's part of the illusion of ocean life that my own passage seemed to be the only important thing here. I didn't look back to watch Pitcairn fade on the horizon. Each time I passed the land by it grew easier, and more exhilarating.

The next stage of the voyage was fast and nervous. My destination was Isles Gambier, the most south-easterly group in French Polynesia, three hundred miles from Pitcairn. The wind climbed steadily through the first afternoon. At midnight there was a forty-five-knot squall. By dawn the following morning I was running north-west at over six knots. A double reef hung from the boom, occasionally cracking in the wind. In the large easterly swell the wave crests broke with a wet thud under the transom. With each one the boat rushed onwards in a burst of speed.

In the tropics these conditions are usually reinforced trade winds that can last for many days. The trade is steady at up to thirty knots, making for a fast and furious ride, with luck in strong sunshine.

The sky that morning was sleet grey, though, and patches of glancing rain came over the eastern horizon. In the cockpit I ducked from unpredictable assaults of both salt spray and rain, but could only tell one from the other when the heavy flecks landed near my mouth. Worse, I recorded in the log the lowest readings for barometric pressure since leaving the coast of Patagonia. It seemed that these were not trade winds generated by high pressure to the south, but an easterly on the underside of a depression somewhere to my north, near the Marquesas. Depressions in the tropics are bad news. That made me nervous.

There had been reports on the radio all summer of freak weather around the globe. South-east Asia had suffered months of drought; bush fires raged in Sumatra, Borneo and Malaysia, forcing traffic to use headlights at midday; smoke from the fires drifted across the Indian Ocean to the Maldives. Flooding killed fifty-five people in Poland and sixty in the Czech Republic. Mud-slides destroyed communities from the Mississippi to California.

I listened to these BBC reports with a sailor's smug detachment at first. Over the time I've been at sea, I've spent hundreds of hours sitting beside the radio listening as world history unfolds. I have heard accounts of wars, elections, scandals, genocide, liberation, earthquakes. After weeks on passage through the trade winds, the tropical seas can appear the most benign place on earth by comparison. There is no threat here. I've found a small island that is far removed from both natural disasters and the cruelties of the human race.

Reports of unusual weather right around the world continued through the early months of 1998. By the time I reached the tropics, news agencies were agreed that this was a systematic disruption to global weather. But still I managed for several weeks longer to believe that somehow I was separate from the world beyond the horizon. It was not until late in March that the façade of my island sanctuary began to crack. Almost after the event, I realised that the freak weather in distant parts of the world had started right here: the stretch of ocean I had just crossed, between the coast of South America and the Polynesian islands, is one of the most volatile in the world.

When I first sailed in the Pacific, some sailors scoffed at El Niño: it was a silly name, they said, used by those determined to explain every vagary of global weather. By the late 1990s you seldom heard that attitude any more.

El Niño begins around Christmas time off the coasts of Chile and Peru and is so-named, by the local fishermen, after the infant Jesus. In this season, in a normal year, high pressure over the eastern Pacific generates trade winds from east to west. The trades blow warm equatorial waters in the same direction, allowing colder water to well up from the sea-bed off the coast of Chile and Peru. But for reasons that still are not properly understood, in an El Niño year this pattern is reversed. The pressure is abnormally low in the tropics, the trade winds are interrupted by long periods of calm, the warm water is never pushed from the coast, and sea temperatures are from five to ten degrees Celsius above normal.

From this part of the Pacific, El Niño triggers a domino effect of severe weather around the world. But the local weather is also affected. Cyclones in the South Pacific are generated when depressions form over warm, tropical water. In a normal year the cyclone season lasts from November to March or April, but most storms occur in the western sector, in the Coral Sea and the waters around Fiji. Cyclones in the east, in French Polynesia, are relatively rare. I'd timed my arrival in French Polynesia for the end of March to minimise the risk.

However, the previous major El Niño event of 1982–3 had

seen a different weather pattern. Five cyclones battered eastern French Polynesia in the first four months of the year. The last, Cyclone William, hit Gambier with seventy-five-knot winds in late April. My position now was a little more than two hundred miles from Gambier. The wind was thirty-five knots. The sky over the eastern horizon was black, and barometric pressure was low. All the signs were that there was a depression to my north, deep in the tropics. If sea temperatures were warm enough in this El Niño year, this tropical depression would develop into a cyclone, and track south.

The day before I reached Gambier there were two more squalls with driving rain. In the night the easterly never dropped below gale force and I ran under bare poles. By dawn the swells were steep and breaking. The sea was grey. The skyline alternated between tarry black cloud and the advancing, electric fuzz of rain squalls.

Late that morning I sighted two black triangles on the horizon to the south-west, the pyramid summits of Mt Duff and Mt Mokoto. Gambier is a group of nine small islands, protected by a partial barrier reef fifteen miles across. The enclosed lagoon is mostly navigable, but there are numerous shoals. On the eastern reef are several trailing sand islands, or *motus*; the largest accommodates an airstrip. But the main island, Mangareva, is mountainous, a volcanic knife-edge of rock. At its feet there is lush bush, surrounded by a palm-fringed shore and beaches the colour of cream. The lagoon is turquoise. Sea spray hangs as a veil of mist over the reef.

An hour after sunset I was two miles off the northern point of the reef. It was ten miles to the pass, and the lagoon inside the reef was not navigable in darkness. I had arrived too late, and knew I would not find an anchorage until the following morning.

In the lee of the reef the seas became calmer. Then I sailed into Mangareva's wind shadow and the gale was blocked out, replaced by a dirty offshore flow. In this way the island extended its sphere of influence out over the ocean. I sailed along more quietly now under a double-reefed main, parallel to the shore some three miles away. Off the pass I dropped the sails and lay ahull, drifting on the wind and current. I sat up for two hours, making a meal and watching the rate of drift on the GPS. The boat was heading north-west at about half a knot, away from the island. I lay down on the leeward bunk and set the alarm.

At 1 a.m. I put up reduced sails and beat back towards the reef, then lay ahull again to wait till dawn. I slept little that night, anxious about this interruption in the voyage and the thought of leaving the sea life I had practised so hard. But unlike Easter Island and Pitcairn, there was no alternative to this stop at Gambier. I'd been offshore for a month, and needed to fill the tank with water. Even so, this landfall was problematic. If there was a tropical storm in the islands, there were few good anchorages here. The main bay at the village of Rikitea was exposed. The person I had become over the last months said it might be better to stay at sea. But the person I had been for all my life before sailing offshore craved the security of land. At this point, after five months of the voyage, these two irreconcilable instincts were equally strong. So I waited for daybreak, the island invisible but its sheltering forces something I could feel in the wind and the wave pattern all around. I tried to rest under a tartan rug on the bunk, and more than once found an ugly solace in a bottle of Spanish brandy.

At dawn the wind was thirty knots. I motor-sailed through the pass shortly after first light. It was a broad area of shoaling with depths of twenty-five feet. There was an inflowing current. I entered the channel between Mangareva and Taravai. The overfalls here were the steepest I have seen. The two steel buoys marking the channel bucked wildly on heavy chains where steep swells picked up by the east wind met resistance from the tide. It took two hours to short-tack the four miles from the pass. There was little time to take in the islands around me, except for watery impressions of bush at sea level and columns of black rock climbing vertically into the mist and rain. Once clear of the south-east point of the island I could bear away to the north, then follow a second channel through coral heads to the village at Rikitea.

I anchored off a small beach in fifteen feet of cloudy, disturbed water. The wind was fresh and directly onshore, though the anchorage was partly protected by reefs. Beyond, the surface of the lagoon was almost completely white with breaking water. Ashore, palms crashed and reared in the wind, their fronds blown submissively outwards like umbrellas in a gale. The houses along the water's edge were protected by a rough coral sea wall, but spray still reached their walls. The shutters were closed. On a hill above the village I could see a large, white church. Above this the island was lost in rain cloud.

From the dinghy I set a second anchor. The boat was nodding heavily on the regular chop. This done, I lifted the oars and let the wind blow me ashore. I landed on a tiny beach, only a few paces long. The coral sand was coarse and glassy. I tied the painter to the trunk of a mango tree. A disposable nappy was neatly folded into the crook of two branches.

A muddy road ran parallel to the water's edge between weather-board cottages, their gardens shaded by breadfruit and sour-sop trees. Bougainvillaea climbed over trellised porches. The *gendarme* was a young French import in tight blue nylon shorts and a white shirt. His eyes lit up when he saw me. 'What about the World Cup?' he beamed. 'Only three months now, but England has no one to feed Shearer.'

I hadn't spoken to anyone for four weeks. I told the *gendarme* I had been worried about the weather. 'The sun certainly will not shine on the England team,' he said, pushing a piece of paper and a pen across the desk. I wrote my details on the page, which he said would be faxed to Tahiti. The formalities were now complete.

I walked up through the village. A large women in a floral print dress, completely sodden with rain, skidded past on a motor-scooter, splattering mud behind. The *gendarme* had directed me towards the island's meteorological office. I came to a barn of a building on the hillside beyond the last houses, knocked, and stepped inside. It appeared to be an empty warehouse, then I saw someone wave from a desk at the far end. The meteorologist was called Henri. Charts and weather maps were pinned to the walls above his desk. There was a set of wind instruments and a baro-graph. Otherwise, the building was filled with the sound of wind pummelling the corrugated iron walls and torrents of squally rain on the roof. Henri handed me the latest weather fax. The chart showed the spiralling form of a deep depression spread across the page, centred five hundred miles north of Gambier. I asked Henri what he thought was going to happen. 'England will lose,' he said innocently. I said I meant about the weather, what was going to happen with the depression? He said not to worry. The depres-sion had filled already and was moving to the west. The wind would stay strong, but was unlikely to get worse.

It was raining more persistently by the time I got back to the village. The street was deserted. I walked slowly past the houses. There was a post office and a hall. I'd hoped there might be a bar, somewhere to hang out. Now that my feet were on land, I hated the idea of going back to the pitching boat.

When I reached the first of the two shops I went inside and asked the Chinese owner if he would let me have some water. He took me out the back to look at the rain water tank. As I admired it, he touched my arm and asked if I had any bullets. My French didn't stretch to 'bullets', so this was achieved by him mimicking shooting me in the face. I told him I didn't have any bullets. He said I could not have any water.

The shop was next to the beach. I walked back dejectedly and stood beside the dinghy. The boat was still bobbing into the seas coming off the lagoon. The anchorage was churned up and messy. I decided to look elsewhere for water.

As I turned back towards the road I saw several faces staring at me from the shadows of a building nearby. They waved, so I walked over. The building was open-sided, a storage shed for milled timber. About ten young men, dressed in damp *pareus*, were lying around on the planks, drinking Hinano, the Tahitian beer. They made a place for me to sit and put a bottle in my hands. The boys were brash and drunk. Laughter boomed from figures I could barely see in the half-light. The guy next to me was called Matai. His arms and legs were covered in the raised scars of coral cuts, almost white against his brown skin. His black hair was matted and chalky with salt. Matai wore a scarlet singlet showing a Polynesian god springing from a cloudburst carrying an AK47. By late afternoon he was off his face, banging on about Nostradamus. I walked out to the beach several times to see if conditions had improved in the lagoon, and stood pushing my feet through the sand until the rain forced me to make a decision: return to the boat, or stay ashore. I always went back to the timber shed. It was warm and comfortable inside, and the company of drunks seemed a blessed relief after the passage. Matai took me to his home and his sister provided a meal. It was after dark before I returned to the beach.

One September evening in 1834 three Picpus Fathers gladly quit the ship that had carried them for the last four weeks from the coast of Chile, hoisted their cassocks around their thighs, and waded through the warm shoal water to a beach in the Gambier group. They had landed at Akamaru, a small island on the windward side of the lagoon. Their leader, Father Louis Laval, gathered Father Caret and Brother Murphy around him, gave thanks for their safe landfall, and prayed for the fortunes of the Order of the Sacred Hearts of Jesus and Mary and the Perpetual Adoration of the Blessed Sacrament, at last established in the South Seas.

Gambier was an independent kingdom at the time of the missionaries' arrival. There were *maraes* on each of the main islands in the group, adorned with idols to Polynesian gods. The people were reputed to be among the most fierce in the South Pacific. Human sacrifice was practised and cannibalism was widespread. Corpses of loved ones were only preserved by being buried in the deepest part of the lagoon, beyond the reach of even the fittest divers. The king, Maputeoa, initially refused Father Laval access to the main island of Mangareva, so the missionaries set to work on the smaller islands in the group.

Within a year there were mass baptisms at Taravai, Aukena and Akamuru. During Lent, stone images of the god Tu were smashed. Stone churches were built on the sites of *maraes*. Christian marriage was introduced. The islanders were taught the concept of original sin, and given calico tunics to preserve their modesty. Despite this success, Father Laval describes living in a wretched grass hut on Akamuru. Father Caret kept a small garden and Brother Murphy distilled alcohol from the *ti* plant. The missionaries enjoyed a glass after dinner.

The Picpus Fathers were the fundamentalists of their day. They believed the perfect mission to be a replica of a medieval settlement, governed by Catholic orthodoxy, with a priest at its centre, propped up by the native monarchy and nobility. Laval was twenty-five years old, working on a mission in Chile, when he heard about the South Seas. Making the trade wind passage to Polynesia and building a remote island theocracy in a pagan ocean was to be his life's work.

After some months the king began to appear at mass. The missionaries had been in Gambier for two years when Maputeoa agreed to the destruction of the Te Keika *marae*, the largest in the group, built on terraces above the village of Rikitea. In its place Laval began work on the vast St Michel cathedral. It was the largest church in the French Pacific, on one of the smallest islands.

By this time the missionaries had been joined by Count

Alphonse de Latour de Clamouze, a minor aristocrat with some skill as a draughtsman who was largely responsible for an extraordinary series of building projects that transformed the timber and grass villages into imposing settlements of coral and rock. The stone was quarried from Mt Duff and carried on the islanders' backs to the village. Coral was cut from the reef at Kamaka, then brought to Mangareva by boat and burned to make lime. On the waterfront beneath the temple Laval built a stone palace with conical dining towers and follies. Triumphal stone archways guarded the paved avenue that led from the wharf to the cathedral door.

At Rourou, on the slopes of Mt Duff, a great stone convent was established. Two hundred nuns filled the cells, and many of the island's unmarried women were compelled to take up residence and tend the convent gardens. Virtually the whole population worked as forced labour for the quarrying and building programme. Some died of starvation, and many fled on passing ships. One estimate, based on a study of Gambier's records of births and deaths, suggests that the population fell from 11,000 to just 500 during the period of Laval's rule.

Father Laval introduced the 'Mangarevan Code', a system of religious laws governing all aspects of life in the islands, based on those operating in a Jesuit convent. There were plans to build a monastery, so that men and women could live completely separate lives. Many islanders took vows of chastity. Impure thoughts were punishable by imprisonment. A religious police force was established to implement the Code. Laval was supreme judge in the islands, by virtue of his powers of excommunication.

The islanders were taught that sailors were devils. At the first sight of a ship in the lagoon the women and girls were instructed to run and hide in the convent. Laval described one captain, a pearl trader named Jean Pignon, as having been his nightmare for twenty years. Trading captains, used to receiving favours from local women and living wild in the outer islands, bitterly resented

Laval's puritanical creed. When Jean Pignon's nephew Jean Dupuy refused to sign the Mangarevan Code he was sentenced to fifteen months' imprisonment. On his return to Tahiti, Dupuy joined forces with Pignon and together they laid a complaint. Finally, the Catholic Bishop of Tahiti recalled Father Laval to Papeete. A report by the French Commandant in Papeete, M. Motte-Rouge, described Laval as unstable and authoritarian, carried away by religious zealotry, from having lived in isolation from the world for thirty-five years on a remote island. It was also found that the Picpus Fathers had conducted a highly profitable trade in nacre shell – mother-of-pearl – to finance their projects. Laval died in Papeete in 1880, from a cat scratch that went septic.

Part of Matai's drunken rambling on my first afternoon in the woodshed concerned the island of Taravai. He and his friend Paul had a pearl farm in the lagoon there. Matai described the island as paradise, repeatedly. He seemed to assume that, as a European in the South Seas, I had to be searching for paradise.

When I landed the dinghy on the beach the following morning I found the Chinese shop-keeper had had a change of heart. He was now kindness itself, and insisted I take as much water as I needed. I spent the next hour filling jerry cans and shuttling them out to the boat. The wind was still fresh off the lagoon, and by the end I was soaked with spray from rowing through the choppy water. When I again landed on the beach I met Matai and Paul. They said they were going to Taravai in an island boat, and invited me to come and visit them there.

The passage across the lagoon to Taravai took only half an hour. The island was shapely, three miles long and about one wide, its central ridge a thousand feet above the sea. Occasional squalls still rolled in over the reef to the east. The grassy slopes of the island were the softest olive green in the watery sunshine. The colour of the lagoon alternated between black and sky blue as cloud obscured the sun. The tiny village was on the windward side. There was no tenable anchorage here in this wind, so I ran down behind the island's lee and anchored in a deep horseshoe bay fringed by palms. The wind was almost still here. Hardly a frond rustled.

That afternoon I climbed up to the central ridge, then bush-whacked down to the village through *aeho* grass, chest-high, and thickets of bamboo.

There were four houses in the village. Only one family lived here full-time. It was a simple and lovely place. The houses stood beneath palms and breadfruit trees at the water's edge. A grassy track, the only road of any sort on the island, now overgrown knee-high, followed the shoreline, flanked by white orchids and *maire* ferns. Inland, yellow-flowered *purau* trees sheltered the old gardens. I caught the scent of vanilla. At the head of the track stood the whitewashed church built by Father Laval, the bell tower climbing above the palms, dazzling in the sun. Inside, the domed ceiling was inlaid with rosewood. Blue stained-glass filled the windows. Sunlight the colour of the ocean flooded in. Prayer must have reminded the islanders of swimming underwater.

Outside the church was a large grassy rectangle of reclaimed land pushing out into the lagoon, trussed up with coral boulders to break the seas. At the centre of this plaza stood a forbidding stone archway thirty feet high. The volcanic rock was black, now much covered with moss, but the masonry was in good condi-tion. Laval had placed the archway here to dominate all access to the island, as this was also the wharf. He had turned the island into a theatre of forced devotion. But today, since this was the only area of clear, levelled land, Matai and Paul used the archway as the goal-post for their afternoon soccer practice.

I spent a week on Taravai. The weather cleared, though the wind never dropped below twenty knots. Three times I slept in the village, the other nights I battled back to the anchorage on the leeward side. We left before dawn one morning to hunt wild pigs with dogs and a .22 rifle. The kill was butchered on the spot, the carcass carried back to the village in old postal sacks, blood dripping down our backs. We trolled for fish along the southern reef in a pirogue, and slept in the sun at the pearl farm.

One night Paul and I went fishing after dark, once the moon was high. He laid a net in the lagoon, then we dived to retrieve the catch. In the moonlight the water was a deep, emerald green. I could just see Paul working beneath me, his body like a trail of emulsion in the water. Beneath the waves he moved with a different grace and agility, as if he would never come back. He showed me how to bite the fish on the head before pulling them from the net. This stunned them long enough to thread a cord through the gills.

On my last morning at Taravai a boat-load of picnickers arrived from Mangareva. We made a long table in the clearing. The picnickers were led by a feisty old woman named Marie. Marie was small and uncommonly gaunt, wrapped in a vivid purple *pareu* and matching headscarf. She called me 'little one', though her head barely reached my ribs. They had brought fish, some raw, some baked, some marinated in coconut milk and lime. Also pots of taro, yams, sweet potatoes, and flagons of wine. Bananas and pomelos were picked from nearby trees.

About fifteen people sat down to lunch. A few of the oldest ones lay out on woven pandanus mats in the shade. Toddlers ran screaming in and out of the waves. Sitting opposite me was a French guy from Toulouse, now married to a Mangarevan woman. He was a civilian technician on Mururoa Atoll, the French nuclear test site, two hundred and fifty miles from Gambier. Until the test site was decommissioned the year before my visit, the whole surrounding area had been off-limits to yachts. When I asked about his work the technician said, 'Most of the houses are empty now. It's a beautiful place, like this here.

This talk about nuclear pollution, that the atoll is leaking waste into the ocean – it's all lies. I swim in the lagoon every day.'

I returned to Rikitea on Sunday morning. I planned to buy a few things in the store the following day, then put to sea. I climbed the curving staircase to the cathedral of St Michel for the ten o'clock service. This was the centre-piece of Father Laval's project, a great edifice in coral and rock, with seating for twelve hundred. The entire population of the islands today would fill less than half the pews. Laval is buried in a crypt before the mother-of-pearl altar. That Sunday the congregation numbered thirty, mostly children. Paul was wearing multiple shell necklaces, playing in a ukulele ensemble.

In the afternoon there was a football match. The pitch was just beyond the cathedral, below the site of the present-day mission house. Paul and Matai were playing in the same team. There were about fifty spectators, sitting on cars or scattered around the bank on the inland side. The pitch was completely water-logged: a bog. The ball wouldn't travel any distance unless airborne. As I watched the game I noticed a figure moving slowly through the crowd. I recognised him as the island's French priest. He stopped at each group of spectators, shook a few hands, and sometimes stayed to chat. It was obvious that soon he would get to me.

The priest smiled as he sat down beside me. 'You must come from the yacht,' he said. He didn't take his eyes off the game.

I told him I thought the standard of play was very high.

He said, 'I think we have a real chance this year at the championships in Papeete.'

'It's a shame the ground is so wet.'

He shook his head. 'What we need is a proper playing surface. It must have drainage and good turf. Perhaps if we win the championships. That is something I would like to see here.' The ball had gone into touch and he turned to look at me for a few moments, warming to his theme. 'Le Stade de Gambier – yes, indeed, come back and visit us again in five years. Perhaps we will have built a new stadium by then. But first we must win the championships.'

Eight

THERE IS NOTHING in the world like sailing in to Tahiti. The island is both myth and reality. The myth appears above the horizon many days before landfall. Maybe it has always been there, just beyond the range of vision, hanging over the sea. Perhaps the bow of every boat in history has secretly been pointing, within the sailor's heart, towards some distant and better place.

The myth of an island paradise has been the subject of theological speculation; it has shaped the course of cartographic history, informed philosophical debate, and inspired writers and poets. It also features prominently in coconut confectionary advertisements. Tahiti has that placeless quality, like Samarkand and Xanadu: many of us would probably struggle to find it on the map. Tahiti is the stuff of rainy Sunday afternoons by the fire with tea and toast, a fine B-movie on television, and Errol Flynn in green tights and pixie boots, swinging through the rigging with a jolly cry. Who wouldn't smile? Errol's off for a romp on the beach with a tribe of dusky nymphets, even now limbering up beneath the palms.

Of course, we know it is not really like this. We know about the condoms and hypodermics on the beach, the nuclear colonialism, the techno drowning out the surf. But in the European mind, Tahiti is both an island, and an idea. Where the real island ends and our own imaginary geography begins is a line on the ocean I suspect I have never properly crossed.

It was a fine, tropical morning when I left Gambier. The trade wind was steady at twenty knots. The sky was perfectly clear. I sailed north-west across a bold but even sea, full of the noise of breaking water but seldom a drop of spray. The genoa was poled out to windward, the breeze on the quarter. I'd sailed on variations of this same course and tack since leaving the coast of Patagonia. My ship life seemed to resume automatically as I winched the sails into place, and my view again became that off-shore kaleidoscope of waves, sky, and the foreshortened rig describing a pendulum swing across the sun. When I looked back, my memory of time ashore was closed out by the ocean even before the summits of Mt Mokoto and Mt Duff disappeared beneath the horizon.

The fine weather lasted through the second day as the boat surged calmly onwards at six knots. That night I passed in the lee of Mururoa Atoll. It is a long atoll, about twenty-five miles, but only a few metres high, capped in palms. From offshore the land was invisible, there were no lights. Behind a high island the wind flow is dirty and disrupted, but in the lee of a low-lying atoll the wind is as clean as that blowing over the open ocean. So although I could see nothing of the island, for several hours after midnight I could distinctly smell it. Islands have a smell shadow, a trail of sweet fragrance, the sticky juice of coconuts, breadfruit, pandanus and mangoes, that spreads across the water downwind as a final extension to their territory. It is subtle, this smell; the effects of a fresh wind over such a distance make the perimeters of the area unclear. When I woke at dawn the smell had gone and I sailed again across a sovereign sea.

I saw little of the sun that day. By lunch time the barometer was falling and a sheet of dry cloud filled the sky. The wind freshened to thirty knots and the sea began to fall about. I popped a short seam in the genoa running by the lee, so furled that sail and ran under just the double-reefed mainsail. In the afternoon I passed in the lee of Tematangi Atoll. The island was eight miles to windward when I passed the northern point. From that distance no distinct features of land were visible, only the green fuzz of palm forests forming a broken line along the horizon. By midnight I'd taken in the mainsail. The boat ran under bare poles as the wind rose to gale force. It seemed that a second depression was forming to the north. It was going to be a rough but fast trip.

The wind had moderated to thirty knots the following morning and I re-set the double-reefed mainsail. I ran this way for the next three days. The rain was often heavy, and both the hatches were closed. Time moved slowly in the cabin. I fried breadfruit chips and tried to read, but I was bored. I'd reached a stage in the voyage when, unless conditions were good, I found the sea a trial. I felt that I'd been on passage long enough. The steep roll of the boat seemed to be more intrusive than at any time I could remember. I grew tired of doing everything with only one hand, while the other alternately pushed and pulled against a strong-point in order to keep me upright. This workout never stopped. Wherever I looked, I saw my rigid hand gripped around some bar or handle, arm muscles working in and out like a piston, as if I couldn't have functioned at all unless physically clamped to my environment. Sometimes the struggle to cook meals and give some structure to time seemed quite pointless. The boat was running off a hundred and fifty miles at every noon fix. I would be in Tahiti within a few days. The temptation was simply to crawl into bed and try to sleep it out. My bunk was the best refuge, but still there was no escape from the sound of running water: the constant, pressured rush of ocean parting round the keel; the flop of spray against the washboards; the drumming rain on the coach-roof. The makeshift double-glazing of the three small windows on both sides of the cabin – the sheets of polycarbonate I had bolted over them for security – was dirty now with accumulated salt and sea grime. When I looked out to try to catch sight of the sky, I saw only a sheet of running water over an already cloudy, scaly surface. Even inside the cabin the surfaces were damp. I brought water in on my oilskins. I spilt drinks. Four days out from Gambier the toilet leaked, and the contents sluiced across the already wet and greasy floorboards. In the ocean east of Tahiti, I thought more than once that I might end the voyage there, and stay on the island until they booted me out.

Medieval cartographers assumed that the terrestrial paradise lay beyond a great barrier, perhaps an impassable one, which explained why no one had been there. On some maps this barrier was the ocean, and paradise an island. Fra Mauro's *mappa mundi* shows paradise as an island in the most distant ocean. Likewise, the Hereford map represents Paradise as an island off the coast of Cathay, in an unknown eastern sea.

The myth of a dream island was explored by the Portuguese sailor and poet Luis Vaz de Camoëns. From 1553 to 1570 de Camoëns made landfalls throughout the Indian Ocean, exploiting the legacy left by his forebear, Vasco da Gama, whose voyage around the Cape of Good Hope had pioneered the sea route to the east.

De Camoëns' epic poem *Os Lusiadas* is a vast and passionate tribute to the sea. In it, Vasco da Gama and his crew are rewarded by Venus for their trials on the ocean by being transported to a tropical sea, where they make a magical landfall on an island that rises up over the horizon and moves across the ocean towards them. On golden beaches, in lush valleys filled with waterfalls, fruit, flowers and animals, the sailors frolic with nereids engorged by love. They sleep in palaces, make music, and hunt game. Da Gama and his crew have discovered the sea, they have opened the door to global communication. Now the sailors learn that their voyages can lead to more than commerce and conquest; in the South Seas their souls find peace, they live a life free from pain in an island-garden of other-worldly beauty.

After lunch on the third day I passed a group of three small atolls, the nearest being Nukutepipi. A day later I sailed to windward of Hereheretue. From here my course lay across three hundred miles of open water to Tahiti. I spent much of that afternoon in the cockpit. It was another miserable day, the wind at over thirty knots, the breaking seas remorseless. I wore an oilskin jacket and stood facing the front, holding the spray-hood for support. It was very mild. After several hours my bare legs were still not cold, though they were wet from spray and occasional rain. I was beginning to feel physically tired, my arm and leg muscles always working to maintain balance, and this was what I wanted. I was sick of sitting in the damp cabin. After weeks of easy living in the tropics and free access to the deck, I wondered how I had stuck it out in the cabin for days on end in the Southern Ocean. As I stood in the cockpit that afternoon I made myself promise that I would never go high-latitude sailing again.

The best, but also sometimes the worst, thing about sailing in the tropics is the long nights. In fine weather the tropical sea comes to life at night, but in a gale, or even just in strong winds as I had on that passage to Tahiti, there is little pleasure to be found on deck then. Standing in the cockpit was a workout, which was what I wanted to inflict on myself that afternoon. I wanted to be so tired I would sleep through the long hours of darkness. I wanted to become so exhausted and cold that I could again face the thought of pulling the hatch closed behind me and lying on that worn-out bunk, the thirty-year-old foam mattress collapsed into a permanent hollow, the vinyl cover cracked and falling off in shreds, the feather pillow prickly and damp.

On passage to Tahiti the sun set at 6:15 p.m. Darkness fell very quickly after that. If I cooked and ate slowly I could spin out my meal till eight o'clock. After that it was a very long night, and when the weather was bad there was nowhere to go but bed. Those hours until dawn had passed so slowly over the last days. I hoped that this new strategy might allow for a better night's rest.

I stood stubbornly in the cockpit until sunset. Afterwards, in the cabin, I turned on all the lights and moved through a stained brown glow. My dinner looked and tasted brown. On my bunk I read for an hour, mechanically turning pages I hadn't taken in. Then I killed the last lamp and tried to sleep. It was eight o'clock. I flooded my mind with childhood memories, to suit this child's bedtime. I thought that in this way I might transport myself to another time and place, and sleep till dawn. The rain began again, the sea seemed a little quieter. I pictured go-kart races down the lawn as the boat surfed down the swells. I felt tension spread through my body as the boat balanced precariously for a second with the wind dead astern – risking a gybe – then it raced off with the breeze safely on the quarter, my weight again settling firmly in the lee-cloth. In my thoughts I dallied in tree houses and rock pools, wandered sore-necked in a starchy collar at some golf club function. But I couldn't sleep, or convince myself that this dank cabin was anywhere but here and now. At 10 p.m. I climbed over the lee-cloth, and desperately gulped a mug of rum in the brown cabin light.

In June 1766 the Royal Society sent Wallis and Carteret to search for the Southern Continent. The navigators found no Southland, but in June of the following year Wallis made landfall on

a spectacular volcanic pinnacle in mid Pacific, previously unknown to Europeans. He transcribed the native name as
'Otaheite', so turning the mere mention of the island into an
expression of both longing and sadness: Oh-Tahiti. In his journal
Wallis describes Tahiti as the 'Garden of Eden'. His crew are
thought to have introduced venereal disease there.

But perhaps it was Louis-Antoine de Bougainville's arrival in
Tahiti a year later that, more than any other European landfall in
the Pacific, defined the South Sea islands as an erotic paradise.

After clearing the Magellan Strait and sailing north-west for
the Juan Fernández group, Bougainville searched for the mythical Davis Land in the ocean west of Chile. He then sailed up
into Polynesia. What happened in the days following his landfall
in Tahiti changed the island for good. He wrote: 'As we
approached the land the natives surrounded the ships. The crush
of canoes about the vessel was so heavy that we had trouble
mooring amid the crowd and the noise. They all came shouting
"tayo", which means friend, and giving us a thousand evidences
of it.' Many of the women were naked, and the men

> pressed us to choose a woman, to follow her ashore,
> and unequivocal gestures demonstrated the manner in
> which her acquaintance was to be made ... I ask how
> to keep at work, in the midst of such a spectacle, four
> hundred Frenchmen, young sailors who have seen no
> women for six months?
>
> In spite of all our precautions, one young woman
> came aboard and got onto the poop, and stood by one
> of the hatches above the capstan. This hatch was
> opened to give some air to those who were working.
> The young girl negligently allowed her loincloth to
> fall to the ground, and appeared to all eyes such as
> Venus showed herself to the Phrygian shepherd. She
> had the Goddess's celestial form. Sailors and soldiers

hurried to get to the hatchway, and never was the capstan heaved with such speed.

Bougainville named his discovery 'Nouvelle-Cythère', after the island home of Aphrodite, the Greek goddess of love. Acts of possession were buried in thirteen different places ashore.

One of Bougainville's crew was a young aristocrat, Prince Charles Nicholas Othon de Nassau-Siegen. One day, caught on the island in a squall, he took shelter in a house. Here he found six beautiful young girls who helped him undress. He wrote, 'The whiteness of a European body ravished them ... They hastened to see if I was formed like the inhabitants of their land.' During the sex that followed an audience of up to fifty islanders gathered to watch, complete with nose-flute players. The expedition naturalist was Philibert Commerson. While the ships were still at sea he wrote a letter home which was published in the *Mercure de France* in November 1769. Commerson wrote that the Tahitians knew 'no other god but love; every day is consecrated to it, the whole island is its temple, all women are its idols, all men its worshippers'.

The artist on Captain Cook's second voyage to the Pacific, William Hodges, depicted the Tahitian men as statuesque heroes and the women as classical nymphs. Europeans often expressed astonishment at how fair-skinned the Tahitians were. Hodges drew them as almost white, and transformed their tapa-cloth cloaks, called '*ahu*, into flowing robes like togas. Cook's botanist was a wealthy amateur, Joseph Banks. He described Tahiti as 'Arcadia', a land where 'we were to be kings'. He gave the Tahitians Greek names like Hercules, Ajax and Lycurgus.

Both Bougainville and Cook returned from Tahiti with a native islander to show off in their respective capitals. Aotourou voyaged to Paris, Omai to London. Both men made a remarkable impact, being presented at court, attending balls and the opera. The Theatre Royal in Covent Garden produced a play about Omai. After Cook's return a cult of all things Polynesian developed in Europe. Tahitian wallpaper, jewellery and toys were manufactured. Country estates were remodelled to include Tahitian verandas and lakes. Dr Johnson's friend Mrs Thrale delighted fashion-conscious ladies by appearing in an island dress made from the tapa cloth of Huahine. Brothels performed Tahitian dances. Women were said to adore both Aotourou and Omai. While he was in London Omai was painted by Sir Joshua Reynolds. The portrait is a caricature of the exotic, Omai dressed in a robe, his dark curly hair wrapped in an outlandish turban decorated with East Indian feather plumes and a jewelled Persian crescent. Later, he was safely returned to Tahiti, but the expedition carrying Aotourou back to the islands met disaster and he died in Madagascar, possibly of venereal disease.

I made landfall on Tahiti shortly after noon on the sixth day out from Gambier. There was very little to see. There had been no change in the weather over the previous days. The wind was still in the south-east at near gale force. Visibility was five miles, but less in the rain, and it rained frequently. I first saw the land from three miles offshore. As another rain squall moved away a dark wall appeared over the sea. The east coast of Tahiti is largely uninhabited, an area of precipitous bush with barrier reefs up to a mile offshore. From my position the coastline was featureless. It appeared as a vast lump of black rock rising from the ocean, disappearing in cloud two hundred metres above the sea.

In the afternoon the land fell away out of sight to the south-west. With the island to one side now the seas evened out a little, the sky lightened above the boat. It was an easy afternoon speeding north-west on a regular, powerful swell. At sunset I saw the lights of Mahaena and of settlements along the coast road nearby. In the distance ahead I picked up the lighthouse at

Pointe Vénus. Then the rain began again. Within a few minutes it was torrential. I sailed west for the next hour, navigating by GPS as the rain was blinding on deck. Every twenty minutes I picked up the GPS from its bracket under the spray-hood, then pushed back the hatch and scrambled over the washboards chased by the rain. I sat in a puddle on the engine box, pulled off my dripping jacket and carefully dried my face and arms with a tea-towel before plotting the position, so as to preserve the paper chart. The wind and sea would ease in the lee of the island, but if the rain continued like this I wondered if I would be able to pick up the leading lights to take me through the reef passage and into the harbour at Papeete. When I rounded Pointe Vénus the seas heaped up and began to break. A wave crashed out of the darkness behind me, filling the cockpit to the level of my calves. I stood gripping the spray-hood, shaking with surprise, the sheets floating like tangled guts around my shins. But as the boat tumbled into the lee of the peninsula the rain eased and the wind was blocked out by the mountains.

Within a short time I saw the crawling red and yellow strip of Papeete two miles to the south, and its wet reflection in the night above. In the cityscape ashore everything was dripping. Along the docks street lamps oozed yellow light into the darkness. Beneath them the harbour was a sheet of gold. Headlights spun in crazy circles on the highway. I found the leading lights into the harbour very easily, and slipped through the reef pass. In the loom from the city nearby I saw white breakers over the coral on either side. I motored across the lagoon, the wind falling about in gusts, the surface of the water rippled and slapping against the hull. Within minutes the sounds of the sea were drowned out as the city's hum covered the water. Soon I couldn't even hear the engine of the boat as I glided along the quay-side, mixing it with cars and lovers and dudes on blades.

There's no cushion in Papeete: landfall is immediate. One minute I was at sea, the next I had ducked ashore and was walking along the boulevard Pomare beside a strip of cafés and bars. There were drunken Scandinavian sailors, crew-cut Légionnaires, transvestites, junkies, tattooed bouncers, back-packers, stevedores, bewildered passengers from a cruise ship, and beautiful women in platform boots and leather jump-suits, brown arms frozen in the strobe-light.

I followed the waterfront to an area of food stalls near the port. On land the gale had colour. The rain was illuminated by fairy lights, awnings slapped in the wind as palms thrashed overhead, and diners called for more *tartare*. A Chinese cook hustled me onto a stool at the counter. I ate a meal, then re-crossed the Boulevard to a bar under the trees. I sat drinking beer until my eyelids began to droop – probably about half an hour. Then I wandered back to my bunk.

The head-spin never really stopped in Tahiti. My impressions that first evening, of a heaving dance floor and rain drumming on the terrace, of strobe lights and neon, an island nightclub in the ocean, persisted until I sailed on west. However, I see from the log that I actually arrived in Papeete on a Sunday evening. Relatively speaking, it was probably a quiet night.

I woke early the next morning. It was difficult to sleep in Tahiti. The buzz of the city seemed to last all night. After the few, repetitive sounds of a boat at sea, I was woken that first morning by the warbling drone of what appeared to be a thousand noises, merging over Papeete harbour. Container ships were tied up at Motu Uta, the *Empress Explorer* from Nassau, *Pacific Star III* from Panama. Their generators ran all night. Ferries to and from Moorea passed every twenty minutes, their wash sending the anchored boat into a violent roll. I rowed ashore. Papeete is a long, thin city, pressed out onto the coastal strip. Today cloud hung above the tiled roof-tops and wind and rain fell in blasts from the mountains. The tree-lined boulevard Pomare snaked along the waterfront, four lanes of traffic running day and night. Headlights had flashed into the boat's cabin long before dawn. Tyres hissed on flooded tarmac. A café awning had broken free and was flying like a streamer in the gale.

I walked beside the traffic. It was still early in the season but already thirty foreign yachts were tied up stern to the quay. Bronzed figures were stepping back on board with pawpaw and baguettes for breakfast. A few of the French boats looked like they'd been here a long time: louvred windows were built into the wheel-houses and herb gardens stood in tubs on deck. The rain in Papeete seemed glutinous, almost the consistency of potter's slip. Boom awnings sagged under great pools of water. The boats looked wetter than they ever did at sea. Two seventy-foot catamarans, hulls like bullets, waited for better weather to take tourists to Marlon Brando's atoll retreat of Tetiaroa. The last bonito boats readied their lines – most of the fleet had already left. And in the heart of the city the cruise ship *Paul Gauguin* towered over the palms and food stalls and waiting coaches. The *Gauguin* was much the tallest structure in town.

I cleared customs and immigration, then devoted the rest of the day to sitting in cafés and wandering the streets, depending on the weather. On the inland side of the boulevard a web of back-streets surrounds the market, each full of Chinese trade stores and pearl dealers. As I approached the market the rain set in again. Crowds ran for the shelter of its ornate verandas, hanging off the wrought iron pillars like passengers on an Indian train. I pushed through into the main hall, and nearly tripped over twin babies asleep in a barrow of watermelons.

In the rue Dumont d'Urville a truck was being loaded with sacks of vegetables and crates of dried milk. Three guys worked in the rain, stripped to the waist. A fourth man was dressed in a floral print frock, wearing lipstick and several days' beard. His brawny arms were covered in mud as he hurled a sack to the next man in the chain.

Papeete was slippery as an eel. People pushed and jostled. Scooters altered course to try to hit me (I'm sure). I walked back along the boulevard to the post office to make a phone call and stood at the outside booth waiting for the man ahead of me to finish. He was obviously off a yacht, wearing a red oilskin jacket against the rain, his hair matted, his eyes red. He looked exhausted. I guessed he had just arrived after a rough passage through the gale. He had a broad Yorkshire accent. I couldn't help but overhear as he bellowed into the telephone over the noise of the traffic. 'Unbelievable! You can hardly hear yourself think. The racket goes on day and night. We've been here a week and we're more fooking knackered than when we arrived!'

Landfall in Tahiti is different from any other in the Pacific. Particularly when you've come from the outer islands, having been the only yacht in the bay, the crush of the city serves to prick the sailor's ego. At lunch time I took a table at a café beside the park and ordered steak and wine. Later I ventured a smile at a woman sitting alone at a table nearby. Her reaction was to stare in comic disbelief, and snap her fork down on the table as if to say, 'Oh, for God's sake, get a shower, a hair cut, and some proper clothes.' This was the same attitude I met wherever I went on the island, in the harbour-master's office and the bank, on buses and in the market. It seemed that the Tahitians had long ago forgotten to be impressed every time another sailor turned up in the bay uninvited.

In *Lord Jim*, Joseph Conrad describes the profession of the water-clerks who operated in the larger ports of the Far East in the Age of Sail. As a water-clerk, Jim represents the firm of De Jongh, ship-chandlers. It is his job to claim each incoming vessel for his own firm. To do this he must sail far offshore in a skiff, often in foul weather, further and faster than any of the competition from rival chandlers. The first water-clerk to reach an inbound vessel secures for his firm the business of providing that ship with everything it needs while in port.

Jim's profession is essentially still alive, though it operates rather less formally nowadays. In the West Indies, where it's most prolific, these people are called 'boat boys'. As I approached the island of Dominica in 1991 I was accosted by a boy of no more than twelve who came over the waves on a bare windsurfer board half a mile offshore, kneeling down and paddling with his hands. He came crashing alongside, looking wild with exhaustion, said determinedly 'I'm the first', then clung to the stanchion while I towed him into Prince Rupert Bay. In the larger anchorages, where there might be more than a hundred yachts, these people did a thriving trade, fetching ice or fresh fruit, taking rubbish ashore, and supplying island produce that wasn't available in conventional retail outlets. They solicited business so industriously that it wasn't uncommon for the whole anchorage to be disturbed by some puffed-up skipper shrieking abuse at them.

That first afternoon in Papeete I moved the boat from its anchorage and tied up stern to the town quay. My berth was the last of a long line of boats, opposite a small garden with an orange pebble-dash monument to General de Gaulle. By July there would be three times as many yachts in the harbour, packed side by side along the beach to the west of the avenue Bruat on very long shorelines, a raft of reclaimed land following the shape of the shoreline.

As I reversed in towards the quay I saw a young Tahitian man working out between the bollards. He had folded his *pareu* neatly over a standpipe and was doing sit-ups on the rough concrete, his breaths short and loud through tight lips, oblivious to the rain. When I got closer he stood up and put out one arm to indicate that I should throw my shore lines. He tied these off for me, then went silently back to his exercises.

The quay in Papeete was a wild place. Tahitians came down to the water's edge as they always had, and simply ignored the flotilla of foreign yachts. They cast fishing lines between us, boys peed ostentatiously from rocks, children dived and bombed all around, then hung dripping from the shorelines. If they saw me watching through the companionway they dived back into the oily water. Being tied to the quay in Papeete was like dropping anchor in a municipal swimming pool.

When I went ashore later that afternoon the guy had stopped his workout. He took the painter and tied it to a tree. Then he asked me if I had any spare rope. It turned out he offered the same array of services as the boat boys in the West Indies and their counterparts throughout the larger ports in the tropics. His name was Ata. He had been born in Moorea. He had spent time in prison. Now he lived right here on the quay. Did I want a tart?

I got him a couple of lengths of cord off the boat. He used one for skipping. The other he stretched between a railing and a tree. When he worked out now, he hung his *pareu* over this second rope, occasionally stopping to make sure it was hanging without a crease. As far as I could see this *pareu* was the only thing he owned. After dark he moved back from the quay and slept beneath the statue of de Gaulle. He never once touted for business. In fact, he was so cool, so dignified, so wholly Tahitian that he could only just be bothered with me between his sit-ups and leg-kicks and crossover skipping routines.

When the weather finally cleared, the heat and humidity in Papeete became suffocating. There was not a breath of wind in the harbour, and without the sound of rainfall to soften the island's clamour the noise seemed to spread from the shoreline and fill the whole lagoon.

In the afternoon I walked out of town through the eastern suburbs of Papeete. After passing the hospital I turned inland up the Fautaua valley, a ravine cut deep into the slopes of Mt Aorai. The valley floor was sweltering and airless, home to concrete housing projects daubed in graffiti, and exhausted palm trees dying in the ground. A chain-mail bridge spanned the black Fautaua River, clogged with kitchen appliances and rubbish. The rainbow patterns of oil floating on the surface looked surprisingly beautiful amid the swamp grass. Nearby, tin-roofed shacks were all but buried beneath greying breadfruit and banana trees. The trapped heat in the valley made the whole landscape melt into a mirage, as several days of heavy rainfall was evaporated by the sun. High overhead the white-washed villas of Tahiti's élite clung to the cool ridges.

After an hour's walk I passed the last houses and came out at Loti's Pool. The river was deep and clear here. A dozen scooters were lined up along the bank. I sat down between the worn flukes of a mapé tree, its bark ingrained with dust and mud. More scooters whined up into the clearing and groups of teenagers disappeared yelling into the bush. The pool itself was shaped like a quarter-moon, beneath a treacherous muddy bank. Steps had been cut into the bank and a small jumping platform carved out. Young bucks in bermuda shorts did somersaults into the water while their girlfriends looked studiously unimpressed. Alpha Blondie droned from a ghetto-blaster, the echoing bass-line trapped beneath the trees.

The pool was named after the French writer Pierre Loti (Louis Marie Julien Viaud). It was here that Loti fell in love with Rarahu, a beautiful young girl from Bora Bora, and succumbed to the South Seas myth. In *The Marriage of Loti*, his autobiographical novel, he described the Tahitian landscape as one 'where misery is unknown and work useless, where each has his place in the sun and the shade, his place in the water and his food in the woods'.

Loti was a member of a group of literati who transformed Tahiti into one of the great fictional landscapes. Herman Melville described Tahiti as a 'fairy land'. According to one biographer, Melville believed Tahiti should have been the place for the Coming of Christ. In 1842 Melville had jumped from the whaleship *Acushnet* in the Marquesas and fled to the cannibal valley of Typee. In his fictionalised account of this episode, called *Typee*, Melville rekindled the spirit of Rousseau's noble savage in describing his love, Fayaway, as 'a child of nature ... breathing from infancy an atmosphere of perpetual summer, and nurtured by the simple fruits of the earth'.

Jack London came to French Polynesia in search of Melville's paradise valley, and left disgusted by what he saw as the corrupting influence of the white man. Robert Louis Stevenson, Somerset Maugham and Rupert Brooke all answered the siren call of the South Seas. James Michener was annoyed when his account of serving in Polynesia during the Second World War, which was intended to counter the myth of the islands as a romantic paradise, was later adapted by Rogers and Hammerstein into the musical *South Pacific*.

Yet perhaps more than any writer it was the French painter Paul Gauguin who left the most enduring images of Nouvelle Cythère. Gauguin used the south to turn his life upside-down. In his early thirties he abandoned what he called his filthy bourgeois existence as a stockbroker's agent, deserted his Danish wife Mette, his five children and his home, and travelled first to the West Indies and then to Tahiti in search of an island paradise he could reproduce in paint. Inevitably, the Tahiti in Gauguin's mind was very different from the reality. He despised the genteel white settler community of the Papeete of the 1890s and went bush to live with a thirteen-year-old girl, Tehaamana, whom he often painted as an Eve figure. Mostly Gauguin portrayed the island women as impenetrable children of nature, but in the painting *Matamua* he harked back to the classical imagery of the first Europeans in Tahiti with the figure of Hina, another resident of mythical Cythera.

This on-going saga of Tahitian fantasy has a strong connection to the sea, as indeed does almost everything else in Tahiti: it is a sailor's island, and has been ever since the first migratory

Polynesian canoes came in off the ocean. Pierre Loti was a midshipman, and arrived in Papeete serving on a naval ship. Herman Melville fled his middle-class home for the sea aged nineteen, and two years later voyaged on a whaleship around Cape Horn to Polynesia. Jack London also worked as a seaman early in his life. He sailed his own boat, the *Snark*, to Tahiti in 1907. Robert Louis Stevenson chartered a seventy-ton topsail schooner, *Casco*, in California and voyaged to Tahiti in 1888. Even Gauguin had had experience at sea. Apparently his eyes were blue-green, very hard and cold: he said this was because as a young man he'd voyaged in high latitudes and his eyes had frozen over. There was some truth in this. Gauguin served as a *pilotin* – a novice on a merchant ship – and later did his national service on the French imperial yacht in the North Sea. So these men had one thing in common: they didn't simply arrive in Tahiti, they made landfall here. (Also, obviously, they were men. Women writers don't seem to have been very interested in the South Seas.)

Late in the afternoon it began to rain. Swarms of mosquitoes circled my knees and ankles. I thought I might leave. The ghettoblaster was put in a plastic bag and hidden imperfectly under one of the scooters. The scooter-riders were all in the water now. The girls were still in shorts and T-shirts, wading imperiously. The boys were becoming ever more energetic in their efforts to impress. Couples looped warily around each other as if in some sort of ritual dance. The boys' faces were daubed with mud. One couple half swam, half paddled, with their hands on the riverbed, to another, smaller pool downstream where they could be alone. As the rain became a downpour they sheltered beneath the surface, only their heads above the water, angled forwards to keep the explosive drops from their eyes.

On my last visit to Tahiti, eight years earlier, I had bussed to distant parts of the coastline to see various sights. I'd also walked the two-day track through the island's vertiginous core. It was easy to see why the first Europeans had described Tahiti as a garden. On either side of the track gullies were choked with the red berries of *mati* and *puarata*, while ahead emerald slopes of *anuhe* ferns, acacias, guavas and lantana swept down to the turquoise lagoon.

But this visit was very different. I made little effort to explore the island, or even venture out of Papeete, except for the short walk to Loti's Pool. I felt little inclined to witness further scenes of natural beauty. Instead, I woke each morning craving the din and exhaust fumes of the city, the jostling crowds, the tropical filth and an espresso. After the ocean, Papeete was a breath of fresh air. I ate in the food stalls around the port and in cafés along the waterfront. I bought clothes, shoes, and books. But mostly I just ate and drank. I stayed less than a week in the city, and filled my time with an orgy of consumption.

In this, at least, I was in good company. Bougainville spent just nine days at Tahiti, and was criticised on his return for the poverty of the data he gathered relating to the island and its people. Wallis managed a more extended stay of five weeks, and conducted various expeditions into the island's interior. None the less, it was Bougainville's voyage that received all the publicity.

Although I spent most of each day in the town, I tried to return to the boat for a time in the early evening. By then the cabin was cooler, and the children who played on the quay during the day had gone home.

The sunset hour in Papeete was bewitching. Flashing lights from the container port and neon from bars ashore rippled weakly in the water as the scent of copra drifted over the lagoon. The last ferry to Moorea slipped through the pass, twin trails of smoke from its funnels just darker than the sky. Breakers on the reef were all that was visible of the sea. On the long beach to the west, polished outrigger racing canoes were pulled from racks. Their crews stood at the water's edge wearing only a scrap of *pareu*, a single wooden paddle held across their shoulders like a yoke, stretching the muscles of their backs. As they pushed off from the beach a faint chant was heard above the traffic, then a deep pump and sigh as they came rhythmically towards me across the harbour, like great multi-limbed insects stepping lightly on the surface. As the last yacht on the quay, I was the finish-point for these informal canoe races. The crews drifted around just in front of the boat, slumped forwards, breathing hard, splashing water across their backs and chests. 'Hooooh!' bellowed the helmsman, and each crew sat up stiffly in one movement, then deeply pawed the water for the run home. As their chant receded into the west, the last of the sun cast Moorea's rocky peaks and spires into an outrageous silhouette.

Every morning the yachts in Papeete held a 'Net', a kind of radio love-in which is an institution in every large tropical anchorage. At 8 a.m. the radio would crackle into life: 'Good morning to you all, this is the Papeete cruisers' Net on VHF channel 12. I'm Steve off of *Serendipity*. Okay, who we got out there today? Check in now, please.' Then those boats participating checked in by giving their name: *Symphony. Sanctuary. Southerly*'s in Papeete today. *Jonah. Kristiansund. Blue Horizon* here, morning everyone. *Easy Rider. Superannuity . . .*'

'Great turn-out, guys. And any boats leaving Papeete today? Go now . . .'

A couple of boats gave their names and destinations.

'Well, you guys, have fair winds and fast passages and I know we'll be seeing you further down the line. Any new arrivals – check in now please.'

'*Down Tide*, Joy and Peter, fifteen days from Hawaii. *Safari*, Zed and Becky, two days from Rangiroa, hi Steve, hi everyone.'

'Well, it's good to have you in port. Welcome to Papeete. Okay, so moving on to the first thing we got today, that's the

Weather.' The depression south of the Marquesas had drifted east and was filling. A ridge of high pressure was building south of Rarotonga and there was a shallow trough west of the northern Cooks. 'Any comeback on the weather?'

'Steve, this is Diane on *Sanctity*.'

'Go ahead, Diane.'

'I got a weak front on my chart kinda connected to that trough and lying west of the Societies. We could expect that here in Papeete within twenty-four hours. You copy?'

'Sure, Diane. Nice contribution.'

The good weather was short-lived. Towards the end of April Steve off of *Serendipity* announced on the Net that a tropical depression had formed north-west of Tahiti. That morning the system was upgraded to a tropical storm, named cyclone Alan. During the afternoon the wind rose and it started to rain. But conditions in the harbour were not too bad at this stage. The cyclone was generating easterly winds at Tahiti, so here in Papeete we were sheltered in the lee of the mountains, which rose two thousand metres within five miles of the coast. The wind was gusty and glanced through the city in blasts. But the effect on the anchorage was little worse than during the gale in the first days after my arrival. Any future threat was dependent on the course the storm now took, and changes in wind direction that came as a result. A north wind would blow straight into the harbour. I, like every other boat, put out extra shorelines to bollards ashore, a cat's-cradle of cordage that sagged and pulled in the intermittent gale.

It blew hard all that night, the wind very hot, and mostly dry. On the radio I listened to reports of damage in Tahaa and Raiatea, two islands a hundred miles north-west of Tahiti that bore the brunt of the storm. Lives were lost in mud-slides, and five yachts were destroyed. We spent an anxious night in Papeete, as at one point the storm was forecast to come directly our way. But by evening on the second day the threat had lifted:

the system was filling, and moving out over the open ocean to the south.

Two days later a yacht called *Salamander* arrived in Papeete. They had radioed ahead: the engine was down and the sails damaged. A powerful tender from one of the boats on the wharf towed *Salamander* through the pass into the lagoon. They had been on passage from the Marquesas to Tahiti when the tropical storm struck. The trip had been difficult. I watched the dinghy and yacht convoy move slowly up the harbour towards me. There were three children on the foredeck: two girls sitting on the coach-roof and a boy perched in the pulpit, the damaged genoa furled with long strips of torn sail cloth hanging above his head. Their parents were both in the cockpit. When they reached my boat I rowed ashore and walked apace along the quay.

Salamander was manoeuvred into an empty slot on the quay by means of an ever-growing network of shorelines, boat hooks and helping hands. Several friends stepped aboard. The mother was now sitting on the cockpit bench, her face stained with tears. Another woman was hugging her. The father was standing behind the wheel, his eyes on stalks. In the near darkness the children were too far away for me to see their faces. But in the other sailors standing around me I saw something I hardly recognised. They were mostly middle-aged couples, retirees. What I saw was a sense of mortality, the eyes of the hunted, seldom evident among tropical sailors.

I caught sight of the family from *Salamander* the next day, sitting in a café behind the boulevard Pomare. The kids were eating ice-cream, the girls' blonde hair now plaited down their deeply tanned necks. Mom wore a crêpe-cotton sundress and sandals. She was reading the *Washington Post*, and the shades in her hair still had the price tag attached, in case she changed her mind. Pop was in a lurid Hawaiian shirt, counting bank notes, smiling happily. They were surrounded by a pile of shopping bags.

★

My only previous experience near a cyclone had been seven years earlier. I arrived in Vava'u in the north of Tonga in November, the start of the cyclone season. The inner harbour there is reasonably well protected and I planned to spend the next six months based in the group. Nine other boats had made the same decision. As the remainder of the fleet left Vava'u for places outside the cyclone region, our decision to stay behind seemed portentous for the first time: the anchorage suddenly looked bigger and more exposed, the prospect of six months in these melancholy islands much longer than it had.

The town of Neiafu was sleepy and dusty. The ubiquitous South Seas trading company of Burns Philp maintained a store on the main street. Gangs of schoolgirls with matching ribbons in their hair ate ice-creams on the veranda. Inside were a few tinned goods, boxes of powdered milk, and freezer-burnt cuts of lamb and sausage meat. It wasn't long before some of the boats began to complain about the limited diet. Early in December a fifty-foot ketch, *Flying Cloud,* left for Pago Pago to stock up on food. It was a three-day trip across open ocean. There were two crew on the boat. They planned to spend a short time in American Samoa, where there were large US supermarkets, then return to Vava'u before Christmas with full lockers.

On the third morning after *Flying Cloud* left the anchorage, the sky above Vava'u went black from horizon to horizon. It was blowing a severe gale and seas were breaking in the lagoon. We heard on the radio that a tropical storm, cyclone Val, had developed north of Samoa and that those islands were being battered by 130-knot winds, with most arable crops destroyed and two-thirds of buildings structurally damaged. A long-line tuna boat had met *Flying Cloud* at sea and radioed to warn of the approaching storm. The skipper of the yacht, Steve, replied that they were only eight hours from Pago Pago, the best natural harbour in the South Seas, and would reach a safe anchorage before the storm struck. Nothing was heard from *Flying Cloud* again, and no trace of the boat was ever found. In Vava'u, the waiting was the hardest part. At present the wind was not dangerous, but this group lay on the track that the system was most likely to take. We could only listen to the radio reports of damage in islands further north, knowing that soon we might be getting the same thing.

On the second day I wanted to go into Neiafu to see if there was any news and buy food. It was too rough to cross the lagoon so I took the land route, which involved a journey of some six miles. I walked through taro and pumpkin plantations as palm fronds were torn from the trees overhead, then hitched a lift in a pick-up truck when I reached the road. There were four of us sitting on the floor in the back of the truck. Above us a tarpaulin was stretched over a heavy steel frame: it squeaked and swayed with every pothole. At the southern end of the lagoon the road passes over a causeway two hundred metres long, with open water on both sides. Midway across the causeway the wind lifted one side of the frame cover off the back of the truck. It hovered there for an agonising moment, then the wind got right underneath and tore the hood from the truck, frame and all. We watched it sail off for some distance, then land in the lagoon. The truck bumped to a halt as the hood sank beneath the surface. We continued wordlessly into the town, our eyes now streaming with tears from the wind, our faces covered in dust.

We were lucky: cyclone Val took a more easterly course, over open ocean, and did not reach Vava'u. The islanders seemed unconcerned, and among the sailors, too, there was a superficial calm. Things continued much as before in our small community, including the daily radio Net, run by a man named John. With only nine boats in the anchorage we knew each other only too well: the Net was redundant, but John wasn't worried about that. His catamaran was anchored just behind me. Some mornings at eight o'clock I heard John practising. His voice wafted over when the wind was light: 'Good morning, cruisers.' Eh-hem ... 'GOOD morning, cruisers.' Then the radio clicked and he came on air through the speaker: Good MORNING, cruisers.' No one bothered to check in any more, and John did not ask if there were 'Any boats leaving?': after what had happened to *Flying Cloud*, it was hardly likely before the end of the cyclone season. He did the weather, then ran through the usual categories.

'Okay, first up is Services Offered or Needed.'

Silence.

'Well, okay, what about Island Information? Places to Go, Places to Avoid.'

Silence.

'Let's move to Hints, Tips, New Ideas or Old Ones You're Willing to Share ...'

In the end, someone hinted that he should abandon the Net until the new boats started to arrive in May. So we waited the months out until the end of the season. As time passed, most things returned to normal. We even began to gossip about the missing yacht. Apparently Steve's crew on *Flying Cloud* was an ex-US Navy seal known as Dave Canada; they were carrying more than a hundred thousand dollars in cash, trusted to them by various individuals here to buy expensive items in Pago Pago. Some suggested they had somehow got ashore and disappeared with the money. But no one much believed this. We had all seen the black sky and felt the gale, though we were some three hundred miles from the storm's centre. I sometimes saw in the faces of the other sailors that same look I later recognised on the quay in Papeete: a frozen, hunted stare, as if old certainties had just dissolved. This island life of palm trees and sunset drinks had revealed a darker side. Cyclones were the one thing that all the sailors agreed they were scared of.

At the end of the cyclone season I made the passage north-east to Samoa. It was only a short trip, but the trade was forward of the beam and the seas large. I reached the east point of Upolu at dawn on the fourth day. In the lee of the island the wind fell still, but the east swell was running high: I motored laboriously down the coast, the boat rolling from gunwale to gunwale, the heat stifling. The harbour at Apia is formed by a deep recess in the reef and an open bay, exposed to any wind or swell from the north. Robert Louis Stevenson was so unimpressed by it that he referred to the 'so-called harbour at Apia'. Since Stevenson's day it had been improved by the addition of a short breakwater from the eastern point, but as I approached I saw that all that remained of this structure now was a small section awash in the middle of the harbour entrance: the rest had been carried away by cyclone Val. On the far side of the entrance a bank of sand and coral rubble the size of a runway had been thrown up by the seas. Ashore, many houses had lost their roofs. Whole walls had been stove in. A warehouse complex on the east side had disappeared. On the south coast, where once had been beaches of yellow sand, sheets of smooth black rock now led down to the sea, the sand washed away by vast breaking swells. And in the hills inland, thousands of trees rose without branches or foliage, like a forest of telegraph poles, or a scene from the trenches.

Robert Louis Stevenson also arrived in Apia in the aftermath of a cyclone. This was in the days before such events were given names, and this one is generally referred to simply as the 'great hurricane of 1889'. In mid March seven foreign warships were anchored in Apia harbour, together with six other merchant vessels. The storm came on during the night. By dawn, as Stevenson wrote in *A Footnote to History*, 'In the pressure of the squalls, the bay was obscured as if by midnight, but between them a great part of it was clearly if darkly visible amid driving mist and rain.' The *Eber* was first to drag her anchors, and foundered on the reef with the loss of eighty lives. By the time the wind abated, eleven more ships had been destroyed; only the *Calliope* managed to limp out to sea, and survive in open water. The beach was 'heaped high with the debris of ships and the wreck of mountain forests', and 'a horde of castaways'.

One other vessel in Samoan waters at the time of the cyclone also survived. A sixty-four-ton trading schooner named *Equator* rode out the storm at sea, then put in at Pago Pago with all sails and spars intact. The skipper was a young Scot named Edwin Reid, who arrived in Apia in the days after the storm, wearing a Highland bonnet and carrying a cargo of pigs to relieve the settlement. Stevenson, in Hawaii, was so impressed when he heard of Reid's seamanship that he chartered the schooner *Equator* to carry the Stevenson family on their last Pacific cruise, to Apia.

Though Reid was only twenty-seven years old, it seems that Stevenson had great faith in his abilities. On the cruise south from Hawaii through the Gilbert Islands the two men discussed going into the copra trade together under the name 'Jekyll, Hyde & Co.' Specifically Stevenson picked Reid because the *Equator* had survived the great cyclone at Samoa when so many other, larger ships had not. He is believed to have had a particular fear of Pacific cyclones. Critics recognise that whereas Melville characterised the threat of the sea in terms of the creatures that inhabited it, Stevenson's fear of tropical storms is a constant theme in his Pacific writings. He would only trust a skipper who had brought his command safely through a cyclone. He wrote: 'I have always feared the sound of the wind beyond everything. In my hell it would always blow a gale.'

After the cyclone scare in Papeete no one left the anchorage for several days. There were several other boats on the quay I had met before: the rotating nature of winds and currents means that people are recycled. I heard on the Net one morning that *Carpe Diem* had charts for sale ('Buy, Sell, Trade, or Part Exchange'). I had previously met four boats named *Carpe Diem*, and this was one of them: we had shared an anchorage several times in the Marquesas, seven years earlier. It was a heavy, double-ended cruising boat popular with Californians. An aluminium gangplank led onto the stern. The winches and instruments were covered in beige canvas, the spray-hood and awnings matched. A chandelier of green bananas hung from the boom.

Zack climbed through the companionway and crushed my hand. In the cabin, Mary was watching a video. She said, 'You look beat up, Miles. Get some rest. Eat some.' She pushed a plate of doughnuts across the table towards me. Zack showed me the charts and I asked the price. 'I don't want your money, son. You keep the charts. We got plenty. These bloodsuckers will soon be charging you harbour fees, and the taxi drivers will take the rest. It's all greed here.' The sailors were often generous towards their own kind, but distrustful of people ashore. Zack and I had cleared into Papeete at the same time, standing in line together in the customs, immigration and harbourmaster's offices, and I'd listened to him grumble about the form-filling and bureaucracy that follows each landfall. The government was out to tax you, customs officers to invade your boat, shopkeepers to rip you off, boat boys to hassle you. Like many sailors, Zack had a rifle on the boat. In Papeete you had to hand any weapons over to the police until you left port. I saw Zack shuffling disconsolately along the quayside towards the police station in flip-flops and sun-visor, a gun-bag under his arm. Landfall meant an act of surrender.

Carpe Diem was a big boat, twenty-five tons. All three sails were on electric furlers. There were two auto-pilots: Zack and Mary never touched the wheel. They had a generator, water-maker, and radar with compatible electronic chart-plotter. They carried charts for the whole world on compact discs, which was why they were happy to give some paper charts to me. Zack and Mary were both in their sixties, and he was able to sail the boat alone. The cabin was air-conditioned, upholstered in leather, with maple trim. The wrap-around galley worktops were formed from a single stainless-steel stamping. Zack told me once that had he been born a generation earlier he wouldn't have been interested in the sea; he would have retired some place like Florida along with everyone else. He thought he was lucky to have witnessed the revolution in boat-building and navigational technology that, in two decades, had opened up the oceans to individuals as never before.

The idea that utopia might be achieved through technology is not new. At the beginning of the nineteenth century Claude Henri de Saint-Simon recognised how communication networks could promote individual freedom. Starting with railways and canals, then telegraphs, telephones, and finally the internet, believers have argued that freedom from tyranny lies most surely in the free flow of people and information. The writer Jules Verne was a Saint-Simonist. Many of his stories concerned ships and the sea, but Verne's sailors were technocrats and scientists; his castaways were engineers who built mines and factories and worked to establish the perfect society.

The first information super-highway was the system of sea routes established in the Age of Discovery. This was a worldwide web of lines of communication that crossed oceans and linked continents as never before. Many of these routes are still sailed today by people like Zack and Mary. While at sea Zack kept an eye on his air-conditioning supply business in San Diego via the internet, which he accessed through short-wave radio. I see the California yachts in the Pacific today as a continuation of a much older wagon train that's just kept rolling west, over the Rockies, beyond the coastline, and out across the ocean, still in search of El Dorado. They play volleyball on the beach, have steel-dome barbecues clipped to the stern rail, and listen to Jimmy Buffet on CD. For them, paradise is not a place, but a time: a point in human evolution when individuals can set off across the ocean to the farthest corners of the earth and still have hair-dryers and *latte*. They are the chosen generation of techno-libertarians, who bank offshore, and live there as well.

I couldn't stay long on *Carpe Diem* that morning. Zack and Mary were going diving. Mary ate the last doughnut while I helped Zack get the dive bottles into the dinghy. Mary said,

'Diving is like flying, that's how it feels – the sea and the sky are the same thing.' There are few goodbyes on boats. Paths cross as the result of a combination of the season, winds, currents, and chance. As I walked home along the quay, six US Navy charts rolled beneath my arm, I saw them motoring towards the barrier reef north of Faaa.

That morning I got a clearance and bought fresh produce at the market. Before noon I was through the pass and heading south-west down the Chenal de Moorea.

Nine

TAHITI AND MOOREA were on the horizon to the north-east when I first suspected that something was wrong. The islands looked one-dimensional, quite black. They had taken on the quality of land in the far distance: seen from the deck of a small yacht, waves from my foreground were already threatening their shores. The land seemed to have become disconnected from whatever once moored it. Floating on the high seas, it would now drift away, or be overrun by the ocean.

I sat down on the cockpit bench and winced as my stomach turned. The weather was set fair. High pressure was re-established south of Rarotonga and the trade was a steady fifteen knots. A strong tropical sun beamed through puff-ball cloud. The pain in my stomach was slight, but I felt listless, increasingly suspicious that all was not well. I wished it was sea-sickness, as that at least would be a known quantity. When I first went blue-water sailing I'd been a sickly crewman, often of little use for the first days of a passage. Even when I left New Zealand for Patagonia, I felt queasy until two hundred miles offshore. But I'd had no problem with motion sickness since then. On the recent passage to Tahiti, running before a big swell, I could sit below, the sealed cabin thick with cigarette smoke and fumes from the stove, frying tinned ham and drinking beer. And although I have never been particularly careful with food on the boat, I had never suffered any sort of poisoning at sea until this point.

In fact, the few illnesses I've experienced while living afloat have resulted from contact with land. Perhaps this isn't surprising. Landfall reveals a filthy sailor on a weary boat, but one that has spent the last weeks sailing a pristine sea. You then step ashore into an urban ocean of viruses and germs, and the weakling seafarer is first to succumb.

I had celebrated my previous landfall in Tahiti in 1991 by going down with a flu-like bug that incapacitated me for nearly a week. All through the anchorage there were sailors in a similar state. When I took my daily stagger along the quayside I saw wan figures curled up beneath awnings in the cockpit. The sailors complained that they were 'land sick'. The morning Net was a litany of disappointments, and cheerful remedies from those already recovered. Papeete was torture for the sick. The light wind was often across the boat, so little breeze came through the hatches. I lay naked and sweating on my bunk. The noise was endless. Crowds wandered along the quay: if they stood on tiptoe and leaned forward, they could just take a peek down into the cabin to check out what was going on. Children were put on shoulders for a better view. Then they dived into the water and splashed round the boat, pulling on the shore-lines so the boat lurched, dragging themselves up over the rail to stare through the windows.

Of course, this threat the islands now pose to a sailor's health is a sad irony. At the time of the first European voyages into the South Seas it was quite the reverse. The population of Tahiti is estimated to have been forty thousand when Wallis made landfall. Within two generations it had fallen to nine thousand, the result of diseases introduced by sailors.

Tahiti was six hours away when I felt the first stomach cramp. With the wind in the south-east it would be easy to turn about and reach back to Papeete. I would need to clear customs again, and the thought of the noise and nosiness on the quay was little comfort. I hoped it might be nothing, or a hangover, and persuaded myself I had drunk more the night before than was in fact the case. I sat self-consciously in the cockpit for two hours, trying to monitor my own body state. I drank a little fruit tea, and was sick. Late in the afternoon I crawled into my bed and lay there shivering.

My other experience of being ill on the boat had also been on my previous voyage, at the end of a series of disasters on the western side of Fiji. The sailing season was coming to an end and most boats were preparing to escape the tropics before the onset of the cyclone season. I was bound for New Zealand, but before I left decided to haul and paint the boat at a new, but already decrepit, small boat-yard at Lautoka. This proved a mistake. The boat was hauled from the water by a flash new crane, and I painted it. Then the boat-yard went bankrupt and the crane, the principal asset, was impounded in a legal wrangle between the receivers and the owners. Twelve boats were marooned, cast away high and dry on the land, while the rest of the fleet sailed out of the cyclone region. The English couple on the boat next to me, who understood such things, went on a PR offensive. We were paraded before television cameras and journalists, the cute children and affable grandparent figures pushed to the front. As a gesture of good will the receivers took us on a picnic, but doubled the guard on the crane. After several weeks and no end of angst we were allowed to bring local cranes onto the site. The bigger boats needed two to lift them; I was picked up by one, and swung with road contractor's verve over the quay. The boat landed with a splash, but without a scratch, and I motored thankfully out to the anchorage. The following day, when I had planned to be buying provisions and getting a clearance, I went down with dengue fever.

Lautoka is a hot and dusty city on the arid western shore of Viti Levu, the coastal plains and hillsides around it planted with sugar cane. The farms are mostly run by Fiji's large ethnic Indian population. Each morning the fires in the harvested cane fields were relit. By afternoon the coast was swathed in smoky cloud and the sunshine was silver. In the evening the sun set crimson over the baked concrete grid of the city and the scorched earth of the hillsides all around.

For three days I could not leave the boat. Getting to the sink to pump out a glass of water left me faint. I lay hopeless on my bunk, often sleeping. The anchorage was exposed to the west and in the afternoons a stiff sea breeze set in, making the boat pitch heavily and snag on its chain. At night the land was an apocalyptic vision of smouldering fires and bursts of flame. When I got ashore after three days to see a doctor, she told me that dengue fever is a mosquito-borne disease: I might be feverish for several more days, and weak for a long time after that. I spent two more days on the boat. The wind was lighter now. In the evening the calm water of the anchorage turned orange with reflected fire. That night the city's windows were filled with candles to celebrate Diwali, the Hindu festival of light. When the fever lifted I sailed three hours south-west to the offshore islands and anchored off the palms. I knew that I should leave the tropics: it was already late in the year. But I felt weak and diffident. I spent many hours each day in a lifejacket and straw hat, drifting round in the lagoon to cool off, frail and afraid.

Now, as the sun went down that first day out of Papeete, the thought of going about and returning to be sick on land held little appeal. Most immediately, it would mean staying awake and sailing back inshore through much of the night, when all I wanted to do was rest. Conditions were very easy that evening. The wind was light and steady, the sea made almost no sound. I slept fitfully, shivering through trips to the toilet, and to the deck to throw up, while the boat sailed on west in a black hush. By dawn I was wearing more bedding than I ever had in the Southern Ocean.

Then I slept for several hours and woke to the late morning heat, soaked in sweat.

I had eaten a steak sandwich for breakfast at a stall on the avenue Bruat shortly before getting a clearance on my last morning in Papeete. Perhaps the food was bad, or I had picked up a bug before leaving the city. But more likely it was the harbour. I'd gone into the water that last morning, to scrub off any weed or gooseneck barnacles attached to the hull before this final passage towards New Zealand. The harbour was brown, full of storm water and no doubt sewage. The local kids swam in it all the time.

When I woke I felt a little better, hot and tired, but no longer nauseous. I drank some water and climbed gingerly to the cock-pit. The strength of the sun beating on my face made me wince. I noted that the boat was still sailing west, the breeze again very light. Really, I needed to hoist the third sail, the lighter number one to be fed by the poled-out genoa. But I made no changes. I was too tired and disinterested to engage the sea. The boat rolled on beneath this reduced 'hospital' rig for the next night and day.

The stomach cramps and vomiting stopped after the first night, but I had a fever for the rest of that second day and felt feeble for some time after that. In truth, there was little urgent need to recover. This was an easy convalescence, the trade wind a reliable nurse. On the second afternoon the breeze freshened a little and I made a slight adjustment to the sails. Otherwise I was free to rest. If I worried now, it was only from seeing how redundant I really was. An invalid could sail this boat through the tropical Pacific.

I usually spent the mornings on my bunk. But in the after-noons, on this westerly course, the small awning was more effec-tive and I often lay on a nest of cushions in the cockpit, pouring glasses of cold fruit tea from a pot wedged in a coiled warp, reading a book. When the boat rolled the sun crept beneath the awning and flared across the page. When the wind demanded, I pinned the leaves back with bulldog clips, so as to free my hands.

Whether sick or in good health, I cannot read at sea in the same way that I read on land. Sitting in my house, I can lose myself in a book. But at sea it is the book that gets lost, constantly put aside pinned open with clips, the story suspended while its reader watches the waves or paces the confines of his small world, making tiny alterations to the sails or fossicking deep in lockers to reassure himself about an item that isn't needed. On the ocean a book becomes fragmented into a thousand different parts. At sea, narrative is reduced to multiple vignettes, some a paragraph in length, others a few pages. The story is seldom sustained for longer than this.

When I scanned the horizon around the boat, the ocean in this part of the Pacific appeared wide and deep. Superficially, the seas were no different from those I had been crossing for weeks past. But there was a different quality to the passage, now. This stretch of water was bounded: the atolls and islands of Polynesia lay beyond the horizon, all around. I would never see the majority of these places, but their presence made a difference – a distant life-belt, but one none the less within reach. I couldn't feel the land in any physical sense, but still I noticed its proximity, in the lighter mood about the boat, and my less cautious footsteps on deck.

When I plotted my course now, I saw the names of islands and reefs stretching away across the sheet: Mauke, Atiu, Takutea, Manuae, Mitiaro. The islands are no bigger than the dot on the i in some of their names, but the names themselves fight for space on the page, curving upward or around to make way for a neighbour. In this way the shape of the islands is distorted by an ungainly echo of nomenclature. When I think of Africa or Australia, I immediately picture the shape of the land in my mind. But when I look at the chart of Polynesia I see only clusters of writing on the water. The land itself is almost invisible, hidden behind the printed word. The sea is full of text: a discourse of ocean.

From the earliest times writers used the idea of an 'upside-down' southern continent as a setting for literary utopias. The Greeks produced allegories describing ideal southern lands with perfect governments.

Bishop Joseph Hall set his *Mundus Alter et Idem* of 1605 in the imaginary Southland. Hall plays heavily on the theme of inversion south of the equator, portraying depravity as prudence and wisdom as idiocy. Included with the text are fictitious maps of the southern continent, which bear a great similarity to the maps being drawn by leading cartographers at the end of the sixteenth century such as Mercator and Ortelius. Hall has his narrator visit the imaginary land of 'Fooliana' in order to satirise what he saw as religious folly. *Mundus* was published in the same year that Quirós set sail in search of Solomon's Ophir, and established New Jerusalem in the tropical South Pacific.

Robert Burton proposed building a revitalised and utopian English state in the southern continent, to be called 'New Atlantis, a poetical commonwealth'. In his *Anatomy of Melancholy*, published in 1621, Burton speculates that the Southland extends 'from the Tropick of Capricorn to the circle of the Antarctic, and lying as it doth in the temperate Zone, cannot choose but yield in time some flourishing Kingdoms to succeeding ages, as America did unto the Spaniards'.

Huguenot writers penned imaginary voyages to the Southland to found perfect societies free from religious persecution. There is an emphasis in this fiction on equality and uniformity: the countryside is regular, and regularly fertile; cities are laid out in symmetrical patterns; languages are totally rational; dress is standardised; education is valued above all else. These were ordered societies, an inverted image of the greed and debauchery of Louis' palace at Versailles.

Most of the imaginary voyages follow a predictable format: the sailors make a long and arduous sea-passage, usually across the equator to the upside-down Southland where social norms are reversed. Here the navigators meet a terrible storm, the ship is wrecked, and castaways are washed up on an unknown shore.

Few of these writers were interested in the process of sailing a boat. Sea travel was a literary device, employed, it sometimes seems, on the assumption that every good voyage ends in a wreck and the sailor only becomes interesting once he is cast away. According to this tradition, voyaging itself becomes an act of baptism, as the sailor inevitably finds himself struggling for survival in stormy water, the ship and all the certainties of his old life destroyed. Landfall is the process of being washed up, naked and alone, on the shores of an unknown world.

In 1569 an imaginary voyager named George is shipwrecked and reaches the coastline of the Southland. George is washed ashore riding astride the ship's bowsprit, an apt piece of phallic imagery given his task ahead. Clinging to the bowsprit with him are the only other survivors of the wreck: the captain's fourteen-year-old daughter, and three more women. The castaways set up camp on the shores of a magical new land. The women each bear between seven and thirteen children to George Pines, who peoples a new land in his own image.

Henry Neville's *Isle of Pines* was published in 1668, and became an immediate success. Neville was a Member of Parliament and a republican. His novel is inspired by the idea of antipodean inversion: George was the captain's servant before the wreck, now he is liberated in a utopian world of opportunity. When a Dutch ship finally makes contact with the group one hundred years later, George's grandson is leader of a society of 1,789 people. None of this group will leave Pines' land. The memory of the old sailor is enough to maintain his creation intact.

My waypoint on this part of the passage was Palmerston Island, a large but remote atoll on the western fringe of the southern Cooks. I made landfall late one afternoon. The trade was moderate and a bright sea was running. There are six main islets at different points around the diamond-shaped coral reef, and the central lagoon is seven miles across. The island was sighted by Captain Cook in 1774, but no landing was made until Cook's third voyage three years later, when it was found to be uninhabited.

Traders in Tahiti learned the co-ordinates of the island, and a Scot named Brander established an agent at Palmerston and occasionally stopped to collect copra and *bêche-de-mer*. There is no deep-water passage through the reef into the lagoon and the ship had to heave-to in the island's lee. When the agent left in 1863 an Englishman named William Marsters, who had been living on Manuae, took up residence with two Polynesian wives. William, a carpenter and cooper by trade, a native of the Midlands, had been a seaman for many years. He soon took a third wife, and fathered seventeen children altogether. He divided the atoll into three and established each wife and her children on a separate group of the tiny islets that surround a lagoon of 3,500 acres, much of it turquoise shoaling. The highest point, called the Mountain, a sand hill six metres high, was where Marsters and his families sought safety during cyclones. He was an absolute ruler, running his island kingdom in accordance with strict religious and judicial laws which banned marriage within one family. Two years after William died, squabbles broke out over his succession. The British Resident at Rarotonga, Colonel Gudgeon, appointed William's eldest son Joel as his agent and magistrate for the island. Today Palmerston is populated by sixty-three people, all named Marsters, who occupy the three original provinces, depending on their family of origin. The anniversary of Father Marsters's arrival is celebrated by competitions between the three families in volleyball, ping-pong, cricket and darts. More than a thousand of William's direct descendants are scattered throughout the Cook Islands and New Zealand.

As I approached the islet at the northern point of the atoll I caught a heavy mahi-mahi and was busy for some time winching it in. After that, engaged in cleaning the fish, I glanced only periodically at the reef and island a mile to the south. When I did I saw a haze of silver palm fronds in the low sun, their trunks hidden by a mist of sea spray over the reef. I looked for long enough to ensure that my course would take me clear of any dangers, then returned to cleaning the fish.

The easy conditions on this passage prompted a few maintenance activities around the boat. I had noticed when hauling the anchor in Papeete that the windlass action was sticky: the grease had dried and gone hard, and the bushes were clogged with salt. The windlass needed to be dismantled and cleaned.

Tasks like this were satisfying at sea: undoing the bolts, cleaning the mechanism with spirit, and then smearing the moving parts with a fresh film of grease. It occupied plenty of time. However, there was one small complication: the windlass casing was firmly gummed down onto its bolts. It would be hard to get the whole mechanism off without applying heat, so I needed to remove all the internal components, the cogs, pins and bushes, take them back to the cockpit where they could be cleaned more easily, then reassemble the unit in situ on the foredeck.

The swell was slight that day, only a handful of white-caps in all the great plain of water bound by the horizon. The motion on the foredeck was an easy, slightly twisted roll. I made many journeys between cockpit and foredeck during the afternoon, to get a tool I'd forgotten, a cigarette, a drink. I moved easily about the hot, dry deck, bare feet finding sure footholds. Certainly I did not think to wear a harness.

When I first sailed alone, I was acutely aware of the danger of falling overboard. In those first weeks, sailing across the Bay of Biscay and down the Portuguese coast, I wore a safety harness all the time, even on calm days. Sometimes I woke at night to an image of me in the water, watching the boat's navigation light disappear into the distance. It was an irrational fear, something that lurked in the ocean all around and crept aboard the boat in the finest weather. I believed that the toe-rail around the deck marked the limit of my life. I sailed into the Pacific still believing it was possible to fall off the edge of my world.

With each successive passage this anxiety diminished. I still wore the harness in heavy weather, and sometimes on squally nights I wore it next to my skin in bed so that I would be ready to walk the deck from the moment of waking. My fetish was a sense of strapped-in security. But by the time I left New Zealand to cross the Southern Ocean I was finding the tether an irritant. As it dragged along the jack-stays behind me, it was liable to get snagged on the jury mast or windlass and pull me up short.

So that fine afternoon, after seven months at sea, the thought of using a safety harness did not enter my mind. Had I been asked, I would have said that I'd learnt to manage my fear of falling over the side. But in fact, that wasn't entirely true. My fear had simply changed its form. The sea can do this. It is not one place with one characteristic: it can reinvent itself, come back to haunt you when you think you have conquered your demons.

I sat cross-legged on the foredeck, my back braced against the front of the coach-roof to combat the roll. As I slid each cog and pin from the windlass and dropped it into a bucket for safe keeping, I had seldom felt more aware of the deep water all around. The last time I had done this job, on my mooring in Auckland, I had dropped a screwdriver over the side. But this was an improvement, as the time before that I had allowed a whole tray of tools to fall into the sea. This was what frightened me now, the thought of dropping things from the boat, partly because I have done it too often and each time I know I'm a klutz, but partly because I feel a moment of panic whenever it happens, panic at seeing the boundaries of my world so sharply defined, and so easily breached. I dread that fumbled transfer of bolt or tool and the subsequent barely audible *plop* above the other noises of the sea, because it brings home the finality of the ocean, more so than any gale.

My track record is not good. In mid Atlantic I released a precious whisker pole into the briny. In the West Indies I dropped a fishing-line and reel. Off Venezuela I lost my grip on the frying pan while cleaning it in the racing swells. I've dropped knives and a spoon, two books, my glasses, my glasses again, and again. In Auckland I lost all three washboards from beneath the spray-hood when the boat heeled-to a gust. Fortunately, the baby sitting next to them did not go astray.

It is true that as I have sailed further, I have dropped less. I sat that afternoon on the foredeck with the bucket gripped securely between my knees while I dismantled the windlass. Nothing slipped from my fingers. In the cockpit I cleaned the parts cautiously, then reassembled the windlass on the foredeck. I have learnt to corral my possessions at sea, to guard them safe in the cabin and cockpit, to distrust myself near the water's edge. I wish to preserve the wake intact. I've beaten the fear that one day I might flounder there in those parting waters behind the boat. I know I have. But in its place, the fear of dropping parts of my life overboard has become disproportionately large. I dread the sight of anything floating into the distance behind the boat. And yet there are things I must throw over the side. Food scraps, for example. I cannot guard them safe onboard the boat, rotting and stinking in the tropical heat. Peels, cores, stones, leaves, remnants must be thrown into the sea. I always watch until they disappear beneath, or behind, the lifting seas.

The first voyages I made in the Pacific were as crew on a fifty-foot Australian ketch. The skipper was of the old school, a ship's pilot from colonial New Guinea. We generated a lot of rubbish, and with two children on the boat there were nappies as well. Plastic bin liners stuffed with rubbish were heaved over the rail without a second thought. While I sat in the cockpit reading a book, drinks bottles, milk cartons and plastic packaging would come sailing up through the companionway and over my head into the sea as the skipper worked in the galley. Rubbish is a perpetual problem on boats. The sailor must choose: to pollute the land, or the sea?

I practise what seafarers call 'clean wake sailing'. Only food scraps go over the side, that material which is biodegradable. Other rubbish is accumulated in carrier bags. When each one is full it is stowed in the lazarette, sometimes for weeks or months. I stockpile my rubbish and take it guiltily ashore when I get the chance. Often this isn't easy: the atolls have nowhere to bury rubbish. You must wait for a high island that has public trash-cans. Near popular yacht anchorages these are often overflow-ing. I arrived in Tahiti with nine bags full of rubbish, the lazarette stuffed to the deck. Now the locker contained only one bag, but the residual stench still lingered. So the single-hander's boat is both his empire and a rubbish barge. I can claim my wake is clean because I dump my garbage on land. I appear to conform to the environmental politics of my generation, I do preserve my wake intact – but in truth I am concerned with something other than pollution.

My original fear, of watching the boat speed on without me, has evolved. It is now hidden behind lesser versions of itself, like dropping the tools I need into the sea, or watching bags of rubbish, each the size of a human head, float away on the wake. This is what the sea has made of me. I am the ultimate retentive, a hoarder, a warder, a gatekeeper. I live a life of ease and splendour, and abject terror. I guard my boundary, patrol the perimeter fence, not to stop an adversary gaining entry to my world but to prevent any-thing escaping it.

I tell myself that I have rationalised my fear. I have become a better sailor, a device of flesh and bone who works the sails, reads sea conditions, draws lines on charts, and completes the log. But the doubt is still there. It comes from an ever-present awareness of the abyss all around, and a terror that anything should fall from this boat. I know how to navigate a course across the abyss, but this hasn't made my consciousness of it fade.

By nightfall the following day the conditions were again too light. That evening the boat struggled to make way in failing airs. Later I dropped the sails to the deck. I wasn't tired. It had been an easy passage from the start, and without the wind to soothe me I struggled to sleep that night, hot and restless.

Before dawn a light trade returned and I re-set the sails. The boat bumped along its course for an hour. The sun exposed a frail sea-scape, the swell slack and shapeless, the wind barely putting weight in the rig. The twenty-four-hour run to noon that day was forty-five miles. I tried to prepare myself for a period of frustration. Sure enough, the passage was soon dogged by calms. I dropped the sails on two consecutive nights. Then I was becalmed for three straight days. When the wind returned, a swirling world of white cloud encircled the boat and I spent the night reaching to the south-west in a powerful, wet sea. The following day the sun was strong, the wind lighter at fifteen knots. The sky cleared of cloud and the boat ran downwind on steep, tight swells. I found other, small maintenance tasks to complete now I'd finished the windlass. Time passed easily. I had seldom felt so proud of my ship – until late in the after-noon, when I dropped a blade over the side while re-lashing the life-lines.

★

As the sun sinks lower in the sky, and the day winds down on the tropical sea, there is little sense of something coming to an end, but rather of a new beginning. A fresh energy seems to be kindled in the boat. I took my bath later, after five o'clock, then put water on the stove to boil. I drank tea as the sun fell from the sky, a whole pot, 1.5 litres exactly. Drinking now, towards the end of the day, was an inelegant process, a functional necessity to re-hydrate after the meridian heat. I took long, deep, gulps from a large mug, forcing the liquid down my throat. There was a sense of expectation: the night is coming again, the passage is moving on, the cycle of life on the ocean is indeed still turning, not stuck forever beneath a burning sun on a harsh, singed sea.

By the time I had finished drinking it was noticeably cooler. The sun no longer had the strength to pinch my skin with the force of its rays. I sat in the cockpit for some time, watching shadows form fleetingly behind waves as the sun closed in on the horizon. Life returned to the boat on the seemingly chill breeze.

The sun sets early in the tropics and the night is long. Sailing west through the Pacific I entered a new time zone every week or so that the boat was on passage. In theory I should have put my watch back one hour each time I did so. If I kept local time, the sun set soon after 6 p.m., and darkness fell quickly after that. I found this made the evenings too long, that I went to bed too early, and was awake by the small hours of the morning. So in the tropics I delayed the onset of night by a couple of hours, ignoring local time and watching the sun set at about 8 p.m. As master of my own domain, I can command darkness and light.

In the early evening I cooked a meal and ate it sitting on the engine box, listening to the radio news. I usually cooked and ate slowly, sometimes with a book open on the chart table as well. In this way the cooking and eating process might last two hours. Between mouthfuls, listening to news headlines and reading pages of the text, I often climbed to the cockpit and watched the ocean world change before my eyes. Ahead of the boat the sun was so large it seemed to quite block the horizon, while directly astern the full moon climbed urgently above the sea. As I ran west along the line of light that these two bodies cast across the water, the true nature of ocean passage-making, as travel on a planetary scale, was revealed. I had grown used to a visual feast being part of my meal.

By the time I had finished eating the last light was fading from the sky. I put my plate and the pot into a bucket and lifted it over the bridge-deck into the cockpit. The swell had subsided during the day and the sea was now calm enough to open the fore-hatch without it being vulnerable to spray. As a result, a steady breeze was blowing right through the boat. It was cooler in the cabin now and I took a T-shirt from the locker behind my bunk. Then I climbed on deck to do the dishes, intending to lie down and rest soon after that.

In the cockpit I saw that the sun was setting, the whole of that sector of the ocean reflecting its light. Astern, the crest of each sea was silver beneath the climbing moon. As I watched, the boat was overtaken by this tide of moonlight advancing towards the western horizon. Twenty minutes passed and I forgot the dishes. Night had fallen and the sky was full of stars. The tropical night has this power: an ability to replace sleep as the only form of rest. I thought I had been tired at mid afternoon, worn out by the long calm, and the boisterous reach the previous night. But now I stood in the cockpit for over an hour, my feet on the benches, holding the steel handles in the spray-hood, the boat lifting to the small seas and gliding westward. It was like riding some great beast across unseen terrain.

When I lie on my bunk during those perfect nights in the trades, I often doze off for periods of time. When I wake and look up, it is to see the wind generator ablaze in the moonlight. I come on deck for five minutes, to check the compass and search the sea for ships, and find myself still standing on the cockpit benches an hour later. When the trade is established and the weather fair, the night is irresistible. Over and over again I am drawn to the cockpit to stand in this world of sea and night sky, feeling the sails pulling cleanly against the rig, and listening to the sounds of progress bubbling up from the sea. I sit astride oceanic currents, ride winds that have circled the Pacific to reach this point, surf the foaming white crescent towards unknown lands beyond the horizon. Perhaps, like a mountain climber who returns again and again to hang over the abyss, the drop is a drug. At sea the drop is everywhere, in three dimensions, while my boat is caught somewhere nameless, held in suspension, as if hanging on strings from heaven's shimmering hand.

It was a broken night's rest, disrupted by a series of journeys to the cockpit to stare out at the sea and sky. But when I woke at dawn I felt no ill-effects from this, only disappointment that the night was over, and another day had begun.

Climbing to the cockpit, I set the fishing-line and brought the wind around more finely over the quarter. The bucket of un-washed dishes was now wedged beneath the spray-hood, last night's food dry and hard in the bowl.

Landfall on a reef is different from any other. From seaward I've so often searched the horizon for mountains and forests, or the formless grey mass of a city with the detail of wharves and ware-houses in the foreground. But when you make landfall on a reef, this moment of revelation never comes. Sometimes at Beveridge Reef it is possible to see the reflection of the lagoon in clouds overhead. But today the only cloud was a bank of torn cirrus far to the south. I heard the surf at almost the same time I saw it, a faint report, like the roar from a stadium many blocks away. The line of breakers appeared as a cleaner, folded crease above the buckled ocean. Behind this line, spray hung immobile in the air.

There is no dry land at Beveridge. It is a ring of coral four miles across, atop a sea-mount in mid ocean. The reef encloses a shallow lagoon, about forty-five feet deep. There is a pass through the reef on the west side, so it is possible to enter the lagoon and anchor in shallow, protected water.

The pass is about fifty metres wide. In a few short moments the seabed rose from five thousand metres to appear as a cracked yellow strip of rock and sand just beneath the keel. The swell foamed over the coral close on either side. There was little current in the pass, and I motored gently inside the reef. The lagoon stretched ahead devoid of scale, a disc of hot light reflected by the shallow sand bottom. The anchorage appeared to be empty.

I had a very tentative arrangement to meet a friend named Pete Atkinson here. Pete was spending that cyclone season in Vava'u, some two hundred and fifty miles to the north-west. I had faxed him from Tahiti to suggest a rendezvous at Beveridge: Pete was an underwater photographer and often worked here. I had received no reply to the fax. From Vava'u it would be an uncomfortable slog to windward.to reach Beveridge. I motored over to the windward side of the lagoon and anchored in the shallows. From the masthead I traced the line of the circular reef around me. As I did so, three black squiggles appeared in the water near the boat: the unmistakable shape of sharks.

I had met Pete eight years earlier in the Marquesas. He sailed a seventy-year-old Fred Shepherd cutter. The boat was impossibly elegant, but kept in workmanlike condition, unpampered. The topsides were painted grey, patches of fresh caulking a newer, lighter shade between pitch-pine planks. The decks were bare, greying teak. It could be a demanding boat to sail. Beating between two atolls in Kiribati, the hull leaked so badly that Pete was forced to jump over the side to nail a lead tingle over the garboard seam.

He tried to come to Beveridge every year. The combination of water clarity, light reflected from the white sand seabed, and the numerous sharks made it a good location for underwater

photography. But now that I had arrived, it seemed more doubtful that Pete would be here at the same time. This place was as
empty and remote as the ocean all around, only more still. I
couldn't picture another boat in the pass, or motoring through
the mirages in the lagoon towards me.

Even if he did come, I didn't know exactly what to expect.
Pete often sailed alone, but not through choice. He once adver-
tised in *Dive* magazine for 'an underwater model: must like
sharks and whales'. He got four replies and took Michelle from
Bridgenorth. I met Michelle when she flew out to Auckland to
join the boat. She was twenty-one years old, bright, pretty, and
had not been sailing before. She had no idea what she was getting
into. Pete told her that the first passage would be an easy island
hop from Auckland to Rarotonga. It is an ocean passage of two
thousand miles. The boat met fifty-knot winds. He lost the self-
steering, and the boom broke. Michelle stayed in bed for twenty
of the twenty-two days it took to complete the trip, and demanded to be put ashore in Rarotonga as soon as the boat was
anchored. Pete was always looking for crew, and you could never
be certain whether he would be alone or not.

That afternoon I took the dinghy over to the reef. It was half-
tide. Patches of bare rock burnt brown in the sun. The surface
of the coral was raised into hundreds of pentagonal formations.
Pools of white water were swelling on the flood. Sixty metres to
windward the surf beat relentlessly on the outer edge of the reef.
The sky spread vast and lopsided across the sea.

I waded along the back-reef margin, snorkelling in the shallows. There were clams here among the coral, their lips twisted
into smiling corrugations. I put several into a bag, then walked
south along the reef towards the wreck of the fishing boat *Nicky
Lou*, from Seattle. The boat had been high and dry for about ten
years. In that time someone had come to Beveridge and blasted

the four-bladed bronze propeller off the boat with explosives, but the superstructure was still largely intact.

I sat in the lee of this great carcass and looked back across the lagoon. The atolls and reefs in the Pacific have a quality that sets them apart. Paradoxically, from the sailor's perspective, it is that landfall here brings so little change. The sea and sky around the boat are the same as when on passage, only there is a scrap of rock to walk along at high tide. Robert Louis Stevenson described the sensation of living on Fakarava Atoll as a kind of slow-release euphoria, an atoll madness that came with living on both the land and the sea at the same time.

It was nearly dark by the time I got back to the boat. I ate the clams marinated in lime juice. At high tide, small swells came right over the reef. The trade was building from the south-east, and the boat began to joggle on a slight chop.

In my fax to Pete I had given him the date I expected to arrive at the reef, and said I would wait here three days. But my passage west through Polynesia had been slow and I was already overdue. The same calms that had held me up would have eased his passage in the opposite direction: he could have motored across flat seas. It seemed unlikely he would arrive now.

I decided to fill my time the following day by making a chart of the reef. On the Admiralty chart Beveridge is shown as a dot to be avoided by navigators. There was no chart of the reef itself. It was a simple drawing to make. With a handheld GPS I found the position at various points around the reef and mapped its shape onto graph paper. The coral formation was fifty to eighty metres wide, the sand-flat behind the back-reef margin about two hundred metres wide. I measured spot-depths in the reef passage and throughout the lagoon and identified a small number of coral heads. The wreck of the *Nicky Lou* was prominent on the windward side.

I drew the reef as it is at low tide. This is the convention on all marine charts: potential hazards like rocks are thus shown at their most dangerous. But it struck me that I had never drawn a chart quite like this one before. At Beveridge, when the slight, tropical tide closed in on the reef, there was no land at all above the water. I had drawn a map of a place that wasn't always there.

In his story 'Of Exactitude in Science' the Argentinian writer Jorge Luis Borges describes the world's first truly accurate map. It is drawn on a scale of 1:1 with the land it represents: 'a map of the empire whose scale was that of the empire, and which coincided point for point with it'. The map was accurate, and useless for any practical purpose because of its great size. Maps are of necessity abstractions. When you condense information, you change it.

Most world maps today are drawn on Mercator's projection. Gerhardus Mercator cracked a problem that had plagued cartographers since Greek times: how to represent a spherical planet on a flat piece of paper. To do this Mercator distorted global geography. In effect, his projection exaggerates the size of countries in the northern part of the northern hemisphere.

World maps have not always been oriented on north. Arab maps were traditionally oriented on south. *Mappae mundi* showed east at the top of the sheet because this was the supposed location of Paradise. In fact there are numerous different ways of projecting the planet onto a flat page. Stab-Werner projection shows the earth as heart-shaped. Fuller's projection is a series of interlocking triangles that can be unfolded in different ways to produce unrecognisably different images of the earth. On one of these sheets the planet appears as just one great ocean with a few scraps of land around the periphery.

The Greeks did not believe it was possible to draw a map of the sea. The first aids to maritime navigation, the classical *periploi*, were textual rather than graphic. There are other examples of non-graphic maps. In the second century, Dionysius recited an Alexandrian world map in the form of a poem. Bruce Chatwin describes in *The Songlines* how Australian aboriginals migrate through the outback by singing a map as they walk. When Robert

Louis Stevenson arrived in the Gilbert Islands in the schooner *Equator* he was given what he assumed was a traditional Micronesian 'stick-map': a woven frame of bamboo twigs with shells sewn into place representing the islands of the South Seas. Today, however, these stick-maps are thought to have been copied from nineteenth-century European sea charts. The Pacific peoples colonised their ocean without the use of maps. These navigators understood which stars followed the same 'path', those that rose in succession from the same point on the horizon and described the same arc across the sky. Thus they knew which direction to steer for a certain island by knowing which stars rose and set above it. The star path was used throughout the South Sea islands. It was known as *kavenga* in the Solomons, *kaveinga* in Tonga, and *'avei'a* in Tahiti. Navigators in the Caroline Islands devised a star path that gave thirty-two directions. Star paths were not represented graphically or in tabular form. Their use meant that navigators committed to memory huge amounts of information, which researchers believe was retrieved by means of complex mnemonic devices: these first ocean sailors chanted their way across the sea towards a featureless horizon.

Today, the most informative maps of the sea are the 'routeing charts'. These charts show the continents around each ocean as well as the principal islands. But routeing charts are mostly crammed with information about the water itself, and conditions prevailing in and above it: average wind strength and direction at numerous fixed points; ocean currents; mean air temperature and pressure; mean sea temperature; percentage frequency of fog and low visibility; tracks of past cyclones; shipping lanes; limits of icebergs. The sea cannot be portrayed in this way on a single sheet. A map of the ocean must defy cartographic conventions. There are twelve routeing charts for each ocean: one sheet for each month of the year. The information contained on each sheet is often very different, depending on seasonal variations. Even so, I have had too many occasions to bemoan the shortcomings of routeing charts: the wind hasn't blown from the promised direction, the supposedly favourable current was non-existent. Routeing charts are still only approximations of certain key characteristics of the ocean important to navigators. They are a brave but not wholly successful attempt to fill the sea with knowledge. Perhaps the ocean can best be recorded only in the form of text: a narrative of a voyage describing a single line of experience that might never be repeated.

But even given the inadequacies of cartography, a map is still the ultimate traveller's trophy: proof that you have been to the places you describe, and know their relation one to the other. So if I were to draw a map of the sea, it wouldn't be complete without some mention of the places sailors have dreamt up to fill the empty ocean. The shorelines of imaginary islands and continents would need to be faint, so as not to confuse practising navigators. I would draw them as a shadow beneath the waves, like the outline of a reef submerged at high tide.

On my last evening at Beveridge, shortly after dark, I took the dinghy over to the reef. I put the anchor in among the corals and let the wind hold the inflatable boat free of the rocks out in the lagoon. The tide was coming in and there was a slight current across the reef, flowing around my legs. The reef's surface was uneven. Mostly I waded through calf-deep water, but at times it came to my knees. Several times I stumbled. I knew that my ankles were bleeding and I began to worry about sharks, especially in the deeper water. I was supposed to be looking for crayfish. I held a torch in one hand and wore a thick glove on the other. I realised I had never looked for crays alone before. Previously, in the atolls, I had gone with the islanders, and listened to their prayers for a good catch whispered beneath the rustling palms before wading out onto the reef.

I made my way slowly down the reef, using a torch to illuminate the path as much as to look for crayfish. The trade was light, the water smooth and silky, warmer than the air above. I came to a deeper channel where the water reached my waist. I waded slowly forwards, half-way between the earth and the sky, the land and the sea. Surf roared and sucked in the distance, the spray in places visible as a ghostly ring around the horizon.

I saw one crayfish, but my lunge was tardy and misdirected. After half an hour I returned empty-handed to the dinghy.

The following morning I gave up on Pete and left Beveridge for the south-west. I found out later that he had got bored in Vava'u several months earlier and set sail for the fleshpots of Suva. He had never received my fax.

Ten

IT IS DIFFICULT to narrate the events of that final passage from Beveridge Reef towards New Zealand. At least, the events themselves are simple enough. But to recreate the logic of the sea after the event is hard.

In the first half of the voyage I had written a daily journal. In Patagonia, too, I kept a detailed record of the places I visited on the journey. But on the return passage through the tropics my journal entries were less frequent. Perhaps I felt more at home crossing tropical seas, so relied less on a diary to process the experience. But also I had by this stage of the voyage grown tired of describing my every feeling and impression. In high latitudes I had used the video camera to record a diary of my thoughts, but I never did this any more. I resented the camera's prying eye, its associations with a stage set. The boat was my home, and I now craved the privacy to lead a normal life at sea. Since leaving Papeete, even my written journal entries had been few. After sufficient time on passage my actions become instinctive. In the tropics there is a narrower range of things which happen to a boat at sea: the squalls, rising wind at sunset, landfall, calms. I had learnt to deal with these things on the basis of reflex actions. When I sat down to write an account I sometimes found there were no thought processes to explore. I was sailing on automatic,

and descriptions of routine work about the deck and cabin became repetitive.

By the time I left Beveridge Reef my journal entries had
stopped altogether. So I have no direct record of my thoughts as
I made the passage towards New Zealand. I have no first-hand
source to help reconstruct the rationale of that voyage, and I distrust the imposition of one from a different time and place: I distrust any voice from the outside when it comes to describing
a difficult event at sea. What I can remember about that last,
strange passage was that my decisions seemed just as obvious as
all the others I had made over the preceding months. At no point
did I think I was sailing untried waters.

On the second night out of Beveridge I skirted south of Meyer
Reef and crossed the International Dateline. Early the next
morning a trough went through with heavy rain from the south
and the boat plunged westward in almost zero visibility. As the
wind backed I put more south in the course and sighted the dark
cliffs of Eua, a southern outpost of the Kingdom of Tonga. On
the third evening I saw the conical island of Ata, rising and
dipping in the swells. In the setting sun Ata appeared as a giant
sail billowing up from beneath the horizon.

My latitude now was close to the Tropic of Capricorn, towards the southern limit of the trade winds. The course ahead
took me through an area of variable winds, the so-called 'horse
latitudes', where calms and shifting breezes once forced square-
rigged ships to throw the horses overboard for want of fresh
water. Every day the colours visible in the ocean world were
changing. The sun had lost its intensity at midday, and when it
set the wind felt chill. In these more temperate waters the sea
was a richer, creamier blue, and seemed fuller, more rounded,
without the glaring reflections of the tropical sun. But when the
sky was full of cloud, that almost forgotten grey colour returned
to the water around the boat.

The one record I do have of those days is my log-book. This

is, in some respects, an interminable document, lists of figures and observations of the weather. But using the log-book and the chart in combination, it is easy to reconstruct the courses I steered and the prevailing conditions. When I was learning navigational theory I was taught to make a log entry every hour the boat was on passage. This theory originated long before the advent of electronic navigation, and only insomniacs are so diligent today. In the tropics I had made about five log entries every twelve hours, rather more on the passage across the Southern Ocean. But these averages are misleading, because my log entries over the voyage were erratic.

Looking at the log, it is easy to see periods of heightened anxiety when my entries were more frequent. In places these entries are hourly, or even more often than that: the first week of the voyage, at times of bad weather in high latitudes, before landfall, in squalls, throughout calms. So, flicking through the pages of the log-book I can see those times when the passage was difficult simply measured in the number of entries. When progress was good and the outlook fine, the pages are almost bare. Indirectly, the log acts as a barograph of my moods.

As I sailed south-west out of the tropics over the 24th parallel my log entries became increasingly detailed. I recorded my position relative to the two Minerva Reefs three times, though I was forty miles to the north and they were of minor navigational importance. The wind was certainly less constant in these waters. Over the course of three days it had shifted from south to north-east, with blustery squalls of rain. Then, six nights out of Beveridge, it died completely. That was a slow night, while the boat pitched and rolled on the still lumpy sea, the cabin filled with noise and restlessness. By morning a southerly had set in, but it was difficult to get the boat established on its course as the wind was light and the sea still awkward. When the seas started to smooth out later that morning, the wind began to shift, tending first west, then back to the south. I recorded each of these details faithfully in the log-book.

Despite this one setback with the weather, progress so far on the passage had mostly been good. If this wind continued I planned to head west-south-west to a waypoint four hundred miles north of New Zealand's North Cape. Around there I might expect a west wind to set in, allowing a south course to be steered. I should reach Auckland in a week.

Thus far on the voyage I had listened only to BBC radio on short-wave, but as I sailed into a more temperate latitude I changed this habit and tuned to local stations. Radio New Zealand International broadcasts to the Pacific, a mix of regional programmes and those lifted from the main domestic station. So I began to hear familiar place names and voices. I was keeping the same time as New Zealand now: I ate breakfast tuned to the same news bulletin I had listened to before the voyage; I heard the same jingle that had once meant it was time to go to work. That life seemed much further than a week away.

I reached my waypoint north of North Cape on the tenth morning. The last few days had been slower, the wind south-west. I put the boat about and sailed close-hauled on starboard tack. This course would put me just to the east of Northland, four days' sailing in this wind, less if things improved.

But the log entries over that day continue to be unnecessarily detailed. Admittedly the wind was gusty. I recorded twenty-five knots at 7 a.m., the boat careering over the swells, the sun catching clouds of golden spray. Two hours later the wind was fifteen knots and the seas were collapsing backwards. I recorded these things with earnest precision. I had been nervous for some time, drinking too much for the last several nights. I did the same again that night, blotting it out with cheap rum, but was shaken from my reverie more than once by the need to reef or un-reef the sails in the gusty wind. At dawn the wind went westerly for several hours, but by mid morning was back in the south-west.

At noon on that final day I recorded beating a hundred miles to windward in the preceding twenty-four hours. Shortly afterwards I heard the long-range weather forecast on Radio New Zealand and recorded the details in the back of the log: a broad trough in the Tasman Sea should maintain a south-west wind, though it would ease. I would make landfall in three days.

The facts are simple enough: two hours later I adjusted the self-steering and sailed the boat away from New Zealand. This new course was east-south-east: it would, eventually, have crossed the empty wastes of the Southern Ocean and reached the coast of Antarctica. But at the time my concerns were more immediate, and related only to the conditions on the boat there and then. I didn't care where I was going; I simply wanted to re-establish the patterns that had prevailed for months past. So I brought the wind round on to the quarter. The sailing now was fast and free, long, lunging rolls as the boat ploughed down the faces of the swells. After eight months of passage-making, twelve thousand miles, it seemed that this was the way it had always been. I had grown used to sailing towards a place that was so far distant I could not picture it in my mind. I had learnt to live only in the present, with no destination other than the sea.

I sailed this new course for the next three days. On the first day I made four entries in the log-book. On the second and third I recorded my position at noon each day, and nothing else. I remember eating well and sleeping well, and smoking and drinking less. I felt that the passage had improved recently. Life was back to normal. Certainly, progress was good. I covered 410 miles in that three-day run.

I understood perfectly well that I could not sail this course forever, or even for very long. In Papeete I had bought sufficient stores to reach New Zealand, with a little in reserve. My supplies of water would also soon begin to dwindle. After three days I decided I must choose the place where I would make landfall. With the wind in the west, New Zealand seemed far distant. The obvious choice was to head for an island group in the tropics. Both Tonga and Fiji would be easy to reach from here. I chose Fiji: I wanted the chaos and the crowds. It was a straightforward passage north, first in westerlies, then in the re-found trade.

I carried no charts of Fiji on the boat. I had not expected to come here on this voyage. My island refuge was not on any map. But Suva is a large commercial harbour, well marked and lit, and I had been here several times before. I picked up the leading lights one night in early June.

The yacht club in Suva is a watering-hole for expatriate soaks who watch rugby on television screens above the bar, and also a way-station for offshore transients like myself. The two groups of patrons rarely interact. The cruising yachts here are different from those in Papeete: there are more rust stains and pot plants in Suva. These boats have been in the islands longer, and some never intend to leave. The club provides facilities and a haven of sorts in the sprawling, shapeless harbour, which is otherwise bordered by commercial wharves, ship-yards, mangrove flats and landfills.

In the club I sent faxes and made phone calls. My friends and family expected me to be in New Zealand by now, I was supposed to be going back to work. I explained that the conditions had been unfavourable, and that I was in Suva. Few of these people knew the geography of the region well. For them, the South Pacific was an unknown ocean of many islands, and the fact that three weeks of my life had passed unaccounted for on an abortive passage to New Zealand went unnoticed.

The following day I received a fax from Pete, the friend I had hoped to meet at Beveridge Reef. He was in Vanua Levu, in the north-east of the Fiji group. He had phoned Auckland hoping to find me home, and my housemates had told him I was in Suva. Pete's fax was typically authoritative: 'I'll be there in three days. Stay there.'

Two days later I saw Pete's boat in the anchorage. Almost

immediately a tall, blonde girl stepped up through the companionway and stood on the fantail counter dressed in a pink *pareu*. Her name was Kirsty. She had been boat-hopping in the western islands when she met Pete. They had been sailing together for several months now, Pete diving in reef passages, Kirsty picking him up in the dinghy when the current had swept him through into the lagoon.

That night we went out for a meal. When Kirsty left the table I told Pete about the passage to New Zealand. I explained that I had abandoned the landfall with only a few hundred miles to go, and instead sailed for three days on a course to nowhere. I said I thought I might have had a breakdown at sea. He didn't stop eating. Then he said, 'It gets a bit like that sometimes. You've been at sea too long.' But he looked worried. It was Pete who had written to me before I started the voyage, suggesting I make a shorter trip, straight up to the tropics. Occasionally in the past I had felt patronised by the way Pete viewed me as an innocent adrift. But I was glad he was in Suva now.

Pete told me he planned to fly back to London, and that Kirsty was going to stay in the islands. He was sailing down to western Viti Levu in a few days' time. There was a marina at Vuda Point, then he would fly out from Nandi. He suggested that I go with him, all the way to London.

It was mid June. The weather in New Zealand is often settled in the autumn: it was not too late to sail down south. But I distrusted myself at sea now, and needed to get off the boat. I wanted to go home, and had to choose between flying to Auckland, or to London. I told Pete I would sail west with him, and fly to London.

We left Suva late in the afternoon and sailed through the Mbengga Channel as the sun set. I watched Pete's navigation light all that night as we followed the reefs off the south coast of the island. At dawn we motored through a mirror calm, then back inside the barrier reef. Pete was standing at the tiller, wearing a white silk balaclava against the sun. Later we anchored in the lagoon at Mana Island.

That afternoon we went for a dive. Most of Pete's underwater photography equipment was home-made. He had built the camera housings from Perspex sheeting cut and glued in place, with a flange turned down on the lathe in his father's garage in Ipswich. The Perspex domes for each housing were made from spare parts for marine compasses. The arms for the flashguns were microphone goosenecks covered in heat-shrink tube. When I had first met Pete seven years before, photography was only a hobby and he supported himself by doing odd jobs, including a stint as a dredger operator. Making his own equipment had been a necessity. Since then, though, he had started to make a good living from photography. He could afford to buy the best equipment. But Pete, like some others afloat, still persisted in the cast-away mentality, whereby sailors preferred to make things rather than buy them. Robinson Crusoe invented DIY. The fictional castaway started by fashioning his own pots and plates, then he made clothes, shoes, a table and chair. After that he built a house, dug a garden for his crops, built a boat, and finally a fortress to defend his island home. Pete did have one concession to modernity on his boat, a Roland EP85 digital piano. He was fond of playing Bach's Toccata and Fugue in D minor on clear nights in the trades, with all the hatches open and moonlight flooding into the cabin. The piano was an exception, though. That afternoon he filled our dive bottles using an ancient Briggs and Stratton compressor he had found in a skip and rebuilt.

We dived on a reef known for its sharks, called the 'Supermarket'. The first animals appeared before we reached the coral head, two grey reef sharks gliding in from the deeper water to the south. The shot he was working on that afternoon was a close-up of a shark's mouth. We had both caught fish at twilight the night before. He now opened a bag of fish bits and scattered pieces of flesh in the water. Kneeling on the seabed he threw a small piece of meat into the water above his head. The camera was pre-focused on about a foot. When the shark came in to take the meat he pushed the camera towards its mouth and hit the motor-drive. The shot showed the silky white belly of the shark, a gaping pink mouth at centre, backed by sunbursts, breaking waves and cloud. Two days later I was waiting for a tube at Heathrow.

Pete only stayed in the UK a few weeks. When he returned to the islands I got a fax saying the boat was fine: the bilges dry, the shorelines secure. I knew I should be worried about the boat. Leaving it in the water over a cyclone season in the tropics wasn't a very good idea. But over that period I spent in London I found it easy to put the ocean from my mind.

I arrived in late June and spent the rest of that summer working at a school in Hendon. I slept on the floor of my sister's flat in Kentish Town. As winter set in I got another job, at a school in Covent Garden. And it was easy to wonder now if the wheel had come full circle.

Before I left London to make the voyage to New Zealand eight years earlier I had worked for a publishing company in Henrietta Street. Each day now I walked past their now-defunct offices. I went to the same sandwich shop on Bedford Street to buy lunch. Little had changed, except that I was older and poorer. I found a quiet corner of the Piazza where I could sit and eat, away from the buskers, jugglers, fire-eaters, Whirling Dervishes and troupes of acrobatic dwarfs. And the stories I had read of castaway sailors washed up in fabled cities that appeared as strange reflections of the places from which they had started their journeys didn't seem so entertaining any more.

I enjoyed the cold and dark which seemed to be the only defining features of the endless winter months. They were a sobering therapy after the South Seas. Before Christmas Pete paid another visit to London to attend a wildlife photography dinner. We went out for a meal in Soho, together with his most recent crew. They were bronzed and bleached, creatures from another world. It has not been my experience that single-handed sailing represents a voyage of self-discovery. When I thought of the sea now, of those last days of the passage from Beveridge Reef towards New Zealand, I saw the image of a person I did not know.

At the beginning of February I was offered the use of a cottage in Cornwall for a couple of months. I took a train to Truro and began trying to write an account of the voyage. It was a good place to work. There were few distractions – none, really.

Within only a few days I missed London. There had been something familiar about it: the unpredictability of journey-making, the physical toil, the piles of rubbish bags at the garden gate, sudden eruptions of street violence, scenes of majesty and history. The roving forces of the great city were the closest thing here to being at sea.

By February I had been in England for the same length of time I had spent on the boat in the Pacific. I did not know any more if these were two separate entities, or one continuous voyage of sixteen months' duration. It is difficult to say when a voyage truly ends. I had once assumed I could turn the water off when I was finished with it. I thought the history of the south, its literature and cartography, were things I could read about and then put aside. But as I sailed the waters of the South Seas these aspects of its past, these strands of its vast tapestry, became bound up with the thread of my own voyage, to form a single cloth.

I suspect that even at sea, I am still a drifter. The idea that on the ocean I determined my own course, made landfalls of my own choosing, was partly an illusion. I followed winds and currents around the planet; when they failed, the passage faltered. Flotsam could have made the voyages I have made. If the tracks of every ship in history were drawn onto a single world map, they would coincide with the diagrams of ocean winds and currents found in Admiralty publications. European voyaging, and the discovery of our planet, has been an organic process in this respect, regulated by the global climate as much as by the will of human-kind. In this great swathe of tracks drawn by ships at sea, however, there would be one marked exception. The Pacific peoples did not follow the forces of nature around the ocean. The Micronesians, Melanesians and Polynesians sailed westward, six thousand miles against the trade winds, at a time when northern Europeans were struggling to keep coracles afloat.

My voyaging in the Pacific has been a journey to the ocean's periphery. I was drawn to that place where the land and sea meet. I went in search of unknown coastlines, uncharted canals, fictional continents, island myths, the vigias which may or may not exist. I went where the water is cloudy and disturbed, and where new homelands rise out of the sea to fill the map. I thought I could navigate these waters, but was wrecked on the dangerous shoaling of the lone sailor's state of mind.

In Cornwall, I decided to return to the Pacific and complete what I had started, by making landfall on my home city in New Zealand. I made the decision quickly, with no regrets. At the beginning of April I caught a flight to Nandi.

The marina at Vuda Point is a small basin with concrete walls, carved into the land behind the mangroves, with a long channel blasted through the coral out to deep water. The plane landed at dawn and I caught a taxi down to the compound.

At first glance the decks of the boat looked clean. But as I moved about I found everything covered in a film of something I couldn't immediately identify. It's a kind of tropical goo, a combination of torrential rain, baking sun, and dust and soot from the cane fields inland, that builds up as these forces alternately dominate the environment.

I spent three days working on the boat. The basin was airless, the humidity intense. I worked pouring with sweat, my white skin tingling in the sun. All the winches needed to be stripped and cleaned, the engine cooling was clogged. The self-steering had seized almost solid. When I released the lashings from the wind generator, it too was gummed motionless. Even the genoa, which had been below-decks, had suffered. Some of the stitching had been so weakened by the trapped heat that it failed as soon as I handled the sail. I sat for several hours on the foredeck re-sewing lengths of seam. Only the anchor windlass was still in working order, having been serviced more recently.

On 7 April I caught a bus in to Lautoka to get a clearance, and arrived back at the marina mid morning. When I put the engine astern to motor out of the berth the boat began to vibrate and the tiller was shaking in my hand. In the nine months I had been gone a small eco-system of barnacles and weed had grown on the propeller, reducing its efficiency many times. Even at full revs I was only just able to move the boat through the water. For a moment I considered re-tying the shorelines and going over the side to scrape the propeller clean. But the thought of this filthy basin and the bugs I might contract on the eve of the passage to New Zealand made me delay. I decided to try something else.

There was no apparent wind in the marina basin itself, but when I came out of the channel into Nandi Water a sea breeze was blowing cross-shore at fifteen knots. I put on flippers, a mask and snorkel and took a wire brush into the water. The boat was pitching and rolling on the short seas, white-caps occasionally breaking over my head. As I dived on the propeller, the self-steering paddle was chopping up and down dangerously in the water behind me. It was hard to get my hands on the propeller for long, and I was not able to remove all the growth. In fact, I was more concerned with just getting back on the boat. With no sails up it was lying beam-on to the slight sea, but the wind in the rig was moving it slowly through the water. As I worked on the propeller I also had to swim forwards in order to keep up. When I tried to get back over the rail I failed several times, floundering against the topsides, unable to get a proper grip with my flippered feet, before finally slithering into the cockpit. It was probably the worst piece of seamanship I have to my name.

I ran with the sea breeze on the quarter that afternoon, south-west to the islands on the barrier reef. Here I could clean the whole hull properly, and watch the weather. I began the passage home to New Zealand late the following day.

Sources

I have tried to rely on original sources as far as possible. However, this book has also been both inspired and informed by the following (all titles were published in London unless otherwise specified):

J. O. Bailey, 'Sources for Poe's Arthur Gordon Pym', in *Publication of Modern Languages Association* 57 (1942)

M. Baker, *The Folklore of the Sea* (Newton Abbot, David and Charles, 1979)

J. C. Beaglehole, *The Exploration of the Pacific* (Adam and Charles Black, 1966)

The Life of Captain James Cook (Adam and Charles Black, 1974)

P. Bellwood, *The Polynesians: Prehistory of an Island People* (London, Thames and Hudson, 1978)

S. Berthon & A. Robinson, *The Shape of the World* (Guild Publishing, 1991)

C. Blacker, *Ancient Cosmologies* (Allen and Unwin, 1975)

T. B. Clark, *Omai: The First Polynesian Ambassador to London* (Honolulu, University of Hawaii Press, 1969)

J. M. Cohen, *The Four Voyages of Christopher Columbus* (Cresset Library, 1988)

D. Cosgrove (ed.), *Mappings* (Reaktion Books, 1999)

B. Danielsson, *Gauguin in the South Seas* (Allen and Unwin, 1965)

G. Daws, *A Dream of Islands* (New York, Norton, 1980)

I. Donaldson (ed.), 'Australia and the European Imagination' – Papers from a conference at the Humanities Research Centre, Australian National University, 1981

J. Dunmore, *French Explorers in the Pacific* (Oxford, Clarendon Press, 1965)

R. L. Eskridge, *Manga Reva, The Forgotten Islands* (Indianapolis, Bobbs-Merrill, 1931)

D. Fausett, *Writing the New World: Imaginary Voyages and Utopias of the Great Southern Land* (New York, Syracuse University Press, 1993)

The Strange, Surprising Sources of Robinson Crusoe (Amsterdam, Rodopi, 1994)

B. R. Finney (ed.), *Pacific Navigation and Voyaging* (Wellington, The Polynesian Society, 1976)

V. Flint, *The Imaginative Landscape of Christopher Columbus* (New Jersey, Princeton University Press, 1992)

H. Fry, *Alexander Dalrymple and the Expansion of British Trade* (Royal Commonwealth Society, 1970)

J. Garret, *To Live Among the Stars: Christian Origins in Oceania* (Suva, University of the South Pacific, 1982)

A. Giamatti, *The Earthly Paradise and the Renaissance Epic* (New York, Norton, 1989)

R. Gibson, *The Diminishing Paradise: Changing Literary Perceptions of Australia* (Sydney, Sirius Books, 1984)

P. B. Gove, *The Imaginary Voyage in Prose Fiction* (Holland Press, 1961)

M. Green, *The Robinson Crusoe Story* (University Park, Pennsylvania State University Press, 1990)

H. Henningsen, *Crossing the Equator* (Copenhagen, Munskgaard, 1961)

K. Huntress, 'Another Source for Poe's Narrative of Arthur Gordon Pym', in *American Literature* 16 (1944)

E. Hutchins, 'Understanding Micronesian Navigation', in Gentner & Stevens (eds), *Mental Models* (New Jersey, L. Erlbaum Associates, 1983)

D. Lewis, *The Voyaging Stars* (Sydney, William Collins, 1978)

J. Macmillan Brown, *The Riddle of the Pacific* (New York, AMS Press, 1979)

D. M. McKeithan, 'Two Sources for Poe's Narrative of Arthur Gordon Pym', in *University of Texas Bulletin*, 13 (1933)

F. McLynn, *Robert Louis Stevenson* (Hutchinson, 1993)

J. Moore, 'The Geography of Gulliver's Travels', in *Journal of English and Germanic Philology* 40 (1941)

J. H. Parry, *The Discovery of the Sea* (Berkeley, University of California Press, 1981)

S. Rogers, *Crusoes and Castaways* (Harrap and Co., 1932)

M. Stannard, 'The "South-east Point of New Holland" as No-place: A Possible Solution to a Textual Problem in the Fourth Voyage of Gulliver's Travels', in *Notes and Queries*, September 1996

P. Whitfield, *The Charting of the Oceans* (The British Library, 1996)

J. N. Wilford, *The Mapmakers* (New York, Knopf, 1981)

G. Williams & A. Frost, *Terra Australis to Australia* (Melbourne, Oxford University Press, 1988)

R. Wiseman, *The Spanish Discovery of New Zealand* (Auckland, Discovery Press, 1996)

L. Wroth, Early *Cartography of the Pacific* (Papers of the Bibliographical Society of America vol. 38 No. 2, New York, 1944)

Her Majesty's Stationery and UK Hydrographic Office, Taunton, *The Mariner's Handbook* (1979)

——*South America Pilot*, volume III (1987)

——*Pacific Islands Pilot*, volume III (1982)

——*Ocean Passages For The World* (1973)

Acknowledgements

A big thank you to Maggy Staples for drawing the maps, and to Pete Atkinson for supplying the photographs numbered 10, 11, 13, 15 and 16, and also the jacket photograph.

Extracts from the *Mariner's Handbook* and *South America Pilot*, volume III, are reproduced by kind permission of the Controller of Her Majesty's Stationery and UK Hydrographic Office.